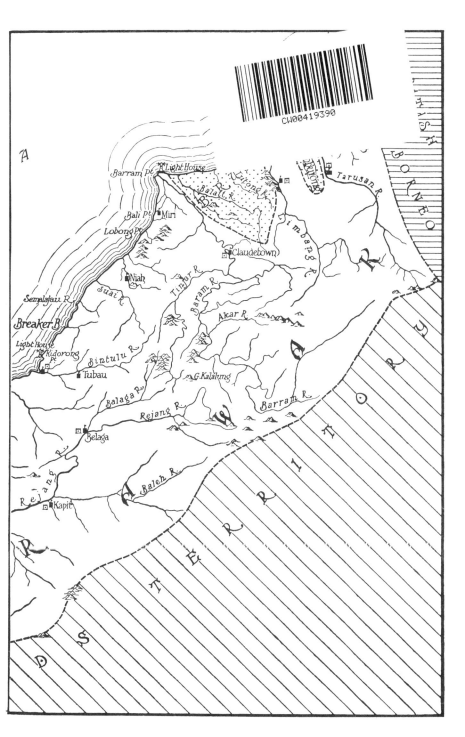

H.H. THE RAJAH OF SARAWAK

MY LIFE IN SARAWAK

MY LIFE
IN SARAWAK

BY

THE RANEE OF SARAWAK

PREFACE BY

SIR FRANK SWETTENHAM, G.C.M.G.
GOVERNOR OF THE STRAITS COLONY
HIGH COMMISSIONER FOR THE FEDERATED MALAY STATES AND
LATE CONSUL-GENERAL FOR BORNEO

WITH TWENTY-SEVEN ILLUSTRATIONS AND A MAP

KUALA LUMPUR
OXFORD UNIVERSITY PRESS
OXFORD SINGAPORE NEW YORK

Oxford University Press

Oxford New York
Athens Auckland Bangkok Bombay
Calcutta Cape Town Dar es Salaam Delhi
Florence Hong Kong Istanbul Karachi
Madras Madrid Melbourne Mexico City
Nairobi Paris Shah Alam Singapore
Taipei Tokyo Toronto

and associated companies in
Berlin Ibadan

Oxford is a trade mark of Oxford University Press

Originally published by Methuen & Co. Ltd., London 1913
First issued as an Oxford University Press paperback 1986
Eighth impression 1996

ISBN 0 19 582663 9

Printed by KHL Co. (S) Pte. Ltd., Singapore
Published by the South-East Asian Publishing Unit,
a division of Penerbit Fajar Bakti Sdn. Bhd.,
under licence from Oxford University Press,
4 Jalan U1/15, Seksyen U1, 40000 Shah Alam,
Selangor Darul Ehsan, Malaysia

DEDICATED TO THE MEMORY

OF

MY GREAT FRIEND

DATU ISA

PREFACE

IT is well for the Malay races of Sarawak that they should find an advocate in their Ranee, for she loves them. To know Ranee Brooke is to know that, and those who read her *Life in Sarawak* will realize this fact to the full, and will feel that, in the years she spent with these simple people, she must have proved it to them and won their confidence by her sympathy. That is the only way to get at the hearts of a Malay people, and though the native population of this section of Borneo is divided into at least two sections,—Malays and Dyaks,—differing widely in religion, customs, and language, they are still members of the great Malay family which is spread over the Malay Peninsula, Sumatra, Java, Borneo, the islands of the Archipelago, and farther afield. It is well for any of the Malay race that they should find a sympathetic writer to tell the world something of their little lives, for they are a silent and exclusive people. They do not understand publicity, they do not want it, so long as they are fairly and justly treated ; indeed, superficial observers might think that Malays do not really care how they are governed, and that it is a matter of indifference to them whether they are treated well or ill. Those who take the trouble to win his regard know that the Malay is as keenly interested in his own and his country's affairs as are those of other nationalities. He is humble about his own capacity, and that of his fellow-countrymen, to organize and endeavour, to frame a scheme of righteous government and to ensue it. He will, if properly approached and considerately handled by Europeans, be the first to admit that they understand the business better, that they are more trustworthy in matters of justice and money, and that they have a conception of duty, of method, and especially a power of continuous application to work, which is foreign and irksome— indeed well-nigh impossible — to him. Treat him fairly, reasonably, justly, remember that he represents the people of the country for whose benefit, as Lord Curzon of Kedleston said, the white man is there, and, though the white man retains in his own hands the principal offices, the real power, and the work which is his burden, the Malay will give him admiration, gratitude, and loyal support, and show no sign of jealousy or impatience. If one bears in mind, as indeed one must, that the growth of the white man's influence, and the adoption of that advice which we say makes for good government, mean always the lessening of the Malay's authority and the curtailment or abolition of his privileges,—very often bad privileges in our opinion,—it is surely rather wonderful and rather admirable that he should accept his fate with such a good, often even a charming, grace. The Malay does not always approve of our methods, and sometimes they are really indefensible, but, though he disapproves, what is he to say? To whom is he to complain, and how? We sometimes learn his language, because that is necessary for our benefit; we even take trouble to inquire about his customs and other matters concerning him and his life; but very, very rarely does he learn either our language, or enough of our customs, to make himself heard effectively. He realizes this better than almost any other thing, and therefore, being a fatalist, he accepts what comes because he knows there is no other way. Given his nature, his traditions, his way of life through all the generations, and his present disabilities, how is he to do otherwise? When you have handed over to others the control of everything you once had, can you complain to them of breach of faith, or even of little things like the neglect of your interests when they happen to clash with your controllers' wishes or ambitions? Western people, in humble or subordinate positions, sometimes find it difficult to assert themselves, or what they believe to be their rights; to the Malay it is impossible.

That being so, one would imagine that every white man who comes into a position of authority amongst such a people, so circumstanced, will be doubly and trebly careful to remember that the greater his power, the more need there is not only to seek, with single purpose, the benefit of " the people

of the country," but to champion their cause—when
he knows it is right—against all comers, and if need
be to his own detriment.   To betray Malays, is like
taking a mean advantage of a blind man who has
put his hand in yours, in the firm belief that he is
safe in his blind trust of you.   To take advantage of
that trust should be unthinkable.   I am not writing
of the customs of what is called business, nor even of
the ways of rival powers ; for in both these cases the
means employed are less regarded than the end to be
gained, and success justifies all things.   I am only
dealing with the mission of the white man when, for
any reason whatever, he undertakes to administer
the affairs of a people who possess a possibly rich
territory, but are unskilled in the art of administration.   That was the case of Sarawak when Sir
James Brooke undertook its pacification and develop-
ment in 1841.   This is not the place to describe the
task set before the first white Rajah of Sarawak, but
it is, I think, the opportunity to point the moral of an
achievement which probably has no parallel.   James
Brooke must have been a man for whom the soft
life of cities had no attraction, but he did not
approach the problem of enforcing peace in a greatly
disturbed province of Borneo as large as England,
and suppressing piracy on its coasts, in the spirit
of an adventurer ; he described his objects in the
following words : " It is a grand experiment, which, if
it succeeds, will bestow a blessing on these poor
people ; and their children's children shall bless

me. If it please God to permit me to give a stamp to this country which shall last after I am no more, I shall have lived a life which emperors might envy. If by dedicating myself to the task I am able to introduce better customs and settled laws, and to raise the feeling of the people so that their rights can never in future be wantonly infringed, I shall indeed be content and happy."

Those were his intentions, and to that end he worked for twenty-six years with a success as remarkable as his own devotion and abnegation of self-interest. When James Brooke died in 1868 he left to his nephew and appointed successor, the present Rajah of Sarawak, a peaceful and contented country, the hearts of whose people he had won by studying them, their interests, their customs, their peculiarities, and their happiness, and to them he gave his life and energy and everything he possessed. It was a remarkable achievement, and he left to the country of his adoption the "stamp" of his heart's desire. Much more than that, he established a precedent on which his successor has acted with unswerving consistency for the last forty-six years; it is the stamp of Brooke rule, and so long as it lasts all will be well with Sarawak.

Interesting and successful as were the methods of administration introduced and established in Sarawak by Sir James Brooke and the present Rajah, I cannot go into them. It is sufficient to say that Sarawak has been ruled by the Brookes "for the benefit of the people of the country," and Mr. Alleyne Ireland, who was well qualified to form a sound judgment, wrote in 1905, after spending two months in travelling up and down the coast and in the interior : " I find myself unable to express the high opinion I have formed of the administration of the country without a fear that I shall lay myself open to the charge of exaggeration. With such knowledge of administrative systems in the tropics as may be gained by actual observation in almost every part of the British Empire except the African Colonies, I can say that in no country which I have ever visited are there to be observed so many signs of a wise and generous rule, such abundant indications of good government, as are to be seen on every hand in Sarawak." Again, in the same book, *Far Eastern Tropics*, Mr. Ireland wrote : " The impression of the country which I carry away with me is that of a land full of contentment and prosperity, a land in which neither the native nor the white man has pushed his views of life to their logical conclusion, but where each has been willing to yield to the other something of his extreme conviction. There has been here a tacit understanding on both sides that those qualities which alone can ensure the *permanence* of good government in the State are to be found in the white man and not in the native ; and the final control remains, therefore, in European hands, although every opportunity is taken of consulting the natives and of benefiting by their intimate knowledge of the country and of the people." That is high praise from an experienced critic, but not too high, and the last words of Mr. Ireland's sentence cannot be insisted upon too urgently when dealing with Malays. In Sarawak, the fact which is most striking and which must command the admiration of every man, especially of those who have been associated intimately with the administration of Eastern peoples and their lands, is that throughout the long years from 1841 to the present time, the two white Rajahs of Sarawak spent practically their whole lives in this remote corner of Asia, devoting their best energies to the prosperity and the happiness of their subjects, whilst taking from the country, of which they were the absolute Rulers, only the most modest income. That has been the admirable and unusual "stamp" of Brooke rule: to live with the people, to make their happiness the first consideration, and to refuse wealth at their expense. Nothing would have been easier—certainly for the present Rajah—than to live at ease in some pleasant Western land, with perhaps an occasional visit to Sarawak, and to devote to his own use revenues which he has spent for the benefit of Sarawak and its people. The State is rich in resources, mineral and agricultural; to many it would have seemed most natural to fill the place with Chinese or to grant concessions to Europeans Either of these courses would have meant a large accession of revenue, and no one would have thought it strange had the Ruler of the country spent whatever proportion seemed good to him on himself. Only the people of the country would have suffered; but they, probably, would have considered that it was perfectly natural, and, had they thought otherwise, it would have made no difference, for it is not their habit to complain publicly of the doings of their Rulers. The Rajahs of Sarawak have made "the benefit of the people of the country" the business of their lives; all honour to them for their high purpose. That the tradition they have established by seventy-two years of devotion, of personal care of the affairs of Sarawak, should be continued and perpetuated must be the prayer of all who love Malays.

I make a final quotation from Mr. Ireland's book. It is this: "Nothing could better serve to exhibit at once the strength and the weakness of a despotic form of government than the present condition of Sarawak, for if it be true that the wisdom, tolerance, and sympathy of the present Rajah have moulded the country to the extraordinary state of tranquil prosperity which it now enjoys, the power of an unwise or wicked ruler to throw the country back into a condition of barbarism must be admitted as a necessary corollary. The advent of such a ruler is, however, in the highest degree improbable."

Every one must hope that a departure from the Brooke tradition is impossible, and as the matter is wholly within the discretion of the present Rajah, who knows better than anyone else what is necessary to secure the objects set out by his predecessor, and confirmed and secured by his own rule, there is no reason to fear for the future of Sarawak. Any real man would be proud to take up and help to perpetuate so great an inheritance. When the time comes, he will remember the words of the first Rajah Brooke: " If it please God to permit me to give a stamp to this country which shall last after I am no more, I shall have lived a life which emperors might envy," and he will begin his rule with the knowledge that his predecessor spent his whole life in making good the promise of those words.

F. A. S.

LONDON, 22nd September 1913

INTRODUCTION

EVERY ONE has heard of Rajah Brooke. He was my husband's uncle, and this is how he became ruler of Sarawak.

Borneo is one of the largest islands of the world. The Dutch occupy three parts of its territory. The British North Borneo Company, a group of Englishmen, have established themselves in the north, and Sarawak, with its five hundred miles of coast-line and its fifty thousand square miles of land, is situated on the north-west. Until some four hundred years ago, at the time of Pigafetta's visit to Brunei, Borneo was almost unknown to Europe, but ever since then, at various periods, Dutch, Portuguese, and English have attempted to gain a footing in the island. The Dutch, however, were the most successful, for it was only in 1839 that the English obtained a firm hold of a portion of this much disputed land. It must be remembered that owing to the murders of Englishmen who attempted to trade with Brunei in 1788, 1803, and 1806, the Admiralty issued a warning as to the dangers attendant upon English merchants engaging in commercial ventures with the Sultan of Brunei and his people. About forty years went by without

English people making further attempts to trade in that part of the world, until one day, in August 1839, James Brooke, the future white Rajah of Sarawak, appeared upon the scene, and it was due to his bold but vague designs that peace, prosperity, and just government were subsequently established in a country hitherto torn with dissension and strife. James Brooke had always felt a great interest in those lands of the Malayan Archipelago. As a very young man he had held a commission in the army of the British East India Company, and had seen active service in Burmah. He was seriously wounded during the Burmese war, invalided home, and finally resigned his commission. He then made two voyages to the Strait Settlements and to China, and it is to be supposed that his interest in that part of the world dates from that period of his life. At his father's death, he inherited a small fortune, which he invested in the purchase of a yacht of 140 tons, in which he set sail in 1838 for the Eastern Archipelago. In those days, the Sultan of Brunei owned the extreme north of the island, and his territory stretched as far as what is called Cape Datu, now belonging to the Rajah. Whilst staying at Singapore, James Brooke heard rumours of a rebellion by the Malays of Sarawak against their Sultan, for both the Sultan and his Brunei nobles (many of whom were of Arabic descent), in order to enrich themselves, had instituted a tyrannous and oppressive government against the people. When Brooke

arrived in Sarawak, he made the acquaintance of the
Sultan's Viceroy, Rajah Muda Hassim, who was an
uncle of the Sultan of Brunei, and the acknowledged
heir to the Sultanate. Hence his title Rajah Muda
and Sultan Muda, meaning heir - apparent. They
made friends, when the Malay Governor confided
in Brooke and besought his help in quelling the
rebellion. Brooke consented, and the rebellion was
soon at an end. The rebels, determined not to fall
back under the yoke of their former tyrants and
oppressors, implored Brooke to become their Rajah
and Governor. Rajah Muda Hassim was favourable to the people's request, and in 1841 Brooke
was proclaimed Rajah of Sarawak amidst the rejoicing of its population. Rajah Muda Hassim, as
representative of the Sultan, signed a document
resigning his title and authority to the Englishman,
and in 1842 Brooke, being desirous of obtaining
from the Sultan himself an additional proof of his
goodwill towards his position in Sarawak, visited
the potentate in Brunei, when the Sultan confirmed his title as independent Rajah of Sarawak.
On the other hand, it is interesting to realize that
Rajah Muda Hassim was never in any sense Rajah
of Sarawak, that country then not being a Raj, but a
simple province misruled by Brunei Governors who
never bore the title of Rajah, for after all Rajah
Muda Hassim did not abdicate in favour of Brooke,
but it was the people themselves who insisted on
Sarawak being independent of the Sultan's and his

emissaries' authority, and chose Brooke as their own Rajah, thus regaining their former independence.

When James Brooke first became Rajah of Sarawak in 1841, the area of his country known as Sarawak proper comprised some seven thousand square miles in extent.

It might be as well to give a short account of the manner in which the first white ruler of Sarawak organized his Government. The Sarawak Malay nobles, the Datus or chiefs that governed the State before James Brooke's accession to power, and who had been superseded and driven into rebellion by the Brunei nobles, the Sultan's emissaries, were recalled by James Brooke and chosen to help in carrying out his Government. When in the course of years these nobles died, their sons or members of the same aristocratic families (but always with the approval of the people) were, and are, chosen to fill the vacant places. The first of these chiefs who helped to inaugurate and establish James Brooke's Government was a gallant Malay gentleman called Datu Patinggi Ali, who was a direct descendant of Rajah Jarum, the founder of Sarawak, who led his people against the oppression of Brunei, and found death by the side of James Brooke, sword in hand, fighting for his and his people's cause. His son, the Datu Bandar, Haji Bua Hassan, held office for sixty years, and died a few years ago in Kuching, over one hundred years of age. He was a brave and upright man; intelligent and wide-minded in

Council, and a true friend of the Rajah's, of our sons, and of mine. Datu Isa, to whose memory I have dedicated this book, was his wife, and I only wish it were in my power to put into words her charming, sympathetic personality, and make it understood how, in her blameless useful life, she set a high standard of conduct amongst the Malay women of Kuching.

The present Datu Bandar, Muhammad Kasim, and the Datu Imaum, Haji Muhammad Ali, are the sons of the late Datu Bandar and of Datu Isa. These four great Malay officials are members of the Supreme Council and assistant judges of the Supreme Court. The Datu Bandar, premier Datu and Malay magistrate, is president of the Muhammadan Probate Divorce Court. The Datu Imaum is the religious head of the Muhammadan community. The Datu Tumanggong's title, signifying that of Commander-in-Chief or fighting Datu, is no longer employed in that capacity, but ranks next to the Bandar as peaceful member of the Council, whilst the Datu Hakim is adviser in Muhammadan law.

Now that a very short account has been given as to the principal Malayan officials in Sarawak, we must turn back to the year 1841 and take up the thread of our story. At that time the more northern rivers outside Sarawak were infested by pirates, who, under the leadership of Brunei nobles, devastated adjacent lands. The first Rajah, backed by his loyal subjects, made many expeditions against these criminal tribes. In 1849, Her Majesty's ship *Dido*, commanded by Sir Harry Keppel, came to his aid, when the combined forces of Malays and Dyaks, strengthened by the crew of Her Majesty's ship, completely scoured out the nests of the redoubtable piratical hordes, and an end was put to their devastation in those regions. Little by little the authority and strength of the white Rajah's government became acknowledged, even by the ci-devant miscreants themselves, and the inhabitants of the more northern rivers, realizing that after all honesty is the best policy, willingly laid down their arms and clamoured to be enrolled in the territory of the great white chief.

Being monarch of all he surveyed, unfettered by tradition, and owning no obedience to the red-tapeism of Europe, Rajah Brooke laid the foundations of one of the most original and, so far as justice goes, successful Governments that perhaps has ever been known, its most salient feature being that from its very beginning the natives of the place were represented by their own people, and had the right to vote for and against any law that was made by their Government. Brooke established stations in the mouths of the principal rivers, and in each of these stations were appointed one or two English officials to represent the white ruler. Billian or iron wood forts were built in each of these settlements, and a small force of Malays, armed with muskets and small cannons, was placed there in order to enforce obedience to the laws of the new Government and to inspire confidence in its supporters. The duty of these officials, called Governors or Residents, was to protect the people from the tyranny of some of the higher classes of Malays, to prevent head-hunting, and to discourage disorder. The co-operation of local chiefs and headmen was elicited to help in this good work, and one cannot repeat too often that such native co-adjutors have been the mainstay of the Rajah's Government, and so they must always remain. The present Rajah and his uncle have strictly adhered to this excellent policy of associating the natives with the government of their country. James Brooke began his law codes in respecting and maintaining whatever was not positively detrimental in the laws and customs as he found them. Instead of imposing European made laws upon the people, Muhammadan law and custom has been maintained whenever it affects Muhammadanism. No favouritism is allowed, and any white man infringing the laws of the country would be treated in exactly the same way as would be the natives of the soil. In the *Sarawak Gazette* of 1872, the present Rajah at the beginning of his reign wrote these words: "A Government such as that of Sarawak may start from things as we find them, putting its veto on what is dangerous or unjust, and supporting what is fair and equitable in the usages of the natives, and letting system and legislation wait upon oc-

casion. When new wants are felt, it examines and
provides for them by measures rather made on the
spot than imported from abroad ; and, to ensure that
these shall not be contrary to native customs, the
consent of the people is gained for them before they
are put in force. The white man's so-called privilege
of class is made little of, and the rulers of government
are framed with greater care for the interests of the
majority who are not Europeans, than for those of
the minority of superior race."

The Supreme Council consists of four Malay
officials, together with three or four of the principal
European officers ; the Rajah presides over all its de-
liberations. The Malay members of the Council always
take an active and prominent part in its decisions.
Every three years a State Council meets at Kuching,
under the presidency of the Rajah, consisting of the
members of the Supreme Council, the European
Residents in charge of the more important districts,
and the principal native chiefs, some seventy in
number, who come from all the important districts of
the principality. At this meeting questions of general
interest as to the government of the country are
discussed ; the members are informed of any recent
question relating to public affairs, and are told of the
general progress achieved in the Government, or of
anything pertaining to the State since the Council's
last meeting. Each member is formally sworn in and
takes an oath of loyalty to the Rajah and his Government. It would be very tempting to anyone who is

as interested as I am in the prosperity of the country
to give more details regarding the incessant work
required in order that each law as it is made should
be satisfactory and meet the requirements of the
whole of the Sarawak people; suffice it to say that
the Rajah, his English officers, and his Malay chiefs
are indefatigable in their endeavours to promote
trade and commerce, peace and prosperity amongst
the people. I have only a short space in which
to speak of these more important matters, and I
can only hope that the very slight sketch I have
given in the limited space at my disposal of the past
and present history of Sarawak may induce those
whom it interests to seek further information in the
many volumes that have already been written on the
subject. It might perhaps not be amiss to mention
the two last books published on Sarawak, these being
The White Rajahs of Sarawak, by Messrs. Bampfylde and Baring-Gould, and *The Pagan Tribes of
Borneo*, by those two well-known English scientists
—Dr. Hose and Mr. McDougall. It must be remembered that Mr. Bampfylde and Dr. Hose
occupied for years very important posts in the Rajah's
Government, and on that account their experience of
the people and the country must be invaluable.

LIST OF ILLUSTRATIONS

xxvi

MY LIFE IN SARAWAK

CHAPTER I

WHEN I remember Sarawak, its remoteness, the dreamy loveliness of its landscape, the childlike confidence its people have in their rulers, I long to take the first ship back to it, never to leave it again. How it happened that as a young English girl I came into intimate contact with the people of Sarawak is as follows: In 1868, on the death of the first English Rajah of Sarawak, his nephew and successor came to England and visited my mother, who was his cousin. On his return to Borneo in the early seventies, I accompanied him as his wife.

Looking over the diaries I kept in those days, they throw little light upon the new surroundings in which I found myself. I had received the limited education given to girls in that mid-Victorian period; I had been taught music, dancing, and could speak two or three European languages; but as regards the important things in life, these had never been thought of consequence to my education.

I was sea-sick almost the whole way from Mar-

seilles to Singapore, so that when we stayed at the
various ports on our way out — Aden, Ceylon,
Penang, etc —I was much too ill to take any interest
in them.   I remember that in Singapore we received
invitations from the Governor and from the residents
of the place to stay with them on our way to Sarawak; but I felt ill, and the Rajah and I thought it
best to take up our quarters at an hotel.   However, we
dined with the Governor and his wife, Sir Harry and
Lady Ord, and I do not think I had ever met kinder
people.   The Chief Justice and his wife, Sir Benson
and Lady Maxwell, were also charming to us, asking
us to spend a day with them at their country house
near Singapore.   This we did, and it was all delightful and lovely, barring the fact that I met none of
the Singapore natives on these occasions.

It was at Singapore that I first tasted tropical
fruits—mangoes, mangosteens, a fruit called the sour-
sop, tasting like cotton wool dipped in vinegar and
sugar; also many other kinds—all of which, under
the distempered state of my mind, owing to the
journey, I thought positively repulsive.   As to the
delights of first impressions in the tropics, I must say
I did not share in those feelings.   I hated the heat,
the damp clammy feel of those equatorial regions,
and I then thought that I should never find happiness
in such countries.

After a few days spent in Singapore, we embarked
in the Rajah's yacht, the *Heartsease*.   She was a
wooden gunboat of 250 tons, and her admirers had

THE AUTHOR

FROM A PAINTING BY MRS. ALFRED SOTHEBY

told me she was as lively as a duck in the water. This behaviour on her part was exceedingly annoying to me during the passage to Kuching, a journey which took two days. It was on board the *Heartsease* that I had my first experience of cockroaches and rats, and these kept me in a perpetual state of terror at night. Cockroaches are like black beetles, only much larger, flatter, and tawny brown in colour. At the approach of rain they are particularly lively, and as rain falls daily in this region, their habits are offensive to human beings. They fly or spring from great distances, and alight on their victims. I remember how they startled me by jumping on to my face, arms and hands, as I lay in my bunk trying to get to sleep. The tiny prick of their spiky, spindly legs was a hateful experience.

Every one must be familiar with rats more or less at a distance, but the *Heartsease's* rats were disconcertingly friendly. They glided up and down the floor of my cabin, sometimes scratching at my pillow, which did not add to my comfort.

It was on the third morning after leaving Singapore, that I suddenly felt the ship moving in absolutely smooth waters. This encouraged me to crawl up on deck, and look around me at the scenery. It was the most beautiful I had ever seen. The tide was on the turn, and the morning mist was still hanging about the watery forests on the banks and about the high mountains of the interior, and as it swept across the river it brought with it that curious, sweet, indefinable smell, half-aromatic and half-sickly, making one think unaccountably of malaria. I remember that I felt very cold, for everything I touched was dripping with dew. I could see the high mountain of Santubong, a great green cliff rising almost out of the water to a height of about three thousand feet, covered to its summit with luxuriant forests. At the foot of the mountain was a great expanse of sand, over which enormous brown boulders were scattered, as though giants had been disturbed at a game of ninepins. At the back of the sandy shore grew groves of Casuarina trees (the natives call them "talking trees," from the sound they make when a breeze stirs their lace-like branches), looking as though the slightest puff might blow them all away in clouds of dark green smoke.

Brown huts, made of dried palm leaves and built on poles, dotted the beach, ands mall canoes tethered to the shore held little brown naked children, playing and baling out the water. Women were washing clothes on the river-banks. They were clothed in one long, clinging garment, folded and tucked under their armpits, and their straight, long, black hair was drawn into huge knots at the nape of their necks. All this I saw as in a vision; the people were too far off for me to distinguish their features, and the incoming tide was carrying us up the river at a swift pace.

Here and there, on our way up, we met Chinamen standing in the stern of swift, small, narrow canoes, propelling their boats gondolier fashion, with cargoes of fish for the Kuching market. We passed boats of all sorts and sizes, from the small sampan scooped out of a single tree trunk, with its solitary paddler, to the larger house-boats belonging to Malays, filled with women and children. These were roofed in to shelter their inmates from the rain or sun, and were usually propelled by old men sitting in the bows cross-legged, wearing dirty white cotton drawers and jauntily placed conical hats, which sometimes allowed the folds of turbans to be seen, these showing that the wearers had been to Mecca. My attention was attracted by one very small canoe, for I saw, sitting amidships, an old woman huddled up in a cotton scarf. A tiny boy, perfectly naked, was bravely paddling her along, whilst he shouted insults to his poor old lady passenger as our steamer passed by.

It was on this morning also, that I made the acquaintance of the Malay crew of our yacht. Like all people suddenly finding themselves for the first time in the midst of an alien race, I thought the sailors all looked alike. I elicited from the Rajah that some were young and some were old, but whether aged eighteen or fifty, I could see no difference in them at all. They all had the same almost bridgeless noses, wide nostrils, thick lips, dark restless eyes, and the lanky hair belonging to their Mongolian race. I tried to make up to them in a feeble way ; I looked at them and smiled as they went to and fro, but they only bent double as they passed, paying no more

attention to my friendly advances than they did to
my cane chair.   They were the gentlest moving
things I had ever seen; yet apparently, their work
did not suffer, for I was told that they were as
efficient as any ordinary European crew.

The Rajah was accompanied on the occasion by
one of his officers who had come to meet us at
Singapore.   As we three sat on deck, I thought they
were the most silent pair I had ever come across.
I wanted to know about the country, and asked
questions, but no satisfactory answer could be
obtained, and I was gently made to understand that
I had better find things out for myself.   I wanted to
know about the mangroves which grew in the mud,
and which at high tide stand "knee-deep in the
flood."   I wanted to know about those great forests
of nipa palms, like gigantic hearse plumes, fringing
the river-banks, and from which I had been told in
Singapore that sixteen different and most useful
products to commerce could be obtained.   I wanted
to know the names of long, slender palms towering
over the other vegetation farther inland, whose glossy
fronds swaying in the morning breeze looked like
green and graceful diadems.   Then I saw great
things like logs of wood lying on the mud, and when
these moved, and went with a sickening flop into the
water, I had to find out for myself that they were the
first crocodiles of my acquaintance.   I saw the black
and mobile faces of monkeys peering at us from
between the branches overhanging the water,

grimacing like angry old men at our intrusion into their solitude, and to my inquiry as to what kind of monkeys they were, the usual indifferent answer was given. I remember trying to make friends with the English officer from Sarawak, with the object of eliciting from him some facts about the place, but my questions did not meet with any very interesting responses, and I soon found out that I should have to make my own discoveries about the country, and from that moment I simply panted to understand the Malay language and make friends with the people belonging to the place.

Although here and there we met a few boats coming up the river, some of the reaches were deserted and silent as the grave. I was exceedingly lonely, and felt as though I had fallen into a phantom land, in the midst of a lost and silent world. But even in such out-of-the-way places people have to be fed, and I remember my first meal in Sarawak, brought to me by the Chinese steward. There were captain's biscuits, lumps of tinned butter slipping about the plate like oil, one boiled egg which had seen its best days, and the cup of Chinese tea, innocent of milk, which the Rajah and his friend seemed to enjoy, but which I thought extremely nasty. The quiet, matter-of-fact way in which they participated in this unpalatable meal surprised me, but I thought that perhaps I, too, might in time look upon such things as mere trifles.

At last, after steaming in silence for about two and

a half hours up the Sarawak River, I heard the boom-
ing of guns—the salute fired to the Rajah on his
return from England—and rounding the last reach
leading up to Kuching, the capital, I saw the Fort
on the right-hand bank on a hill covered with closely
cropped grass. I also saw the flagstaff from which
was flying the Sarawak flag. On the opposite bank
to where the Fort was situated stood a bungalow,
rather a homely looking house, with gables and
green-and-white blinds, the sight of which comforted
me. I was told that this was the house of the agent
of the Borneo Company, Ltd. This gives me an
opportunity of acknowledging, at the outset of my
book, the loyal, and at the same time civilizing
influence which this group of Scotchmen, members of
the firm, have always exerted in their dealings with
Sarawak and its people. This house once out of
sight, we steamed on past the Bazaar on the river's
edge, containing the principal shops of the town, and,
a little farther on, the same side as the Fort, I saw
the Astana,[1] composed of three long low bungalows,
roofed with wooden shingles, built on brick pillars
with a castellated tower forming the entrance.

On the steps of the landing-stage at the bottom
of the garden a great many people were standing.
These were the officials, English and native, and the
principal merchants of the place come to meet the
Rajah on his return. I saw four Malay chiefs, and
was told that they were prominent members in the

---

[1] Malay word meaning palace.

THE RAJAH'S ARRIVAL AT ASTANA AFTER A VISIT TO EUROPE

Rajah's Government. They wore turbans twisted in great folds round their heads, long flowing robes of black or dark-coloured cloth opening on to white robes embroidered with gold. Their feet were shod with sandals, and they carried long staves tipped with great golden knobs. Then I saw Chinamen, traders in the town, with their long pigtails, almond-shaped eyes, fat, comfortable-looking faces, all smiles, dressed in blue silk jackets and wide black trousers. There were also a few Dyak chiefs of neighbouring rivers, with beads and bangles on their legs and arms, and gaily coloured waistcloths of red and yellow and white. I saw about eight or ten Europeans in white uniforms and helmets, and two ladies, also dressed in white, the only European ladies then resident in the place.

As the *Heartsease's* anchor was dropped, a large green barge,[1] used on State occasions, covered with an awning and manned by about twenty Malays and Dyaks in white uniforms faced with black, their paddles painted in the Sarawak colours—yellow, black, and red—came to the companion-ladder to take us on shore. I remember the rhythmical noise made by their paddles as they rowed us the short distance to the landing-stage. When we stepped on land, all the people came forward and shook hands with the Rajah, who presented them to me. It took about ten to fifteen minutes to shake hands with them all.

---

[1] The barge was presented by the King of Siam to the late Rajah in 1851.

Then a strange thing happened, for which I was not prepared. A very picturesque old man, rather taller than the other Malays, dressed in a jacket embroidered with gold, black trousers with a gold band, his head enveloped in a handkerchief tied in a jaunty fashion, with two ends standing up over his left ear, came forward with a large yellow satin umbrella, fringed all round, which he opened with great solemnity and held over the Rajah's head. His name was Subu, and, as I learned, he occupied a great position in Sarawak: that of Umbrella Bearer to the Rajah and Executioner to the State. The Rajah trudged forward, the umbrella held over him, up the steps from the landing-place, and across the broad gravel path, lined with a guard of honour, leading to the house. At the entrance the umbrella was folded up with great reverence by Subu, who carried IT back to ITS home the other side of the river. I followed with the principal European officer present, and the other people who had met us came after us, up the path, and on to the verandah of the Astana. There we seated ourselves on cane chairs prepared for the occasion: the Rajah and myself in the middle of the company. For some minutes we all looked at one another in dead silence: then the oldest Malay chief present, the Datu Bandar, leaning forward with his head on one side and an intent expression, inquired, "Tuan Rajah baik?" (Rajah well?). The Rajah nodded assent. Then more silence: suddenly, the Rajah jumped up and

held out his hand as a signal of dismissal. Every
one took the hint, got up, shook hands with the
Rajah, then with me, and departed down the steps
and garden path to the boats waiting to convey them
to their homes.

I stood on the verandah and watched them go,
the Rajah standing by me. I turned to him.
"Where are the women?" I said. "What women?"
he answered. "The only English ladies staying
in the place came to meet you." "Oh," I replied,
"they do not matter. I mean the women of the
place, where are they?—the chiefs' wives and the
Malay women, why have they not come to meet
me?" "Malay women," replied the Rajah, "never
accompany the men on public occasions. It is not
their custom." "But," I said, "you are their Rajah.
What is the use of my coming here if I am not to see
the women of the place?" "Well," said the Rajah,
with a smile, "we shall see; things may be different
by and by."

In the evening the Rajah took me in his comfortable boat for a turn on the river. Three Malay
boat-boys sent us along; their paddles as they
struck the water were as rhythmic as a march tune.
We floated past the Malay portion of the town with
its brown houses made of palm leaves, their roofs
and walls so frail that "you might anywhere break
them open with your finger!" Moving westwards
we faced the great mountain called Matang, which
bars the sunset, its wooded sides and ravines

changing every moment of the day under the brilliant sunlight or passing clouds. The sunset behind Matang on that first evening I spent in Kuching was a memorable one. The dark purple mass seemed palpitating with mystery, standing out as it did against a background of crimson and rose and yellow.

CHAPTER II

SARAWAK is a land of mountains, of trees, and of water. Steaming from Singapore on your way to Kuching, you enter a great crescent-shaped bay called Datu. The most important rivers of Sarawak flow into this bay. At its southern end stands Tanjong Datu, rising to a height of 700 feet; and across sixty miles of sea in a northerly direction, almost opposite to this green cliff, is Tanjong Sirik, from whence the low and sandy coast runs in an almost straight line as far as Brunei. Harbourless and unprotected, this coast is lashed by the surf during the north-east wind from September to the end of March. During the south-west monsoon, which blows for the remainder of the year, fairer weather prevails, making easier communication between these river mouths and the rest of the world. If you approach Sarawak in the early morning, you can see from the deck of a steamer, cobalt blue mountains hanging baseless between earth and sky. Mists, white as snow-wreaths, encircle their wooded peaks only to melt away at the first rays of the sun and return to the land in refreshing showers later in the afternoon. Cascades born in the mountains, fed by daily rains, tear down their wooded ravines, rolling stones and trees and soil from their banks in their headlong course. Impetuous and irresistible, they widen as they go, until they become mighty rivers tamed by their passage through muddy plains, where they meander in sluggish ways.

The river-banks are lined with nipa palms and mangroves. At low tide you can see the mangroves, standing on trestles of black woody roots, looking like snakes writhing in the mud. Upon these pedestals, a crown of bright green leaves, thirty to forty feet in height, form aquatic forests at the mouth of the rivers all along the coast. Each branch is weighed down by a fruit, which, when ripe, drops into the mud and starts a new tree. The nipa palm has matted roots which easily retain the flotsam and jetsam carried down by the unceasing current of the waters; it has an angular fruit which, like that of the mangrove, sinks into the mud and forms forests on its own account. The incessant action of these encroaching trees add continually to the land. Indeed, there are certain aged natives who have been heard to say that part of the coast near Sirik, although exposed to the constant surf of the north-east monsoon, has encroached on the sea for two miles or more, during their lifetime. When the land reclaimed by the mangroves and nipa palms becomes dryer, the trees die, and give place to other tropical vegetation. On my travels in and out of these rivers, I have often seen, especially on a hot sunny day, the distant line of coast just before it recedes into the

DATU BAY NEAR SANTUBONG

horizon, looking as though it were lifted high up in the air, when, between the line of verdure and the sea, appeared a space of light as though the trees stood on rays of silvery transparency.

The rivers Lundu, Sarawak, Sadong, Batang Lupar, Saribas, Kalaka, and Rejang flow into the Bay of Sarawak. The rivers Oya and Muka (from which two rivers an important trade with sago is carried on), Bintulu and Baram, are situated in the more northern portion of the territory. Owing to the perpetual strife between land and water, these rivers have bars at their mouths, but the bar across the Baram is the most formidable amongst the rivers of the country.

Malays and Milanoes have their settlements on or near the coast, within reach of the tide. Malays are expert fishermen, and excel in boat building. They are Muhammadans, and are the most civilized of the Rajah's subjects. Milanoes inhabit the Rejang delta, the river-banks of Matu, Oya, Muka, and Bintulu, and are the sago workers of the country. Though mostly Muhammadans, they have a curious superstitious religion of their own. Land Dyaks dwell amongst the mountains and hills south of Kuching; Sea Dyaks frequent the Batang Lupar, Saribas, Kalaka, and the Rejang Rivers; Kayans live more inland, and their tribes are supposed to have settlements right across from west to east of the northern portion of Borneo; nor must we forget the Chinese immigrants who have settlements all over the princi-

pality, and who invade it in increasing numbers with
every succeeding year, greatly adding to the prosperity of the country. All these people are, as it
were, sprinkled over the land. If one could imagine
a giant sower dipping into a bag filled with the seeds
of mankind and flinging it out haphazard by handfuls,
some by the sea, and some by the inland rivers and
forests, it might give an idea of the manner in which
the population of Sarawak is scattered over the
country. The different tribes hold themselves
entirely aloof from one another; one never meets
with Dyaks residing in Malay settlements, or *vice
versa*, nor do the Chinese build among people of an
alien race.

It must be remembered that there are very few
roads in Sarawak, and as yet no railways; for it
can well be understood that road-making or laying
down railway lines would be a costly undertaking
in this country, intersected as it is by marshes, hills,
mountains, and almost unbridgeable rivers. Commerce and trade, however, thrive without the help
of such accessories, for Borneo is known to be one of
the best-watered countries in the world, and the produce of its jungles and its forests find an easy passage
down the numberless canals and rivers which nature
has provided through this watery land. Indeed,
it seems to me that there are three things one
cannot escape from in Sarawak : these being mountains, trees, and water. The sound of water is heard
everywhere; houses are built for the most part on

the banks of rivers or streams, so that the tide, as it swishes backwards and forwards, is heard by day and night; daily showers drip on to one's habitation, and the noise of paddles—for the people use the river as Europeans use their streets—is never lacking. Even the animals seem to imitate the sound of water in their morning and evening cries. For instance, the little monkeys, called wah-wahs, give vent, at the first approach of the sun, to liquid sounds, which, whenever I heard them, made me think of the Spirit of the rain pouring refreshing streams through the trees in which these monkeys congregate.

It is seldom that flowers form an important feature in the landscape of tropical countries. It is true there are flowers in profusion, but they are mostly hidden in the hearts of virgin forests. The purple blossoms of the lagerstremia, the golden cups of the allamanda, scarlet rhododendrons, and convolvuli, mauve and pink and white and yellow, sometimes star with flashes of colour the river-banks more inland; but orchids, pitcher plants, and flowering parasites are generally entangled and hidden in the branches of forest trees, for, like everything lovely, delicate, and perfumed, these have to be diligently sought for before a closer acquaintance can be made. One of the most ravishing experiences of Sarawak are the mysterious whiffs of perfumes meeting one unexpectedly in one's walks near the forests, or even on journeys up the rivers. These scented currents are messages from unknown blossoms

2

flowering unseen and unsoiled far from mankind. These rare and exquisite visitations always reminded me of the words of Maupassant, "*C'est une sensation de bien être qui est presque du bonheur.*"

Now to my mind the people of Sarawak match their strange and beautiful surroundings. They love sweet scents and flowers, and, above all, they love the neighbourhood of water, in which, as a fact, they live the greater portion of the day. Every man, woman, and child swims about the streams near their homes in the same way as we take our walks in our gardens. Men and women alike manage boats with wonderful skill, and women are often seen alone in canoes, paddling themselves in search of fruits or vegetables to be found on the banks of streams sometimes a great distance from their village. If you happen to throw in your lot with these people, you insensibly become, in the course of years, as fond of the water as they are, so that, like them, you find yourself perpetually bathing, and after any exertion have recourse to a bath, much as they plunge into the river to cool themselves. Moreover, they are perpetually washing their clothes—I have often thought I have seldom met cleaner people.

CHAPTER III

THE Rajah and I had only been a few weeks in Kuching when he had to leave me and go on an expedition to the interior, and I was left alone in the Astana with a maid whom I had brought from England. She was an ordinary sort of woman, with no capacity for enjoying anything that was not European. She left me soon after, for, as she said, she did not like living in such an outlandish place. With this solitary exception there was, at this time, no one in the Astana with whom I could speak, as I did not know Malay. There was, however, the Rajah's butler, a Sarawak Malay, who had been with the first Rajah Brooke for some years. At the Rajah's death, my husband took this man into his service. He was called Talip (a name signifying light). Talip knew a few words of English, and he and I became great friends. He was good-looking, taller than most Malays, with dark, intelligent eyes, a black moustache, and an abundant crop of hair forming a short curly fringe under his head-handkerchief, which he folded round his head with consummate skill. He was a bit of a dandy, and very neat in appearance. He wore a white jacket, under which appeared the folds of his yellow-and black sarong, white trousers, and he walked about with bare feet. He was a favourite with all

classes in Kuching, for his many years in the first
Rajah's service had endeared him to the people.

During the Rajah's absence I got a great deal of
information out of Talip, and the way he managed to
make himself understood in his broken English was
wonderful.   One day I said to him, " I want to see the
Malay women of Kuching.   Ask them to come here."
Talip answered, "Certainly.   I bring my two wives
play with you!"   I gently suggested that, together with
the two wives, the ministers' and chiefs' wives and
daughters might be included in the invitation.   After
talking the matter over, Talip and I settled that I should
hold a reception—my first reception in Sarawak—and
that he should be the chamberlain on the occasion and
invite, in my name, the principal women of the place.

My life now began to be interesting, for Talip and
I had a great many preparations to make and plans
to talk over.   The dining-room of the Astana was
large, and could accommodate about two hundred and
fifty guests.   I kept impressing on Talip that none of
the ministers' and chiefs' lady relations should be
forgotten, as it would never do to create jealousy on
this my first introduction to the women of the country.
I found out that the Datu Bandar, the Datu Imaum,
the Datu Temanggong, and the other chiefs all had
wives, sons, daughters, and grandchildren galore.
" They must all be invited," I said ; "for I must know
them and make friends with them."   I was then
initiated by Talip into the proper manner of giving
parties in Malayland.

First of all, the question of refreshments had to be considered. Talip invested in dozens and dozens of eggs, pounds and pounds of sugar, and I cannot remember the bewildering quantity of cocoa-nuts and of various other ingredients he deemed necessary for making Malay cakes. These he judiciously parcelled out to the houses of the people I was going to invite, so that they could make the cakes with which I was to present them when they came to call. Talip also borrowed from them cups, saucers, plates, and many other things wanted for such an important occasion.

Some days before the party, on looking out of my sitting-room window towards the landing-place and the path leading up from it to our door, I saw a number of little boys staggering under the weight of numerous round, red lacquer boxes. These were very large, and I sent for Talip and asked him what they were. He informed me that they were to be used for the various cakes and fruit in the same way as we use silver dishes. Talip arranged that on this great occasion we should all sit on the floor round the room, and that the place occupied by the chiefs' wives, with myself in their midst, should be set out with piles of gorgeous cushions covered with gold brocade—also borrowed from the houses of my guests.[1] A fortnight or so was occupied in the preparations, and at last the day came to which I had been looking forward so

---

[1] There is no greater pleasure one can give Malays than that of borrowing their things. Women, however, ungrudgingly lend their golden ornaments to each other, and the same may be said of their crockery, their furniture, their clothes, etc.

much. I glanced into the dining-room in the morning, and thought how pretty a meal laid out for Malay
ladies looked—very much prettier than the table
arrangements at our dinner-parties in England.
Great strips of white and red material, bought for the
occasion in the Bazaar, were laid down both sides of
the room with cross pieces at each end. The red
boxes were put at equal distances on these strips,
and between the boxes were dishes with the fruits
of the country—mangosteens, mangoes, oranges, pine-
apples, etc. The red lacquer boxes made beautiful
notes of colour all round the room.

The tea-party was supposed to begin at 4 o'clock,
so accordingly, I dressed myself in my best garments
and was quite ready to enter the dining-room and
receive my guests. I had heard a great deal of noise
going on outside my rooms since 2 o'clock in the
afternoon : the rustle of silks, bare feet pattering up
and down the verandah, and, becoming curious, I
looked over the partitions and saw women in silken
draperies flitting about. But Talip was on guard,
and every time I came out, or even looked over the
partitions, he said to me, "You must not show
yourself too soon." However, at 4 o'clock I was
dressed, and determined to go out, when Talip
again, like the angel with the flaming sword
at the gate of Paradise, waved me back. He
made me understand that I ought not to show myself before 5.30 on account of Malay etiquette, and
went on to explain that the Rajah's subjects should

A ROOM IN THE ASTANA

await my pleasure. In his opinion, 9 o'clock would
have been preferable for our meeting, but considering
my impatience he would allow me to enter the
dining-hall at half-past five! So another hour and
a half went by whilst I patiently waited to make the
acquaintance of my guests, on account of inexorable
Malay etiquette. I felt a little anxious, for I did not
know a word of Malay, so I took Marsden's Dictionary
with me, and armed with the great volume, at 5.30
punctually, made my entrance into the hall. I was
quite taken aback by the charming sight that awaited
me as I entered the dining-hall. The rows of women
and young girls seated on the floor round the room,
with their silken brocades and gauzy veils of rose,
green, blue, and lilac, reminded me of an animated
bed of brightly coloured flowers. I noticed what
beautiful complexions most of these women had, of
the opaque pale yellow kind, like the petals of a fading
gardenia. Their dark eyes and long eyelashes,
their arched eyebrows, their magnificent black hair,
their lovely feet and hands, and their quiet manners,
were to me quite entrancing. As I came into the
room, Talip told them to get up, and the sound of their
rustling silks, all moving together, was like a gentle
wind sighing through the branches of a bamboo forest.
Datu Isa and Datu Siti, the wives of the principal
Malay chiefs, came forward one on each side of me,
and, each placing one hand under my elbows and the
other under my finger-tips, led me to the seat prepared for me against the wall, in the middle of a row

of women.   My pile of cushions was uncomfortably
high, so I asked Talip whether I could not have two
pillows taken away, but he said : "No, that could not
be.   Rajah Ranee must have three cushions more
than the chiefs' wives."   Therefore, once again I gave
way to the conventions of Malaya.

Talip and his satellites appeared with huge jugs
of lukewarm coffee, made sweet as syrup to suit the
taste of my guests.   It was, however, devoid of milk,
as the Malays of Sarawak are unaccustomed to the
use of that liquid.[1]   It took some time to help us all,
but when each guest's cup was full, Talip stood in
the middle of the room and shouted out : "Makan !
la. . . . Minum ! la. . . . Jangan malu !" (Eat.
Drink.   Don't be ashamed).

After coffee, the real business of the day began.
Talip told me to say something to my guests, and that
he would translate my words into Malay.   "Datus,
Daiangs, my friends," I said, "I have sent for you
because I feel lonely without you.   I have come to
live here and to make friends with you all.   I have
waited for this day with great impatience, because I
know we shall love one another, and I feel sure if
women are friends to one another they can never feel
lonely in any country."   Talip translated my speech
at great length, and when he had finished, Datu Isa,
the wife of Datu Bandar the chief minister, bent
forward, her eyes cast down, her hands palm down-

---

[1] Some Malay women confided in me that they would not drink it,
as by so doing they might get to resemble animals.

wards on her knees, and replied, " Rajah Ranee, you are our father, our mother, and our grandmother. We intend to take care of you and to cherish you, but don't forget that you are very young, and that you know nothing, so we look upon you as our child. When the Rajah is away, as I am the oldest woman here, I will look after you. There is one thing you must not do : I have heard of Englishwomen taking the hands of gentlemen by the roadside. Now, Rajah Ranee, you must not do that, and when you are sad you must come to me, and I will help to lighten your heart." Talip translated this to me, and I smiled in response. But all the women kept that gravity which never leaves Malays when they are shy or nervous, or in the presence of strangers. I thought I would try a little conversation on my own account. I looked out some words in Marsden's Dictionary, and meant to inquire of Datu Isa how many sons she had. This remark thawed the ice, for a ripple of laughter went over the room. Instead of saying "sons" I had used the words "baby boys"—the old lady being seventy, no explanation is required! After that, we became very friendly. I consulted Marsden for the rest of the afternoon, and got on beautifully with my guests.

It is strange, even now, how well I remember that party : it might all have happened yesterday. From that eventful day my home-sickness completely vanished, for I felt I had found my friends.

CHAPTER IV

THEN began a very agreeable time, such as usually comes with a new and interesting friendship. I think the Malay women as well as myself were mutually interested in one another, and I encouraged the frequent morning visits that one or another of the chieftains' lady relations paid to me. I somehow managed to make myself understood, although my Malay must have sounded strange to them. Indeed, in their strenuous endeavours to understand what I said, I sometimes noticed a strained—I might almost say painful—expression flit across their faces. They were much too kind, however, to laugh or smile, or even to show a moment's impatience. Little by little matters mended, and in a few weeks I became more fluent.

That mighty question of "chiffons," which is usually thought to belong only to European womenkind, seemed to me to play quite as important a part in the minds of my new friends. One day, as I was admiring their beautiful silks, satins, and golden ornaments, Datu Isa (who was, you remember, the lady who had undertaken the care of me during the Rajah's absence) said to me in a very ceremonious manner,

DATU ISA AND HER GRAND-DAUGHTERS

"You are the wife of our Rajah, and you ought to wear our dress." I was simply delighted, and at once agreed. Lengthy discussions then took place as to what colours I should choose, and where the things should be made. Finally, the matter resolved itself into the Malay ladies joining together, and insisting on providing me with the whole dress, and I must say it was a beautiful one. The garment called "kain tape" (the Malay name for a woman's skirt) consists of a narrow sheath; this was folded and tucked under my armpits, and made to cover my feet. It was woven in red-and-gold brocade. My jacket was of dark blue satin, and had gold rosettes sewn over it. The collar of the jacket was edged with plaques of gold, fastening in front with a larger clasp, shaped like outstretched wings. All down the sleeves of the jacket, which were slashed up to the elbow, were tiny buttons of gold that jingled like bells. A gauzy scarf of white and gold, obtained from Mecca, covered my head, and a wide wrap of green silk and gold brocade was flung over the left shoulder ready to cover my head and face when wearing the dress in my walks abroad. According to Datu Isa, my right eye alone should peep forth from the golden wrap on such occasions.

Datu Isa had a great many things to say as to the wearing of these garments. "You are my child, Rajah Ranee," she said, "and I have thought a good deal as to whether, being a married woman, you ought to wear golden ornaments, because it is the custom in our country for virgins only to be thus decorated, but as you are the wife of our Rajah, I think that your Malay dress should be as splendid as possible, and we all agree that it will suit you well." I did not share in this opinion. I loved wearing the dress, because of its beauty, but if the truth were told, a tall English-woman cannot expect to wear it with the grace which belongs to those tiny frail-looking daughters of the sun. They are all very small indeed, and the noiseless way they move about lends additional beauty to the dress. No European woman, accustomed as she is to freedom, exercise, and somewhat abrupt movements, can possibly imitate with any degree of success the way in which they glide about and manipulate their silken and gauzy draperies.

It is interesting to know the ideas Malay women entertain about the wearing of these clothes. I was somewhat embarrassed with the length of my sarong, ordered by Datu Isa, and arranged by her so that it should fall in folds draggling on the ground. "Never mind, Rajah Ranee," she would say, "you will get accustomed to it by and by, and you must remember that the Rajah's wife never shows her feet." "But why?" I said to Datu Isa. "Because," she answered, "she is never supposed to walk about. She must have servants and subjects at her call every moment of the day. Now, if you wear that dress properly, you would not fasten it in very securely anywhere, but you would sit on cushions almost motionless, because at the slightest movement your clothes would fall off. The wives of the Sultan of Brunei never secure their kain tapes." This was all very well; moreover, it must be remembered that Datu Isa was strictly conservative. Her ideas concerning ceremonial dress and deportment in Sarawak were as rigid as were those of aristocratic old ladies in Early Victorian days. But Datu Isa's daughter-in-law, Daiang Sahada, who is about my own age, reassured me when I felt a little anxious as to whether I could play my part satisfactorily and not derogate from the exalted position Datu Isa was always striving to put me in. " We understand, Rajah Ranee," she would say. " You must not be too anxious; we all know Datu Isa; she is kind and good and you must humour her. Little by little, she will understand, and will not mind if you wear your kain tape so as to allow you to walk a yard or so."

But talking of these sarongs and the wonderful cloths manufactured by the women of Sarawak, it always surprises me when I consider, given the idea that Sarawak was such an uncivilized country when the first Rajah went there, and that its people were sunk in a state of barbarism, how it was possible that the womenkind of the Malay population living in the place evolved the marvellous embroideries and brocades that nearly all the women of Sarawak are capable of weaving.

The patterns on these golden cloths are very similar, for no kain tape worn by the better classes of Sarawak women is considered quite correct unless the stuff, powdered all over its ground of red silk with open rosettes made of gold thread, is divided by a broad band of different pattern marked in gold thread in a series of Vandyck-shaped lines, reminding one of the dog-tooth design. Inside each tooth is an ornament, supposed by some to represent trees of life. This design is apparently to be met with all over Malaya.

Nor is the making of these cloths at all an easy matter. To help to amuse me and to while away the time, Datu Isa and her maidens brought to the Astana a great loom prepared with golden and silk threads, to teach me how to weave these brocades. The loom was so large that one could sit inside it. A sort of pad made of wood supported one's back and acted as a lever with planks at one's feet to keep the thread taut. A shuttle in each hand threw the thread backwards and forwards in the usual manner, but the effort of keeping the thread tight with one's back and feet was a somewhat fatiguing experience. I must confess I never achieved many inches of these cloths, although it interested me much to learn the Malay methods of weaving them.

Datu Isa sometimes brought with her a friend, whom I got to know well. This lady was a Seripa, that is to say, a descendant of the great Prophet himself. Such descendants are numerous all over the Archipelago. I never quite made out how the many Serips[1] and Seripas[1] I met in Sarawak traced their descent from the great founder of Islam, but as their

[1] Arabic : Sherif and Sheripa.

countrymen and women accepted their great position,
it must have been unassailable, and I never attempted
to solve the mystery. Seripa Madjena's husband was
also a Serip, for female descendants of the Prophet
may not marry out of their rank, although Serips may
marry whom they please. Serip Hussin was employed as an overseer at one of the Rajah's coffee
plantations not far from Kuching. Datu Isa told me,
and I found out for myself, that Seripa Madjena could
do most wonderful embroideries. As she was a poor
woman, Datu Isa suggested that she should come so
many hours a day to the Astana to work for me and
to teach me her craft. Most Malay women, as I have
said before, are able to embroider, and their methods
greatly interested me. My first lesson was conducted
in this fashion. The Seripa was seated in the middle
of the floor of my sitting-room, and the lady Datus,
their friends, and I, were seated round her to watch
the proceedings. The Seripa asked for pieces of
foolscap, which she cut into broad bands of about nine
or ten inches wide and about a yard and a half in
length. She then folded them into about five layers,
and with a sharp penknife began punching out the
design through the top layer. The penknife went in
and out, cutting notches here, rounding circles there,
without any preliminary lines to guide it. In fact, the
Seripa was doing free-hand with a penknife! I had
prepared boxes of betel-nut and sirih for the refreshments of my guests. Datu Isa never moved without
her sirih box, and she prepared a mouthful of this

delicacy for me from her own store. She took a leaf of betel-vine, smeared it with a little shell-lime, stuck a small portion of the areca-nut on the lime, wrapped the leaf into a bundle, and presented it to me. "Bagus sekali" (very nice), she said, and watched the effect on me as I began munching at this Malay delicacy. I did not like it, but did my best to appear as though I did. When the ladies present had been presented with betel-nut and sirih, we sat chewing in a silence only broken by ejaculations from the Seripa, together with long-drawn sighs and invocations to Allah. "She is working in earnest," said Datu Isa. We all nodded assent, whilst giving vent to little grunts of approval. The punching went on, and the little scraps of paper lay like snow around the Seripa, who suddenly gave a louder sigh than usual and a more lengthy invocation to Allah, and shaking the pattern free from the cuttings of paper, we saw a delicate and flowing pattern of conventional leaves, of birds and of fishes, rustling itself free from her fingers to the floor. This improvised work over, she laid layers of foolscap one over the other, stuck them together, laid her prepared pattern on the top, and the punchings began afresh with the penknife. When the design was all cut out, the strip was laid over green satin stretched on a long, wooden frame, about a yard in length. We had chosen green, as it is the colour of the Prophet. The perforated pattern was stitched here and there on to the satin, and the Seripa worked gold thread backwards and forwards over the cardboard, until the design stood out from the satin background a compact mass of gold, recalling to my mind certain medieval church embroideries I knew of in Northern Italy, dating from the sixteenth century.

CHAPTER V

THE expedition which had taken the Rajah into the interior was only one among many he had to undertake in order that trade and commerce might be established in safety in remote parts of his kingdom. In Sarawak, epidemics of head-hunting are apt to occur unexpectedly amongst Dyak tribes, just as of late years the plague has unaccountably broken out afresh in different parts of the world.

One of the largest rivers in the country, the Rejang, whose waters are deep enough for 170 miles to float vessels and schooners of moderate size, has ramifications in the smaller tributaries which run in various directions into mountainous districts. On these hills, sometimes two or three thousand feet in height, Dyaks, who dearly love their independence and to feel the importance of being able to undertake skirmishes on their own account, build houses (to which they can retire temporarily for protection) on the precipitous sides of mountains and hills, like eagles' nests clinging to lofty peaks, and to which apparently only birds can soar. These people, however, climb like monkeys; their activity is wonderful, and when one of these tribes ensconces

34

SEA DYAKS IN WAR DRESS

itself in such inaccessible places it is difficult to dislodge and coerce it into moving to lower and more civilized portions of the territory. At the time of which I am writing, one of these tribes had been particularly tiresome. A Dyak chief, named Lintong,[1] had gathered round him a considerable force of followers, entrenched himself at the head of a stream, where he had managed to build a fleet of boats from the enormous forest trees which grew in the neighbourhood. At the head of his fleet, he harassed and plundered the more law-abiding inhabitants of the delta.

Mr. Harry Skelton, one of the Rajah's officers stationed at a place called Sibu, a fortified settlement sixty miles up from the mouth of the Rejang River, had incurred Lintong's displeasure owing to severe sentences he had inflicted on one or two members of the tribe, who had been caught red-handed. This made Lintong exceedingly angry, and one night, about a fortnight after my first arrival in the country, Lintong descended with his fleet of boats, manned by some three thousand men, and attacked Mr. Skelton's Fort just before daybreak. It was nearly taken by surprise, for Dyaks have a way of muffling the sound of their paddles, and although the Fort was built about twenty yards from the river, and the fleet came within earshot of it, no sound was heard by the sentries, notwithstanding that they were on the look out for any

---

[1] His *nom de guerre*, by which he was usually known, was Mua-ari, or the Face of Day.

emergency. "Face of Day" and his men landed, dashed up to the Fort with horrible yells and threw showers of poisoned arrows and pointed bamboo spears at the building. Sarawak Forts are all built on the same pattern—square stockades with watch-towers at each corner, made of planks of iron-wood, which no native missile can penetrate, being bullet proof. The stockade is about twenty feet high, and between that and the roof, to give air and light, is a trellis-work made of the same iron-wood which divides an overhanging roof, made of wooden shingles, from the wooden walls. The shingles are made detachable to prevent fire when the enemy throw lighted brands on the roof.

Sibu Fort was then garrisoned by thirteen Sikhs, under the command of Mr. Skelton. These Sikhs were ci-devant Indian Sepoys, who had been exiled to Sarawak as punishment for the share they had taken in the Indian Mutiny. These men, although rebels, were amongst the lesser offenders in the Mutiny, and subsequently proved themselves to be valuable servants to the Sarawak Government. They were fierce, magnificent-looking beings, very tall, and smartly conspicuous, with great turbans twisted round their heads, black beards carefully tended, and moustaches with aggressively curled ends. There were also staying in the Fort two or three Dyak chiefs and a recently joined English cadet, Mr. Low, son of Sir Hugh Low, who was then Colonial Secretary in Labuan. A few poisoned arrows and barbed bamboo spears found their way through the trellis-work of the Fort, but no one was struck by these missiles. The party in the Fort made a brave resistance, and in a short time the rebels were repulsed and sent flying to their boats on the beach, leaving about a dozen dead and wounded companions under the wooden walls, Lintong's son being amongst the slain.

The account which Mr. Skelton gave me when I saw him afterwards of the manner in which the friendly Dyak chiefs behaved during the skirmish amused me very much, for they did nothing but peer through the lattice-work, and shout Dyak insults at the attacking party, most of whom they knew very well. They made unpleasant remarks about the enemy's mothers, and inquired whether the men themselves belonged to the female sex, as their efforts were so feeble, etc. It appears the noise was terrific, the attacking party yelling, shouting, and screaming whilst the battle lasted.

It was this serious state of things at Sibu that had called the Rajah away from Kuching a few days after my arrival in Sarawak. He gathered round him some seven thousand Dyaks belonging to friendly tribes, and with Mr. Skelton and one or two other English officers led an expedition up the Rejang River into the interior of the country, and reduced the enemy to subjection. He deemed it advisable to remain at Sibu for some weeks in order to restore peace and order in this part of his country.

Meanwhile Lintong and his people were hiding in the head-waters of remote streams in the neighbourhood; and he and all his tribe became outcasts in the land. The Rajah's object was to persuade these people to confess the error of their ways, own themselves vanquished, make peace, and build a new village on the main river under the surveillance of the Rajah's neighbouring Forts. The Rajah's policy on many similar occasions was always the same : when he had succeeded in crushing the head-hunting ambitions of these tribes, the thing then to be done was to turn these people into decent subjects by making them understand that the benefits to be derived from trade and commerce were more satisfactory to their well-being than their methods of murdering and cutting off the heads of their often harmless neighbours.

About a month or six weeks had elapsed since the Rajah's departure from Kuching, when one morning a dispatch boat from the scene of action arrived at our landing-place with a letter from the Rajah, telling me that he would be back in two or three days. He wanted me to return with him to Sibu and stay for a month or so at the Fort. He mentioned that he was bringing one of the chiefs from the interior with him, because he thought it would interest me to see him and make his acquaintance.

I well remember the day of the Rajah's return. I was interested in hearing all the details of the expedition, whilst I had much to tell him about my new women friends. I think he was amused, in the course of my story, at Malay expressions I let fall with great pride and a good deal of ostentation. At the end of my narrative—and I must say I talked a good deal—I was rewarded by his saying, "Why, you have become a real Malay!"

That evening, after dinner, he sent for Apai Minggat, the chief who had accompanied him to Kuching. We were sitting in the dining-room when this individual entered, a middle-aged Sea Dyak chieftain, who had often fought the Rajah's battles by his side and saved his life on more than one occasion, for he was a famous warrior, with a considerable following of fighting men. He seemed to be tread-ing on eggshells, his toes were turned out, and his body bent. A dingy handkerchief was twisted round his head, which was clean-shaven, with the exception of a lock of hair hanging at the back of his neck; this he had retained, like all Sea Dyaks, in a spirit of true courtesy, in case his head were taken by an enemy, when this lock would serve as a handle for them to carry his head by. He had on a waist-cloth, and a dirty plaid covered his shoulders. He put out his hand from the folds of this garment to shake hands with the Rajah and with me.

I was anxious to hear a war yell, and I asked the Rajah to get him to give vent to one of these sounds of gratification heard when any heads are taken by Dyaks without loss to themselves. A curious falsetto sound issued from his lips. It went higher and higher, louder and louder, something between the crowing of a cock and the whistle of a steam-engine, and then it died down into a whisper. Two or three times he repeated this performance, which greatly interested me. It was not so terrible as I had imagined it must be, but the Rajah explained that when heard in a chorus of thousands of men, all yelling at once, as he had heard these sounds of victory after successful skirmishes against the pirates, it was a most terrifying experience, and froze the blood in one's veins.

Mr. Harry Skelton had also returned with the Rajah, and was our guest at dinner: this over, I got up as custom demands, and left the Rajah and his friend at their claret and cigars; but, not wishing to sit by myself, I made signs to the chief and took him with me into the drawing-room. There I sat in one of the arm-chairs, with the old Dyak at my feet. He removed his head-handkerchief, rubbed his head, and gave vent to strange sounds and groans. I sent for Talip, fearing he was ill. Talip, however, informed me, "He say he bad head he wants gin." I was rather shocked at this idea of Talip's, and thought he was maligning the old man. When Talip had left the room, happening to have a scent bottle in my hand filled with eau-de-Cologne, I poured some on my fingers and rubbed it on poor Minggat's head. This he seemed to enjoy, and made signs to me as though he found it soothing. The moment I left off, he signed to me to go on again, so on I went rubbing his head with eau-de-Cologne, and I remember that it smelt of cocoa-nut oil. Busily engaged as I was, I did not notice that the Rajah and Mr. Skelton had suddenly appeared in the room. I am sorry to say that the Rajah was not at all pleased at my token of sympathy with the old chief, and forthwith ordered him out of the room. "Poor old man," I said to the Rajah, "he has a bad head. Why should I not rub it with eau-de-Cologne?" The Rajah, with right on his side, replied, "If you encourage them in this way, how can you expect me to keep them in order?" Mr. Skelton was much amused, but he told me privately that such tokens of sympathy from a Rajah's wife, was not a very tactful way of behaving in an Oriental country.

CHAPTER VI

THE next day we embarked on the *Heartsease* for Sibu. My journey down the river was very different from my voyage to Kuching two or three months before, for everything now interested me. I wanted to talk to every native I came across. I wanted to find out what they thought and how they looked upon the things that we passed. My Malay was not brilliant even then, but still I could manage to make myself understood. We steamed past the Santubong Mountain, out to sea, and, of course, the minute we were bobbing over the waters of the bar (the sea was not rough) down I went into the cabin and took my usual position on such occasions—a mattress laid on the floor, a bucket by my side, and a bottle of champagne to ward off the sea-sickness. The heat was terrific. For five hours, until we got to the other side of the mouth of the Rejang, I was helpless, and the natives and everything else faded from my mind. Sea-sickness is much laughed at, but I know of no discomfort that equals it. However, it came to an end, and the smooth waters of the river on the other side soon put me right again.

When we arrived at Sibu, I was surprised to see

the extraordinary flatness of the land. Mr. Harry Skelton was most kind and considerate. He gave up his rooms to us, and nothing could exceed his hospitality. I well remember the first morning of my stay : it was all so different from the way things were managed on board the *Heartsease*. My breakfast tray was brought in by my Malay maid, who had accompanied me from Kuching. Mr. Skelton had arranged the tray himself : the captain's biscuits were there, but the tea was delicious ; somehow he had managed to get some cows, for there was milk. The boiled egg was new laid, and even the tinned butter was washed and pretended to be fresh. Then, in the middle of the tray, was a little bunch of flowers from his garden, jasmine, plumbago, and gardenia, tied in a ravishing effect of blue and white. I stayed in the Fort about six weeks, and every morning these charming flower tokens of Mr. Skelton's kindness were carried in to me with my breakfast. But what interested me more than anything were our evening walks. There was a Bazaar where the Chinese had, even in those days, a considerable settlement. As the sun set and the air became cooler, the Rajah, Mr. Skelton, and I set out for our walk, but not before Mr. Skelton had sent for the four Sikhs who were to guard us during our constitutional with loaded muskets. We would sally forth round the settlement, in the middle of our four protectors, for there were usually some bad characters about who were discontented at the turn affairs had taken, and Mr. Skelton was not very certain that in the long grass near by there might not be some one hiding, who, in a fit of insanity, might attempt our lives. On the other hand, I rather liked the idea. One felt oneself important being guarded by men with loaded muskets, and I must say I did not believe in the danger, owing, probably, to my scant knowledge of the country.

Two or three days afterwards we went up the river to visit some of the tribes, for, as I have said before, the Rejang is a long river, with villages dotted here and there along its banks. Another surprise was in store for me : when I went on board, I found that wire-netting had been stretched fore and aft the vessel, so as to secure it from any attack. When we were inside, and the wire-netting securely fastened all round us, we must have looked like animals in a cage ! We started early in the morning. The sun had hardly risen, and there was a thick fog which hid the land. There was a freshet coming down the river, the effect of heavy rain of the day before in the mountains farther inland. Our speed did not exceed eight knots an hour. In a very short space of time the fog began to lift, and we could see the flat, marshy land through which we travelled. It was bitterly cold, and I remember that I wrapped three or four railway rugs round my shoulders, over my white muslin dress, prepared as I was for the intense heat with the advent of the sun. Cocoa-nut and a few sago palms were planted on the banks,

for the water here was brackish, but there were no
other signs of cultivation. Near the Fort the river is
about twelve hundred yards wide. There were signs
of jungle everywhere, the ancient sites of cleared
rice lands, with creepers, small trees, and coarse lalang
grass covering the soil. There were no virgin
forests on these banks. In former years these
were the Dyaks' farm grounds, but the people
had long since removed up the river to plant their
paddy in its tributary streams. Farther up, the banana
and sago plants were replaced by the shrub called
rengas, resembling, in the distance, a hedge of clipped
holly; but on closer examination, although its leaves
are dark and shiny, they are more like laurels in
shape with young shoots of brilliant red. The wood
of this shrub is valuable, and is used a good
deal for making furniture by the carpenters in the
Straits. It has peculiar and disagreeable effects on
certain persons. Some natives can lop off its
branches without its doing them the slightest harm,
whilst others, if they but attempt such work, become
swollen, and are sometimes absolutely blinded, or are
made uncomfortable in various other ways for hours,
even if they merely touch or turn aside its branches.
On the other hand, those who are immune from its ill-
effects can approach the plant with impunity, hack it
about as they choose, and can thus obtain its young
shoots, which make an excellent dish when boiled as
a vegetable. After a time we could see nothing
but low, green hills on the edge of the water,

and everlasting masses of driftwood hurrying down
on the freshet to the sea. This kind of landscape continued for another hour or so, when the banks began
to close in, and we saw here and there bright vermilion
patches about the green grass near the water. These
were made by clerodendron blossoms, a flower of
predilection amongst the Sea Dyaks. They have a
kind of reverence regarding it : they decorate the
heads of enemies taken in battle with its spiky
blossoms, for they imagine that by so doing they will
prevent the curses uttered by the victims in the next
world from falling on their heads. They plant its
roots round their houses, so that whenever one sees
these flowers on the banks, it generally denotes that
once the land was occupied by Sea Dyaks. No one is
allowed to cut the flower or injure it in any way, for
it is only used for sacred purposes or during head-
feasts. When I first saw the flowers they were
growing amongst the lalang grass, and looked like
great coral chandeliers set in a background of
malachite. They are called by the Dyaks " Pemula
Sumpah." Then, we passed several tributary streams
famous in Sarawak history for the many expeditions
the Rajah and his officers have led there, for this district was formally the haunt of the most redoubtable
head-hunters. Like all the rivers of Borneo the
Rejang forms a succession of cataracts near its source,
and behind these it was easy for the Dyaks to imagine
themselves safe to indulge in their favourite pastime
of head-hunting. We had been steaming for hours,

when late in the afternoon we passed Kanowit on the left-hand bank of the river. It was at this spot, in 1859, that Messrs. Fox and Steele, two of the first white Rajah's officers, were murdered through the disaffection of a few natives, and at the instigation of Serip Masahor, one of the very few traitors in Sarawak history. This man ended his days in exile at Singapore. We now came to a series of little hills shelving into the water. The formation of these hills is somewhat peculiar : they are regular in outline and, all being of the same height and wooded with jungle growth, with a few ancient forest trees at their summit, it would seem as though a straight line might be drawn all along their tops, each hill touching the line at its highest point. They rise to a height of 750 feet. There was a kind of brushwood growing on the hills whenever farming had been of recent date, and groves of wild bananas grew here and there. I think the long fronds of the banana plant are amongst the loveliest growing things one can see. When the plants find a sheltered position, unmolested by gales of wind, their long leaves are tinted with the most wonderful colours, as though emeralds and sapphires had been melted together and poured over them ; moreover, a certain bloom rests on them, like that seen on grapes and plums. I think this beautiful effect depends on the light in which the plants are growing, for I have noticed the same bloom spread over ferns growing in dells and shady nooks of virgin forests. It might be as well to mention that Malays often use banana fronds to bind up wounds; their coolness, softness, and purity possessing healing properties absent from ordinary poultices.   These wild bananas thrive luxuriantly on recently abandoned paddy lands, until masses of other weeds grow up and choke them.   The plant possesses an excellent fibre, its fruit being bright green, small, and hard.   The look of such deserted farms is exceedingly pathetic as they stretch along the banks of rivers or climb the sides of steep hills. Here and there are trees, once lofty and magnificent, partially turned to tinder, their charred trunks standing brown and shrivelled from out the green vegetation.   Sometimes they become draped with parasites and creepers.   I remember one such charred skeleton, over whose shrivelled remains the bright yellow blossoms of the allamanda flung a curtain of green and gold.

As we proceeded up the river, I remember noticing men in boats fishing inside little creeks, who, I was told, were Sea Dyaks or Kanowits.   These little creeks were barred across from bank to bank with bamboo palisades to prevent the egress of fish into the main river, for the streams had been poisoned with a root called tuba, a method of fishing prevalent all over Borneo.   This root is pounded with pestles, its juice extracted, and thrown into the river at low tide, when the fishes become stupefied, and rise to the surface, so that the natives find no difficulty in netting or spearing them.   These people were drawing up nets full of fish as we passed, but, as is their wont, when they saw the vessel and the Rajah's flag flying at the main, they shouted to us, excitedly inquiring where we had come from and where we were going. I sat on the deck looking about me, and, as I thought, taking most things in, when apparently from out of nowhere a boat suddenly appeared full of Dyaks under our companion ladder, clamouring to be let in for a few words with the Rajah. The Rajah and Mr. Skelton (both of whom knew every one in the district), could distinguish whether the people were friends or enemies. When friends, the engine was stopped, the companion ladder let down, and the chiefs came solemnly on board, after our wire netting had been opened to allow them to enter. The chieftains' followers remained where they were, their canoes drifting astern of our vessel, and were towed up the river while the chiefs held conversation with the Rajah. Before we got to the end of our journey, our ship was towing along a little flotilla of canoes filled with dusky warriors.

A place called Ngmah was our destination, where was a Fort built on the top of a hill. We anchored beneath the hill for a night and then returned to Sibu. Our journey up river, against the freshet and tide, had taken us two days to accomplish ; ten hours sufficed to float us back to our headquarters at Sibu. Then our usual life at Sibu began again for another fortnight—the breakfasts, the little bunches of flowers,

4

and the walks at sunset round the settlement—when the Rajah went up river again. On this occasion he did not take me with him, but he left Mr. Skelton and Mr. Low to look after me in the Fort.

The Rajah had not been gone a week, when one morning, just as day was breaking, I was awakened by the noise of two muskets being fired from the Fort. I got out of my mosquito curtains, just as I was, tied a sarong over my nightgown, and rushed out of the room. I met Mr. Skelton on his way to warn me that in the semi-darkness preceding dawn, the Sikhs on the look out had noticed what seemed to be two long Dyak boats floating down the river. They had not answered to the challenge from the Fort, and, fresh from the previous attack, Mr. Skelton imagined another disturbance was imminent. My room had to be given up to two fortmen, who were posted with armed muskets to defend that portion of the building, and Mr. Skelton, Mr. Low, and myself congregated in the sitting-room. It was an exciting time, for we all thought that at any moment we should hear the yell of the Dyaks rushing up to attack us. I recollect so well Mr. Skelton, fussy and excited, fearing I should be frightened: but I was really rather enjoying all this commotion, never thinking it strange that we should be sitting together in our night garments; indeed, that fact never entered our heads at all. I suggested to Mr. Skelton, as I did not then know how to manage a musket, that I should sit behind the cottage piano I had brought with me from Kuching, as it would serve for a rampart against poisoned arrows or spears that might find their way into the Fort. Mr. Skelton agreed, and I ignominiously took my post behind the piano. We were all on the look out, our nerves strained to the utmost. Daybreak appeared and we could see all round the Fort, but still nothing happened. I hardly like to confess that I was rather disappointed. Every five minutes, Mr. Skelton invited me to partake of some ham which he had just procured from England, and some soda-water, evidently thinking that these would have a soothing effect on my nerves! We waited and waited, and at last I thought I might just as well go back to bed. Then a most delightful incident occurred. Our Chinese cook, whom we had brought from Kuching, anxious to show his zeal and valour, offered Mr. Skelton to take his post at my door with his large carving knife. Of course Mr. Skelton allowed him to do so, and, thus guarded, I turned into my mosquito net and had an hour's sleep. When I awakened the sun was shining, and all fear of the attack had passed. It is a well-known thing that Dyaks always choose the hour just before dawn to raid any settlement. I think Mr. Skelton was rather annoyed at his mistake.

When the Rajah returned from his trip, he was vexed at what had taken place, for he did not think it possible that another tribe of Dyaks up the Rejang River would have dared another attack so soon after the last one.   Moreover, it would have been impossible for them to have done so, as his gunboat *Heartsease*, with himself on board, was at the time stationed in the higher reaches of the Rejang River. I fancy the real truth of the matter was, that Mr. Skelton and his fortmen had become over-anxious, and I imagine my presence on the occasion also had something to do with it.   It was whispered afterwards that two enormous tree trunks, borne down past the Fort by the current (in the semi-darkness just before dawn when it is difficult to distinguish objects at a distance), were the harmless factors of this scare. Nevertheless, I must again repeat, I was disappointed at the tame manner in which the expected attack fizzed out.

CHAPTER VII

THE Rejang River deserves a few words of explanation. It is a magnificent roadway to commerce in the interior, and once the head-hunting propensities of the tribes in its neighbourhood are abolished, it promises to be a great centre of activity and trade. A large number of Kayans and Kenyahs are to be found in its tributaries. These people are, next to the Sea Dyaks, the most important and advanced of the tribes of Sarawak, and are scattered about the country in various rivers. They have attained a fairly high degree of civilization, whilst other tribes consist of primitive people called Punans, Ukits, and Bukitans. These do not cultivate land, but rely on the wild fruits and game they find in the forests. Curiously enough, however, as though to show they have descended from a higher civilization, they are able to manufacture the weapon in use amongst so many Bornean tribes—that thing we call the blow-pipe.[1] The Punans make their temporary homes under leafy shelters, in limestone caves, or in the buttresses of huge trees, called

[1] Nowadays Punans, Bukitans, and most of the Ukits live in houses and do some farming.

Tapangs, which afford shelter to whole families. When they have exhausted the surrounding localities of their fruits and game, they wander off to some other spot, where their life begins afresh. Notwithstanding their wild state, these people weave beautiful mats and baskets from palms gathered in the vicinity. They ornament such articles with patterns which must have been handed down to them from time immemorial—another proof of their probable degradation from a higher form of existence. A favourite pattern of theirs is the Greek "key" pattern. They are very shy, and might perhaps—from fear, but not from malice—kill a stranger wandering near their settlements.

After remaining some weeks in the Rejang, and when peace had been restored amongst the disturbed people, who began to resume work on their farms, the Rajah and I left Sibu and our kind hosts, Mr. Skelton and Mr. Low, for a trip to the Batang Lupar. We embarked once more on the *Heartsease*, and steamed down the left-hand branch of the Rejang, when, on leaving the mouth of the river, we steered due south, passing the mouths of the Kalakah and Saribas Rivers. We had, alas for me, about four hours of sea to negotiate before we found smooth water again, so that I did not see much of the coast. The sea was supposed to be calm, but a hateful swell drove me to the cabin. I went on deck after we had passed over the bar of the Batang Lupar. I could not believe it to be a river; the shores were so far off, with a stretch of four miles of water between them, and this width continued all down the straight reach as far as Lingga.

Lingga was a desolate place. Its Fort was built on a mud-bank. A small Malay village, its houses built on stilts, lined the banks, and were surrounded by cocoa-nut palms, which palms are said to flourish in brackish water. The present Rajah made this place his home for one year, moving from thence in 1854. He resided in this Batang Lupar district for about ten years, whence he led many punitive expeditions into the interior. The old pirate chief, Rentap, who committed so many crimes, murdered so many people, and prevented peace from settling on the land, was entrenched with his miscreant tribe in neighbouring mountains, and was repeatedly attacked by the present Rajah, who finally dislodged him from his fastnesses, and rendered him harmless by his many defeats. It was from the banks of the Batang Lupar River that the Rajah's friendly Dyaks, sometimes numbering twelve to fourteen thousand men, were gathered together to follow their white chief in his many attacks against the pirate's Fort. For years the present Rajah is said never to have slept securely on account of the incessant alarms and attacks on innocent people by this inveterate head-hunting pirate, who, in spite of a very advanced age, managed to work so much havoc in the neighbourhood.

We did not land at Lingga on this occasion, but

went on to a settlement near a place called Banting, where the Society for the Propagation of the Gospel had charge over a thriving community of Christians. Bishop Chambers, whose name can never be forgotten in the annals of Sarawak, here began his work of civilization as a missionary. He was a great friend of the present Rajah, and for many years, these two men, in their different ways, worked unremittingly for the good of the natives. This missionary settlement is about fifteen miles by river from Lingga, and it was here that I had my first experience of travelling in a Dyak war-boat.

These vessels are comfortable enough, being about seven feet wide amidships by about seventy feet in length. A crew, numbering some fifty, paddled us along. A roofed compartment in the middle of the canoe, furnished with mattresses and pillows, afforded us comfortable accommodation, and curtains hanging from the roof kept off the heat and glare from the river in the daytime; whilst the rhythmical noise of the paddles, and occasional wild bursts of songs from the crew helped to make the journey a pleasant one.

As the crew shipped their paddles, I saw a long Dyak house, propped on stilts about forty feet high, planted some yards from the river-bank. As this place was situated within reach of the tide and we arrived at low water, a vast expanse of mud stretched between us and dry land. I could see nothing in the way of a landing-stage to help our way to the house, excepting a few poles dovetailing one another laid across the mud, supported by trestles. I wondered how I was to get across, but not liking to make inquiries of an unpleasant nature, I said nothing; it is better in any emergency to let events take their course with as little fuss as possible, so that when our canoe was pushed by the side of the supported poles, I kept silent. I remember noticing how cleverly our Dyak crew manœuvred our boat, plunging knee-deep into the mud in their efforts, and yet moving about quickly all the time. The Rajah led the way and walked along some six or seven yards of the poles leading to the Dyak village. I admired the way in which he kept his balance, never slipping once during the journey. When my turn came, four Dyaks helped me out of the boat. My progress across the poles was not a graceful one, for I found them to be as slippery as glass. My four supporters, two on each side of me, must have suffered severely, as I slid first on one side and then on the other. However, their kindly efforts prevented me from taking headers into the mud. But my troubles were not yet over. I saw, leaning against the house at a steep angle, another long pole with notches cut in it all the way up to the door of the building. I saw the Rajah hopping up this small cylindrical stairway with the agility of a gazelle. No explanation was given to me, but the Dyaks signed to me that I had to do the same, so I tried to climb the pole. It was only about twenty inches in circumference, so it will be realized that this was a disconcerting sight to a person unaccustomed to acrobatic feats. However, the Rajah seemed to take it as a matter of course, and I tried to do the same, but the difficulty of turning one's feet out to the right angle was very trying at first. I clasped the pole with great fervour as I went up, and one of the Dyaks behind me took hold of my ankles, placing my feet on each notch with great care. A Dyak in front of me held my left hand and with my right I clutched the bamboo pole, and thus, with a good deal of slipping and a great deal of fright, I managed to reach the verandah of the house.

An extraordinary thing happened on this visit. In every Dyak house of note—and this was the residence of a great Dyak chief, called Banting— a portion of the building is assigned entirely to the women of the tribe. On this occasion, the women were anxious that I should visit them in their room, which I did. The room was a large one and was simply crammed. A little stool covered with yellow calico and a fine Dyak mat were prepared for me, and the women and children squatted all round me on the floor. They took hold of my hands and pushed up my sleeves to see if my arms were white all the way up. I had with me one of the Mission people, who acted as interpreter. He told me that the women wanted me to give them medicine to make their noses stand out from their faces as mine did ; they also wanted medicine to make their skin white. Babies were brought to me to touch, and I promised to

SEA DYAK WOMAN WEAVING A COTTON PETTICOAT

send them pills for their various ailments from Kuching. The women gave me a basket they had made for me, and then showed me their mats which they make so cleverly, their hats, and their paddles—much in the same way English women would show their collection of fans. The conversation went on merrily, when suddenly we heard some ominous cracks underneath our feet, and before I knew where I was, the flooring had given way and the women and children, the interpreter, and I, were plunged about four feet through the floor. We hung in bags, as it were, for the mats covering the floor were secured to the sides of the walls, and these prevented us from dropping to the ground below. The Dyak warriors sprang forward and helped me into safety. The women screamed, and I never heard such a noise in all my life. The Rajah, in the distance, sat imperturbably on, as though nothing out of the way was happening. I think he could see there was no great danger and that the mats would support us. When the dignity of the situation allowed him to do so, he came to where the accident had taken place and said to me, " It is all right, the room was overcrowded. You had better come into the verandah and then everything will be quite safe." He was pleased with the manner in which I had taken this catastrophe, and the Dyak chiefs told him it was evident that I knew how to behave in emergencies.

We then returned to our boats. To make a long

story short, I found the return down the notched pole even more difficult than the going up, but it is wonderful how soon one gets accustomed to anything out of the ordinary run of things, and I went away from Banting very much delighted with my experience in the first Dyak house I had visited.

We rejoined the *Heartsease* at Lingga and steamed to Kuching, which we reached the next morning.

CHAPTER VIII

SOME months had gone by since the day of my first arrival in Kuching and, odd as it may seem, Europe and all its ways were relegated as it were to an almost imperceptible background in my memory. The charm of the people, the wonderful beauty of the country, the spaciousness, and the absence of anything like conventionality, all enchanted me. Moreover, the people were my own, and every day that passed—and I am not ashamed to own it—little by little I lost some of my European ideas, and became more of a mixture between a Dyak and a Malay. The extraordinary idea which English people entertain as to an insuperable bar existing between the white and coloured races, even in those days of my youth, appeared to me to be absurd and nonsensical. Here were these people, with hardly any ideas of the ways of Europeans, who came to me as though they were my own brothers and sisters. They must have thought some of my ways curious and strange, but instead of finding fault with them, they gave way to me in everything. I suppose they saw how ready I was to care for them and consider them as members of my family, and as the country became more familiar to me, little by little, much as when one develops photographic plates, some hitherto unperceived trait in their character came out and charmed me.

I wish I could give a description of our home in Kuching as it appeared to me then and as I think of it now. How I delighted in those many hours spent on the broad verandah of our house, watching the life going on in the little town the other side of the river. I think I have said before that at high tide the breadth of the river where it runs under the banks of our garden is as broad as the Thames at Westminster Bridge. The little town looked so neat and fresh and prosperous under the careful jurisdiction of the Rajah and his officers, that it reminded me of a box of painted toys kept scrupulously clean by a child. The Bazaar runs for some distance along the banks of the river, and this quarter of the town is inhabited almost entirely by Chinese traders, with the exception of one or two Hindoo shops. The Chinese shops look very much like those in small towns on the Italian Lakes. Groceries of exotic kinds are laid out on tables near the pavement, from which purchasers make their choice. At the Hindoo shops you can buy silks from India, sarongs from Java, tea from China, and tiles and porcelain from all parts of the world, laid out in picturesque confusion, and overflowing into the street. Awnings from the shops and brick archways protect purchasers from the sun, whilst across the road all kinds of boats are anchored, bringing produce from the interior of Sarawak, from the Dutch Settlement, from Singapore, and from adjacent islands ; these boats are

MAIL STEAMERS' WHARF AND TRADING VESSELS AT ANCHOR NEAR EMBANKMENT IN KUCHING BAZAAR

picturesque in the extreme. The Chinese junks were always a delight to me, with their orange and tawny sails drying in the sun, and the large "eyes" painted in the bows to enable the vessels to see their way during their journeys. Dutch schooners with their horizontally striped flag of blue, white, and red are to be seen, and English, French, and Siamese flags also fluttered amongst the many masts carrying the Sarawak colours. The most important portion of the Bazaar lay behind the wharf, where the mail steamer was moored, then bringing mails every ten days from Singapore. The Chinese houses of the Bazaar are decorated with coloured porcelains; one sees green dragons, pink lotuses, little gods and goddesses in grotesque attitudes, all along their fronts. The roofs are of red tiles, some of these being higher than the rest and having the curious Chinese termination at each end, thus breaking the line and making it more picturesque. Behind the Bazaar rise a succession of hills, on which are situated European bungalows surrounded by pleasant gardens of flowers and fruit. The houses with their white walls and green and white painted blinds make a charming accessory to the background of forest trees. Churches of the different denominations stand out prominently in the landscape, for all Faiths enjoy the same privileges and freedom at the hands of the Sarawak Government. One sees the Roman Catholic and Protestant churches, Chinese temples marvellously decorated, Hindoo shrines, and Muhammadan mosques. Right opposite to the Palace stands the gaol and court-house, the latter a broad, low building with a castellated tower at its entrance.   The Malay town lies towards the west, along the banks of the river, and beyond the town stretch miles and miles of flat forest land.

When I was in Kuching, it seemed to me that the machinery of life was moved by clockwork, the Rajah being the most punctual man alive.   At five o'clock in the morning, just before daybreak (we must remember that in those latitudes there is scarcely any difference in the length of days), a gun was fired from the Fort, at which signal the Rajah jumped out of bed. Wishing to do the same as the Rajah, the Europeans, Malays, Dyaks, and Chinese jumped out of bed too. One had to dress and bathe by lamplight, and just as one came out to drink one's morning tea, the sun rose. At six o'clock, Kuching was fairly astir, and the Rajah and I used to go across in our boat (for there is no bridge anywhere over the river) to the landing-place below the court-house, where our horses were awaiting us. Mounting our animals was occasionally fraught with difficulty.   Our Syces (grooms) in Sarawak were mostly recruited from the Buyan people of an island off Java, who are extraordinarily sympathetic in their treatment of animals.   For instance, my pony had been bought in Labuan, chosen from out a herd of wild ponies which roam about the plains of that more northern portion of Borneo.   The pony had never been broken in properly, according to our European ideas of what a horse's perfect manners should be, and very often as

I approached to mount the animal (he was only about thirteen and a half hands high) he would turn round and round. I would say to the Syce, "Try and keep him still," whereupon the Syce would reply, "He doesn't want to keep still!" Therefore so long as it suited the pony to turn round and round, the Syce turned round and round too. It generally took some time before the pony became amenable, when I would seize the moment and scramble on to his back as best I could. This kind of thing went on nearly every morning before I started for my ride. In those days, with the exception of a few paths in and out of the town, there was only one well-made road extending for about a mile and a half into the country. Up and down this road, the Rajah and I pounded on our horses for the necessary exercise which every one must take, whether in or out of the tropics.

On coming home, we found the gateway into the Palace full of all sorts of people—Malays, Dyaks, and Chinese—anxious to see the Rajah. The Rajah never refused to see any one, and after hearing their complaints, he dismissed them kindly with a few words of advice. The motley morning crowd always reminded me of pictures in the Bible stories of my childhood, for there were turbaned Hajis in their flowing robes, women draped in dingy folds of cotton from head to foot, youths, maidens, and sometimes little children, crawling, walking, running, or jumping down the path after their interviews, but whether chieftains or beggars, Seripas or women of a lower

5

class, there was always an innate dignity belonging to these people ; they could not look common or vulgar however much they might try to do so.

This business over, the Rajah issued forth from the Astana with the yellow satin umbrella held over him by the redoubtable Subu. Four Malay chiefs, dressed in flowing robes and holding their golden-knobbed sticks, accompanied him to the Court, where five days in the week the Rajah dispensed justice from 8 to 10.30. a.m. A retinue of young men and boys, who had paddled the chiefs to the Palace, followed the procession. I used to watch the boats crossing the river to the landing-place, when Subu once again held the umbrella over the Rajah's head to the door of the Court. There, the umbrella was furled, when Subu, the umbrella, the Rajah and his ministers, disappeared from my view into the building.

I then went to my rooms, where I usually found some Malay women waiting to see me. On one occasion, I was sitting with two or three Malay friends having coffee in the morning, when a young Chinese girl, in a cotton sarong and Malay jacket, dashed into the room, followed by one of the Guards. Her face was covered with scratches, her arms were one mass of bruises, and round her neck was a red mark as though she had been half strangled. She rushed up to me, caught hold of both my knees, and said : " I hope in you because you are the Rajah's wife. The place I am in is a wicked one. I am a servant to a

Chinese woman who is jealous of her husband. When her husband goes out, she locks me in a room and beats, scratches, and tortures me in every possible way, because she thinks her husband looks upon me with favour. I will stay with you always, I will not leave you, for if I go back to those people the woman will kill me." The girl was very pretty, with a pale yellow skin and beautiful eyes, and I could quite understand that any woman might feel jealous of such an adjunct to her household. I sent the Guard away, and told the girl she might remain in a corner of my room until the Rajah came back from the Court. Meanwhile, her employers, finding she had run away from their house, had straightway gone to the Court, where the Rajah was then sitting, and an application was made for an order compelling the runaway to return. The Rajah, being told that the girl had gone to the Palace and not knowing the rights of the story, sent some police to bring her to him over the water. When I was told that they were below, the girl took hold of my gown, and said that if she was to go across to the courthouse, I was to go too to protect her. I had with me at the time, the wives of the three chief ministers of the Rajah's Council, so we held a discussion as to what was to be done. They were all on my side, and urged me not to let the girl accompany the police sent by the Rajah. I must say I felt rather nervous. "Never mind," they said: "if our husbands make any difficulty, when they come home they shall know it. You do the same with the Rajah, and let us save the girl if we possibly can. Moreover, when the rights of the matter are known and they see how dreadful the girl looks, they too will not wish to send the girl back to her employers, but will see the justice of our decision." When the Rajah came back from the Court, and heard the details of the story, he decided to keep the girl at the Palace. Meanwhile, the matter was inquired into, and the woman who had been so cruel was punished by having to pay a fine of money to be given to the girl, who became one of my servants, and remained with me some time, until a kind English lady, then living in Kuching, took a fancy to her, and with the Rajah's permission took her into her service as lady's maid. In course of time this victim of unjustifiable jealousy found a Chinese husband, and I believe the couple are still living in Kuching under comfortable circumstances.

A day or two after this incident, a war-boat full of Dyaks, headed by their chief, arrived in Kuching and came to the Astana to see the Rajah. If I remember rightly, these Dyaks had been, until recently, enemies of the Sarawak Government, owing to the usual failing—their love of head-taking. They had come to lay their submission before their ruler, and to express contrition for their misdeeds, whilst promising to behave better in the future. The Rajah wished to hear what the chief had to say, and gave him an audience in his private room. The chief's followers, about fifty in number, who were not wanted at this interview, were left on the verandah, and the Rajah asked me to keep them amused and occupied whilst he was engaged with the chief. As the Rajah and the chief disappeared down the stairway leading to the study, I made signs to the warriors to follow me into our drawing-room, thinking its furniture, so new to them, might prove of interest. They wandered about in a desultory way, and as I could not speak to them (not knowing their language) I opened the piano and struck a note or two. These sounds apparently delighted them, and I made signs to them to sit on the floor whilst I played that ordinary piece of music, the *Danse Nègre*, by Ascher. Grunts of satisfaction and noddings of heads intimated their approval of my performance. As I went on, I noticed that the rhythm of the music acted on them somewhat strangely. They reminded me of a number of marionettes with strings attached to their arms and legs, moved by invisible hands in time to the music. Their bodies, arms, and legs jerked spasmodically, and before I quite realized what was happening, they all sprang to their feet and bounded about the room, yelling and waving their arms in the throes of an animated war-dance. I did not know how to stop them, and felt apprehensive for the safety of the furniture and knick-knacks placed about the room ; indeed, one large palm tree standing in a pot in a corner was nearly hurled to the ground. As the noise grew louder, the bounds higher and higher, and I myself playing louder and louder, I wondered what would happen, when, in the midst of all this turmoil, the Rajah and the chief appeared in the doorway. The warriors stopped suddenly and looked rather sheepish ; some scratched themselves, while others cleared their throats, and they all flopped down in squatting positions on the floor. I went on playing for a little while after the Rajah had come in. The chief said something to his followers, and the Rajah dismissed the company kindly. We all touched one another's hands, and the Dyaks then filed out of the room and disappeared down the verandah. The Rajah was amused and interested at the idea of my rhythmic piano tune having carried the people so completely off their feet, whilst I was rather pleased at the effect of my playing on such a wild audience, and although realizing that my music does not rouse English people to the same frenzy of enthusiasm, I felt that morning I had gained a success that Rubinstein himself might have envied.

CHAPTER IX

DESPITE my love for Sarawak, there were three great drawbacks to my comfort, namely, malaria, mosquitoes, and rats.

One knows that the tropics, especially where the moisture is excessive, are trying to European constitutions. When one remembers the abrupt transitions from wet to dry, the fierce rays of the sun that beat down on the vegetation, the exhalation of myriads and myriads of leaves drawn up by the heat of the day and cast forth again in poisonous perfumes or evil odours into the atmosphere, all these things must have a pernicious effect on the health of Europeans. But we now also know that these things obvious to our senses are not the sole or the whole cause of some of the worst tropical ailments, but that these are due to the invisible life teeming in earth, air, and water. For instance, it is now established that the disease capable of so many variations, called malaria, is due to the sting of my arch-enemy, the striped black-and-white mosquito. This discovery had not been made when I first visited the tropics, but now I do not wonder at my feelings of repulsion whenever I saw these horrible pests feeding on me.

A short time after my arrival in the country, I was seized with a somewhat unusual form of malaria. Now the ordinary malaria is known by almost all Europeans who live in the tropics. The Rajah, for instance, suffers from this ordinary but very trying and sometimes dangerous kind of fever, but the way the pest attacked me was of a kind not often experienced by Europeans. My kind was more prevalent amongst the natives. Its symptoms are disconcerting to your friends, for you feel very bad tempered. The palms of your hands get hot and dry, and a feeling of impending disaster takes hold of you. These preliminaries are painless. Then, all of a sudden, more often at sunset, you feel sick : nothing happens, but a band of iron, as it were, presses round your body, becoming tighter and tighter until you imagine that fingers of steel are twisting you up inside. You retire to bed, propped by pillows, for you can neither hold yourself up nor move in any way, and there you remain gasping for breath until the attack is over. It may last half an hour, or continue for half a day, when it returns the next afternoon at the same hour—the attacks resembling those of angina pectoris. Your complexion turns a bright yellow and your face is covered with an ugly rash. These attacks have lasted off and on for two or three months, when life becomes unbearable. You can neither eat nor drink, and get reduced to a shadow. Our English doctor in Sarawak, who was clever and intelligent, never understood the disease. He prescribed leeches, cupping-glasses, poultices, and fed me up with champagne, brandy, and even port wine, with the result that all these would-be remedies made me very much worse. I became frightfully thin, so that after nearly four years' residence in Sarawak the Rajah decided to take me home, in order to recover my health.

One morning, during the first years of my residence in Sarawak, my Malay maid, Ima, rushed into my room and told me that a friend of hers, living in a house near her own, was lying at the point of death owing to continuous attacks of this disease. I could well sympathize with the woman's sufferings, and although powerless to cure myself in such emergencies, decided to try what I could do to help Ima's friend. I took with me a box of pills, a bottle of meat juice, some milk and arrowroot, and, accompanied by Ima, sallied forth to the sick woman's house. I climbed up the ladder that hencoop fashion led into her room, and pushing open the dried palm-leaf door saw a woman rolling about on the floor in paroxysms of agony. Here were the symptoms I knew so well— the bright yellow complexion and rash all over the face. The woman was so weak she could hardly move. Ima went up to her, and lifting her up in her arms said : "Rajah Ranee, who knows of medicines that will make you well, has come to see you." The woman looked at me, and shook her head. I told her I had brought some marvellous remedies, known only to Europeans, and made her take two pills and a spoonful of Liebig. When her husband came in, I told him to give her a little milk every hour, and forbade her to touch or eat anything besides what I had prescribed for her. She was carried inside her mosquito curtains, bent double as she was, and gasping for breath. The next morning, when I visited her, I found her better, for the attack had not lasted so long as that of the previous day. I was delighted with the result of my doctoring, and for about a fortnight went to see this woman nearly every day. She was very poor, the wife of a man who earned his living by selling fish which he netted in the river and also by doing odd jobs in neighbouring pine-apple gardens. The woman finally recovered and remained quite well whilst I stayed in Kuching.

As I was sitting writing inside my mosquito house in my morning-room, one day, I heard a fuss going on outside. Our sentry was evidently trying to keep back a visitor who wished to see me. I told Ima to let the visitor in, whoever he might be, when an old and wizened personage, without a jacket, and with garments dripping with mud and water, came in, carrying a net bag in which were a number of crawling things. He ran up to me, deposited the bag at my feet, and catching hold of both my knees, said: " Rajah Ranee pitied my wife, made her well with her medicines and incantations. These shrimps are for Rajah Ranee. I caught them in the river. I nothing else to give. Cook make them into curry." I thought this touching on the part of the affectionate husband, and thanked him many times. The sight of the shrimps crawling about in the net, however, greatly disturbed me, for I cannot bear to see animals uncomfortable. I therefore got rid of my grateful friend as soon as I could, and, directly he had left, told Ima (I could not do it myself, for there was a blazing sun outside) to carry the shrimps back to the river whence they had come. I watched her go down the garden path, carrying the net bag, but I question whether she did as I told her. I rather think that she and her husband, Dul, enjoyed shrimp curry that evening. However, I asked no questions—"What the eye does not see the heart does not grieve over!"

This story of the sick woman has a sad ending, for during one of my absences from Sarawak she was again seized with the illness, and died. I was afterwards told that she often used to say: "If Rajah Ranee were here, with her medicines, her visits, and incantations, I should get over it, but I hope no more now, and I know I must die." Until the day of her death, she never wearied extolling my medical skill, and this cure of mine led to some embarrassing situations, for whenever there were serious cases of illness, the people sent for me, begging that I would cure them as I did the fisherman's wife. On one occasion, a poor woman in the Malay town gave birth to twins, both children being born with hare-lips. The morning of their arrival,

Ima came to me with an urgent message from the father of the twins, requesting me to go directly to their house and put the babies' mouths straight. I was sorry to have to refuse, but—unlike a good many medical men and women—I realized my limitations in certain cases!

Now for mosquitoes. Nothing one can say or write can give any idea of the tortures one undergoes by the actual biting of mosquitoes. A great many people imagine that these pests only begin to torment one at sunset. This is a mistaken idea. A certain kind of black mosquito, striped with white, is a most pernicious pest. By day and night it harassed me so much that if I wanted to do anything at all, I had to retire behind the shelter of a mosquito house. My Malay friends did not seem to care whether mosquitoes stung them or not; indeed, they seemed to enjoy the heavy slaps they administered on their faces, hands, or legs, in their attempts to kill the foe. Their methods, however, required a certain amount of skill. The results of their slaps were not pleasant to witness, and when imitating their methods of slaughter, I always had, close by, a basin containing a weak solution of carbolic acid, and a towel. After a bite, the spot was washed, the remains of the mosquito disposed of, and I was ready for another onslaught. Malay women were not so particular, for after killing a mosquito, they would rub off all traces with their coloured handkerchiefs. My paraphernalia of basin, sponge, and towel elicited from them various grunts. They made funny noises in their throats and appealed to Allah at my extraordinary patience in taking these precautions.

I now come to rats, which were a far more serious business. A Malay woman once told me she had watched a detachment of rats, four or five in number, trying to get at some fowls' eggs she had laid by for cake-making. She was inside her house (Malay houses are often rather dark), and in the dim light she saw these swift-gliding creatures hovering near the place where the eggs were stored. She waited to see what would happen, and saw a large rat—large as are Norwegian rats—somehow or other get hold of an egg, roll over on its back, holding the egg firmly on its stomach with its four paws, when the other rats took hold of its tail, and by a series of backward jerks dragged their companion to a hole in the leafy walling of the store, where it disappeared from sight. I believe this particular story is told with variations all over the world.

A great many stories might be related of rats, but the most extraordinary thing I ever saw regarding these animals was a migration which took place one evening at dusk through my bedroom. I was just getting better from a severe attack of malaria, and was lying on the bed inside my mosquito house half awake and half asleep, with my Malay Ayah sitting against the wall in a corner of my room. Suddenly, I saw two or three long objects moving

across the middle of the room, their black bodies
standing out against the pale yellow matting. My
room opened on to verandahs from all sides (as every
one who is acquainted with the architecture of tropical
houses will understand), and it was easy for any
animal to climb over the outer verandah and pass
through the screened doors leading to the opposite
verandah. I watched these crawling creatures, and,
being only half awake, wondered what they were.
At first I thought it was the result of malaria, making
me see things which did not exist, but when the rats
were joined by others coming in at one door and
going out of the other, in numbers of tens, of twenties,
of sixties, then it must have been hundreds, for the
floor was one mass of moving objects, I called to the
Ayah, who sat motionless the other side of the room.
" Don't move," she said ; " they are the rats." I was
too frightened not to move, and I screamed out to the
Rajah, who I knew was in the room next to mine.
As he came in, the rats ran up one side of him,
and I remember the dull thud they made as they
jumped off his shoulder to the floor. Some fortmen,
hearing my screams, also appeared. The Rajah told
me to make as little noise as possible, so I had to
remain still whilst thousands and thousands of rats
passed through my room. This abnormal invasion
lasted for about ten or fifteen minutes, when the rats
began to diminish in number, until there were only a
few stragglers left to follow the main body.

It appears that such migrations are well known all

over Sarawak, and that people fear them because they are accompanied by a certain amount of danger. It is said by the natives that if any one should kill one of these rats, his companions would attack the person in such large numbers that his body would be almost torn to pieces. Looking deeper into the matter, one wonders why these creatures should so migrate, and where they go; but this no one seems to know. Their area of operations is a restricted one, for it appears that on this occasion my bedroom was the only human habitation through which they went.

By the time the last rat passed through my room, and I began to breathe freely again, darkness had come. My room was lit by the dim light of a wick floating in a tumbler of cocoa-nut oil, enclosed in a lantern of glass. The Ayah took up her position again and squatted by the wall without saying a word, nearly petrified with terror at what had happened. I pictured this mass of swiftly-moving, crafty-looking creatures, under the influence of some mysterious force unknown to ourselves, and remembered Cuvier, that great Frenchman, who wrote that when one thinks of the family life of even the most loathsome of creatures, one is inclined to forget any repulsion one may feel towards them.

Rats, however, were a great trouble to me. I have recognized individual rats visiting me on different occasions. I don't know whether they wanted to make friends, one will never know, but they frightened me dreadfully. I often pitied the way the poor creatures were trapped, poisoned, and killed, when after all they were only trying to keep their place in the world, just as we do.

On another occasion, I was fast asleep when I woke up feeling a sort of nip. I opened my eyes and saw a large rat sitting on my arm. I shook it off, and it fell to the ground. Being in my mosquito house, I was curious to discover how the rat had got in, and lighting a candle, found that it had gnawed a hole through the muslin to get at some food placed on a table for me to eat during the night.

As luck would have it, these rat visitations invariably took place when I was ill, so perhaps it magnified the disgust I felt towards these creatures. But thinking on the matter many times since, I have largely got over my loathing for rats, and I do not think nowadays, I should mind their migrating through my room, because I have become more familiar with animals and their ways.

CHAPTER X

THERE are certain animals in Sarawak, very little mentioned by travellers, with which we are always surrounded. These are the lizards which run up and down the walls of all houses in the tropics. They are light grey-green in colour, make a funny little noise, and on this account the natives call them chik-chak. They have the peculiar and rather disagreeable property of shedding their tails; once or twice they have dropped these append-ages on to my head as they ran to and fro on the ceiling. It sometimes happens that if a picture or a piece of furniture standing against a wall is moved, a very large black chik-chak, about twice the size of an ordinary chik-chak, will come out from behind these shelters. I have noticed that a great many rooms are inhabited by one of these black chik-chak ensconced behind such safe retreats, and these giants of the same species are called by Malays, "Rajah chi-chak."

One might also make remarks of an uncompli-mentary nature about centipedes and scorpions, but I know very little about these formidable insects—if they are insects. I only remember on a certain after-noon, when getting up from my usual siesta, I saw on

6

the muslin walls of my mosquito house a large black thing looking like a miniature lobster. I called the Rajah, who at once recognized it as an enormous scorpion. He took hold of a spear leaning against the wall, so as to kill it, well knowing the awful effects of its sting. I could never have believed what a difficult thing it is to kill a scorpion. Its shell is apparently so thick that it takes a long time to give it its death-blow. I hate seeing anything killed (although on this occasion it was absolutely necessary), so I rushed out of the room. Needless to say, the Rajah ultimately dispatched it.

As for snakes, I am not going to say a word against them. They are the most beautiful creatures one can possibly see, and in my experience they are not nearly so deadly or so dangerous as people seem to think. The most deadly snake in Sarawak is the much-feared hamadryad. Its dangerous character comes from its very virtues. Whenever a hamadryad is laying her eggs, her mate looks after her safety, and resents the presence of any human being within yards of where she has her nest. One afternoon, one of our Malay servants came screaming up the steps leading from the garden to our verandah, closely followed by one of these hamadryads, and had not a Guard seen her danger and killed the snake, she must have been dead in three or four seconds.

Although beasts of prey, such as tigers, panthers, etc., are unknown in Sarawak, the most dangerous reptile in the country is without doubt the crocodile.

I do not think that any statistics have been taken of the loss to human life caused by these creatures in Sarawak, but that their victims are numerous is certain, for every one living in the country has known, or has witnessed, the destructive powers of these creatures. I remember when we were at dinner one evening, we heard the most terrible commotion in one of the little streams running around our garden. They came from a man and from the women folk of his house, and we sent to inquire the cause. We were told that the man had gone to bathe in the creek near his house, and had been seized by a crocodile. The man had laid hold of the log which served as a landing-stage, and the crocodile had managed to tear off one of his legs. He was taken to his house, and although our English doctor did all he could for him, he died the next morning.

I have often, in my excursions up and down the river, been followed in our small river boat by these reptiles, and generally the boat boys were the first to see the tiny conical roofs above their eyes—the only portion to be seen above the water—and as these move swiftly towards the boat, you conclude that you are being followed by a crocodile. The experience is not a pleasant one, although it is seldom that the reptile is powerful enough to upset a canoe capable of carrying six or seven people. The danger to the inhabitants of Sarawak lies in the fact that they go about from one house to another on the river-banks in very small canoes, which only hold one person. Sometimes the canoe is so small you can hardly see its wooden sides, and its solitary occupant appears as though he were sitting on the water, paddling himself along. Both men and women are very skilful in the management of any craft on the waters of these rivers, and despite the fact that crocodiles often with a swish of their tails knock the boats in the air, and seize the occupants as they fall back into the river, paddle in hand, the people seem quite indifferent to the risks they run in these small canoes.

A great many years ago, before Kuching became as civilized as it is now, and when it had few steamers on the river, an enormous crocodile, some twenty feet in length, was the terror of the neighbourhood for three or four months during the north-east monsoon —the rainy season of the country. Our Malay quartermaster on board the *Heartsease* was seized by this monster as he was leaving the Rajah's yacht to go to his house, a few yards from the bank, in his little canoe. It was at night that the crocodile seized him, the canoe being found empty the next morning. Although no one had actually witnessed the calamity, it was certain the poor man had been taken by the monster. This was his first victim, but others followed in quick succession. The crocodile could be seen patrolling the river daily, but it is very difficult to catch or shoot such a creature. At length the Rajah, becoming anxious at the turn affairs were taking, issued a proclamation offering a handsome reward to any one who should succeed in catching the crocodile. This proclamation was made with as much importance as possible. The executioner, Subu, bearing the Sarawak flag, was given a large boat, manned by twenty paddles, painted in the Sarawak colours, and sent up and down the river reading the proclamation at the landing-stages of Malay houses. Looking from my window one morning, I saw the boat gaily decorated and looking very important on the river, with the yellow umbrella of office folded inside and the proclamation from the Rajah being read. A few yards behind the boat I imagined I could see, through my opera glasses, the water disturbed by some huge body following it. The natives had noticed this too, and it was absolutely proved that wherever the boat went up or down the river, the monster followed it, as if in derision of the proclamation.

A great deal of etiquette had to be observed after the capture of this crocodile. As it was being towed a captive to the place of execution, the process to be observed required that it should be first brought to ·the Rajah, and until it was safely landed in the Rajah's garden, the most complimentary speeches were made to it: " You are a Rajah "; " You must come and see your brother " ; " You are the light of the day "; " You are the sun and moon shining over the land," etc. These flattering remarks were made by the captors as they dragged the huge scaly thing to its doom, but once it was safely in the presence of the Rajah, it was made a target for the most insulting language. I saw the crocodile as it lay helpless with its paws tied over its back in the Rajah's garden. The Malays were careful to keep out of reach of the switch of its tail, as one blow from it would have seriously injured anyone who went too near. The Rajah having passed sentence, the reptile was dragged off to be killed by having its head cut off. This done, the body was opened, when human remains, together with the rings and clothes of our unfortunate quartermaster, were found, thus proving our surmises as to his death to be correct.

Full of excitement and zeal after what had taken place, the Malays who had captured the crocodile considered that the deceased quartermaster's silver ring, in which was set a diamond of the country, should be presented to me. Therefore, Talip, holding the ring between his thumb and forefinger, with many bows and ceremonious speeches, brought it to me for my acceptance. I am sorry to say that my feelings were too strong for me on the occasion, and I could not possibly touch the thing. I was so sorry, and told Talip I was grateful for such kindness, but that I thought the ring ought to belong to the victim's wife or daughter. I sent my thanks for the kind thought, and was very glad when Talip and the ring disappeared from view. So ended the history of the great crocodile, whose doings are even now spoken of in Sarawak.

As we are on the subject of animals, we must not

forget to talk about those very delightful creatures, the monkeys. A most delicious Gibbon exists in Sarawak, which the natives call the wah-wah; it is the one which imitates the sound of running water in the morning. Wah-wahs are easily tamed, and quickly take to human beings. I was presented with one of these little animals by Datu Isa, wife of the Datu Bandar, and its pathetic little jet black face, its round, beady, frightened eyes, its grey fur fitting its head like the wig of a clown, soft almost as that of the chinchilla but thicker and longer, and its black arms and legs, made it a beautiful little creature. Datu Isa placed the animal in my arms, when it clung to me as children do. The care of this little being, so helpless, so frightened, so full of a want of affection, really made me quite miserable. I tried to give it the food it liked, I took great care of it and kept it always with me when I was in the house, but it went the way of beautiful sensitive animals taken by kind ignorance into the company of human beings. Like most monkeys of its kind in captivity, the poor little wah-wah developed pneumonia a few months after it had been given to me, and died. It was a great grief to me, and I begged my Malay friends, as kindly as I could, not to give me any more such charming and yet such sorrowful presents. The wah-wah cannot live in captivity, for it is the lack of their own natural food that kills these delicate creatures, though they will eat almost anything, even cocoa-nut, which is fatal to them.

A friend of mine, a Malay woman living in the Malay town near our house, possessed an Albino wah-wah. It was considered a powerful " mascotte," and it lived with her people some time. It must have died during one of my visits to England, for I never heard of it again after I left Sarawak for the first time. On my return, I asked my native women friends what had happened to it, but they were very reticent in giving me news of the little creature. At last they said: " It went to another world, and we would rather not talk about it any more."

Another interesting animal in Sarawak is the buffalo. These animals are tiresome when they come into contact with Europeans. In fact, they are dangerous to meet, should they be uncontrolled by natives. Natives, apparently, can do what they like with them. They never ill-treat the animals, but talk to them as though they were human, this treatment making the beasts tame and easy to manage. In one of our settlements, near a coal-mine, where buffaloes were required to drag trucks of coal to and from the mines to the landing-stage, whence it was shipped to Kuching and Singapore, the animals were housed in stables made of palm leaves, and their keepers, who were Boyans, stayed with them. In course of time, the stables became unfit for habitation either for man or beast. The Rajah therefore ordered new stables to be built for the buffaloes and their keepers. When the new stables were finished and ready for their reception, it was noticed that neither the buffaloes nor their keepers made any use of them. The Rajah, hearing this, made inquiries, when the overseer of the coal-mine, a native who wrote English, sent the Rajah a dispatch informing him that the animals were so much annoyed and put out with their new quarters that they absolutely refused to occupy them, and therefore their keepers, not wishing to incur the displeasure of their friends, preferred to stay in the leaky dwellings. In course of time the question was satisfactorily solved, for the Rajah being of a tactful nature, usually surmounts difficulties that may arise with any of his subjects, men or buffaloes.

CHAPTER XI

DURING those first four years of my stay in Sarawak, the advent of a little girl and twin boys served to show still more strongly the affection and devotion of the people for their chief. Looking back to that time, I cannot help remembering with pleasure the way in which the people took my children to their hearts; the funny little jingling toys they made to amuse them when they were quite babies; the solicitude they showed for their health; the many times they invited them to their houses, when I felt that they were even safer in their keeping than in my own. All this often returns to my mind, and makes me feel more of a Malay than ever.

One sad incident I must mention, if only to contradict the common idea that Muhammadans are all fanatics and incapable of sympathy towards the religious feelings of those who are outside their creed. Once, when returning from a journey with the Rajah, I met with a bad accident. I fell down the hold of a steamer, which resulted in one of my children, a son, being born dead. When this happened, the Rajah had been called away by urgent business up some of the far-off rivers of the interior. Naturally, I was very ill, and the four Malay chiefs of the Rajah's Council were anxious to show their sympathy with me. When they heard that the child had never lived, they went to the doctor and asked him where it was to be buried. The doctor naturally referred them to the Bishop, who had no other alternative but to decide that it could not be buried in consecrated ground. But the chiefs thought differently. They came that night to the Astana, bringing with them a coffin and carried the little body to the consecrated ground on our side of the river, where some of the Rajah's relatives are laid. These chiefs dug the grave themselves, and covered it over with a grass mound. I was much too ill at the time to know what was going on, but I was told afterwards that Datu Isa insisted on a tree of frangipani being planted over the spot. I am sorry to say the tree died, but this additional proof of those dear people's sympathy can never fade from my memory.

The Rajah returned to Kuching immediately he heard the news, and in a few weeks I began to mend. When I was well enough, Datu Isa sat with me daily, and she said the event of my recovery must be marked by a thanksgiving ceremony, for which an afternoon had to be set apart. " You must lie quiet all the morning, Rajah Ranee," she said, "and think kind thoughts, so that your mind may be serene. I will appear at three o'clock with my women." I did not in the least know what she was going to do. At three o'clock, according to her promise, Datu Isa headed a long procession of my friends, who came to the door of my room. I was told not to speak, and we were all as silent as the grave. Datu Isa opened the door of my mosquito house; she carried in one hand a piece of something that looked like dried shark's skin, and in her other she held a ring of pure gold. One of her daughters had a basket containing grains of rice dyed with saffron. Datu Isa rubbed the ring against the "something" two or three times, and then traced signs over my forehead with the ring. She scattered a tiny pinch of gold dust on my hair, and threw a handful of the yellow rice over me. "Thanks be to Allah, Rajah Ranee, for you are well again." I was just going to speak, but she motioned me to be quite silent, and she and her women departed. Being somewhat given to superstition, I feel sure that this quaint rite hastened my recovery.

Before I close this chapter of the first years of my stay in Sarawak, it would be ungrateful of me did I not mention the tokens of affection and kindness I received from the English ladies of the place, almost all of them having come to live in Kuching since my first arrival there. Mrs. Crookshank, wife of the Resident of Sarawak; Mrs. Kemp, then the wife of the Protestant Chaplain; indeed, all the ladies then living in Kuching were always charming to me. We saw a great deal of one another, and whenever any of these ladies left the country, their absence from our tiny English society was very much felt.

As regards my relations with the Malay women, the Rajah himself encouraged our friendship; he approved

of my methods regarding them, and sympathized with
them most completely. Owing to his desire to make
the place more agreeable to me, he appointed my
brother, Harry de Windt, his private secretary. This
was a great joy to me, my brother and I being devoted
to one another. I like to imagine that the interest
he took in Sarawak, and the many expeditions on
which he accompanied the Rajah, first inspired the
travelling passion in him and led to his future
achievements in the many world-wide explorations,
for which (though he is my brother) I think I may
rightly say he has become famous. It was also during
his stay in Sarawak that he wrote his first book and
began his career as an author.

So my first four years of residence in Sarawak
passed away as a dream, until it was realized that
malaria and the climate made it impossible for me to
remain in the country without a change to England.
Therefore the Rajah made up his mind to go home for
a year or so, for he himself, with his incessant work,
expeditions, and journeys here and there for the good
of the people, had suffered quite his share of fever.
As we stepped into the *Heartsease*, all my women
friends congregated on the lawn of the Astana to say
good-bye to me. No need now to ask where were the
women, and no need now to send for them lest they
might be too frightened to come of their own accord.
There they were, the best friends I ever had, or ever
hope to possess. I felt inclined to cry as I said good-
bye to them all, and had it not been for ill-health, I

think the idea of a journey to England would have been hateful to me.

It was during this voyage that the first great sorrow since my arrival in Sarawak occurred. The three children we were taking home with us died within six days of one another, and were buried in the Red Sea.

CHAPTER XII

I T might be interesting to explain, as briefly as possible, the position the Rajahs and their people occupied in that great concern we now know under the name of the British Empire. When the first Rajah Brooke undertook the government of the country, he did so, as he thought, temporarily, imagining that the British Government would in time take the country under its protection. Apparently the British Government was not anxious to increase its responsibilities in the Far East, so that for years the first Rajah struggled on protecting his people unsupported and alone. One important fact to be remembered is that ever since the Brooke dynasty has existed in Sarawak, only in very few instances, have the forces of the British Empire been required to help the two Rajahs and their Government against their external enemies, although these were the enemies of the world at large, for it was only in expeditions against pirates who swept those seas, thus hindering commerce, that British guns came to the assistance of the white Rajahs. If we view the matter dispassionately and, shall we say, from the standpoint of the man in the street, the position was without doubt a difficult one, both for the British Government, and for the

Rajahs themselves. Most of us are aware that vast lands of tropical countries—many of them ill-governed by native princes who are only anxious to amass money for themselves, regardless of the welfare of their subjects—have over and over again been exploited for shorter or longer periods by European adventurers. History teaches us that Europeans, from the time of Cortes down to these days, have on different occasions swooped like vultures on almost unknown tropical countries, have gained concessions, the money paid finding its way into the treasuries of the various princes who claimed the soil, and in this way the unfortunate inhabitants, the real owners of the land, have been enslaved and forced by nefarious, cruel, and tyrannical methods to give their very life's blood so that these land-grabbing aliens might become rich.

Being so intimately associated with the Rajah and his people, it is natural I should be the last to hear the opinions of that portion of the British public unacquainted with the methods of these rulers, but I cannot help thinking that very probably then, and even now, the white Rajahs of Sarawak are classed with such adventurers, and on this account they found it so difficult to get proper recognition of their sovereignty from the British Government. Here was a country come suddenly into existence, with all the paraphernalia of a good Government, with its Ministers, its Courts of Justice, its safety for life and commerce, all in English hands, and owned by private individuals. Communication was slow in those days, and the real position of the rulers and their people was only known to very few and inquiring minds amongst the élite of English-speaking people. The Rajahs were, individually, subjects of the British Crown, and, despite of their belonging to an old and very much respected English family, they had few friends at the English Court to push forward their interests.

The full recognition of Sarawak as an independent State by England occurred in 1863, whilst Lord Palmerston was Premier and Lord John Russell Secretary for Foreign Affairs. It was then that the first English Consul was appointed to Sarawak as a formal acknowledgment of its independence. Warships calling at Kuching saluted the Rajah's flag with twenty-one guns, so that within his own country the Rajah was acknowledged by the British Government as an independent ruler. The first Rajah died five years after the appointment of the Consul, for it will be remembered that the present Rajah succeeded his uncle in 1868.

On our first visit to England after our marriage, the Rajah was anxious to pay homage to Her Majesty, which was only an ordinary act of courtesy on his part, considering his position as ruler in a portion of the Malayan Archipelago. When he requested leave to attend one of Her Majesty's levees as Rajah of Sarawak, the answer given by the Secretary of State for Foreign Affairs was somewhat disconcerting, in view

7

of Sarawak having been recognized as an independent
State. The Rajah was informed that Her Majesty's
Government did not see their way to present him to
the Queen as Rajah of Sarawak, but that he could
attend a levee in the private capacity of an English
gentleman, simply as " Mr. Brooke." The difficulties
of the position were obvious, when one remembers
that the Rajah was governing Sarawak for the
benefit of his people, the British Government
having recognized the country over which he ruled.
Owing to the exigencies of his Government, the
Rajah had to employ Englishmen to assist him
in his work; these gentlemen, being nominated by
him and paid out of the Sarawak treasury, owed
no allegiance to the Foreign or Colonial Offices at
home. To ensure success in the Rajah's endeavours,
these English gentlemen were bound to honour and
obey him, and to acknowledge him as their chief,
yet here was the British Government absolutely
refusing to recognize the Rajah of Sarawak in
England as ruler of his own country !

After much correspondence and several interviews
with the heads of the different departments in power,
the Rajah, a most loyal servant of Her Majesty's,
obtained what the Government called the favour of
being presented to Her Majesty as Mr. Brooke. The
officials insisted that *Rajah of Sarawak* should be
placed in brackets, as though in apology for the
Rajah's position !

Very few people even nowadays understand the

TUAN BUNGSU OF SARAWAK WITH HIS
LITTLE SON, JIMMIE BROOKE

H.H. THE RAJAH MUDA OF SARAWAK

TUAN MUDA OF SARAWAK

position of the Brookes in Sarawak, and it is difficult to drive into their heads that the Rajah's wish to be recognized as Rajah of Sarawak had nothing to do with his own personality. No one can gainsay the fact that nothing is so dangerous to the prosperity of a country as the anomalous position of its ruler and its Government. Although I had nothing to do with the politics of my adopted country, I shared in my husband's wishes that the position of Sarawak might be protected, and its ruler's position acknowledged by the Queen, in order to give additional security and stability to its Government and its people. However, in spite of the scant personal recognition shown for many years to the Rajah by the British Government, the country managed to flourish—an obvious testimony to his single-minded and statesmanlike methods.

Notwithstanding these purely political preoccupations, the time we spent in England was wholly delightful. I quickly regained my health, and enjoyed the English life very much, but never for a moment did I forget my land of predilection the other side of the world, for I was always looking forward to the time when I should return there and begin again the life amongst my beloved Malays and Dyaks.

The present Rajah Muda was born during this visit to England, and his arrival telegraphed to Sarawak, elicited from the people many kind and delightful letters. When the time came for our return to our country, our son was six months old, and owing to the sorrowful experience we had had of the dangers of a sea-voyage for young children, we left him in charge of our good friends, Bishop and Mrs. MacDougall. Our baby was to stay with them in England until he had completed his first year, when he was to rejoin us in Sarawak.

CHAPTER XIII

WHEN we returned to Sarawak, I felt, as it were, a giant refreshed. All symptoms of malaria had gone, and, as we steamed under the landing-place of the Astana, I could see on its broad verandahs my Malay women friends waiting for me. We had lots of things to talk about. Datu Isa was the proud possessor of four more grandchildren, and these were duly presented to me, wrapped in the tight swaddling clothes usual to Malayan babies. I was told that Datu Isa and the other chiefs' wives were delighted with the behaviour of their lords and masters during my absence, who had not so much as hinted at the possibility of adding an additional wife to their household. Talip was also radiant at our return, as was the redoubtable Subu, present with the yellow umbrella, splendid, as usual, in his executioner's uniform of gold and green satin shimmering with ornaments. It was about this time, although I do not know just how it came about, that I got to know Subu better than I ever did before. He was an old man then, nearing the end of his career, for he was one of those who had been with the first Rajah Brooke when he was made Rajah of Sarawak. Such stories the old man had to tell of his encounters with pirates, also of the difficulty he had with his wives, for, sad as it may seem to relate, he had embarked on three, one less than the number allowed to good Muhammadans by the great Prophet himself. The youngest wife he had married not so long ago gave him a good deal of trouble. "She will not listen to the exhortations of my wife No. 1," he would tell me. "This troubles my heart; it makes me sick. She is too wilful and arrogant in her youth. She is pretty, it is true, but she need not always be counting my eldest wife's wrinkles. It is not the way young people should behave to those who are older than themselves, for even in old wives lie the wisdom of time; young ones are thoughtless, stupid, and unknowing." Notwithstanding these domestic storms at home, Subu's wives always called on me together. They would come in strictly in their precedence, No. 1, No. 2, and No. 3, and I am bound to say that so long as they remained with me, the No. 2 and the No. 3 wives always asked permission of the No. 1 wife before they ventured on a remark. These women, however, were not brilliant specimens of the womanhood of Malaya, so, to be quite truthful, I preferred Subu's visits unaccompanied by these dames.

He used to sit on the floor of my room, on a mat prepared for him, and tell me of many events, fights, and hairbreadth escapes he had encountered in his chequered career. His most interesting stories, how-

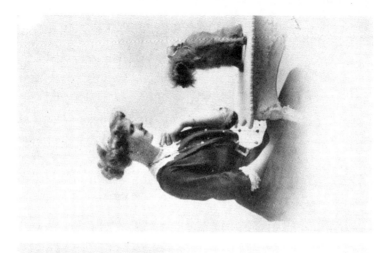

THE DAIANG BUNGSU

H.H. THE RANÉE MUDA

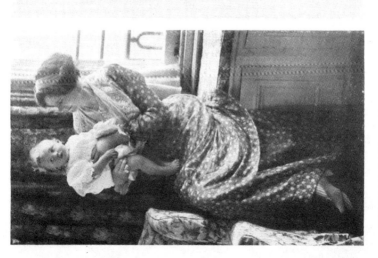

THE DAIANG MUDA AND HER SON
ANTHONY BROOKE

ever, related to the victims whom he had dispatched into the next world. They almost all belonged to the same order of criminals. There were a few Chinese murderers, who had killed people through avarice; Malays, who had slain people on account of jealousy, or through temper; but the greater number of the evildoers were Dyaks who had taken heads on their own account, just for the honour and glory of possessing one of these ghastly trophies. As far as Dyak and Malay malefactors went, it appears the same scene was nearly always enacted, but I had better say at once that no man has ever been executed in Sarawak without the Rajah's sanction, he alone having power over life and death throughout the country. Very often the trial of more serious crimes lasted some days, so thorough were the inquiries set on foot by the Rajah and his ministers.

The trial for murder in Kuching is hedged around by the same precautions when a human life is at stake as it is in the Courts of Law in England. A jury consisting of the culprit's own countrymen is usually empanelled, and the magistrate of the district (an Englishman), the Rajah's ministers (generally three in number), and the Rajah himself, weigh the evidence with the most minute care. When the death sentence has to be passed, it is only after all other resources have failed, and the condemned man is usually led out to his doom the morning after the sentence is passed. The criminals are executed by the kris, with which weapon Subu was wonderfully expert.

A kris is a curious-looking dagger, straight and flat, the blade double-edged, eighteen inches long, with a sharp point. It is inserted in the cavity of the condemned man's right shoulder, and thrust diagonally across the body through the heart, causing instantaneous death. " Do they never tremble ? " I would ask Subu. "No," he said ; "they do not tremble. They smoke cigarettes while their grave is being dug, and sometimes they eat betel-nut and sirih. Then, when I tell them, they sit on the brink of their grave as though they were sitting on the edge of their bed, prepared to take their afternoon sleep. We always parted good friends," said Subu, "and very often we talked all the way to the place of execution."

The condemned men never quite knew when their last moment had come, for they sat placidly smoking until Subu approached from behind them, and with one blow of the kris sent them into eternity. "You white people fret too much about trifles, and that makes you frightened of death," Subu would say. "We take it just as it comes, and consider that Allah has chosen the best moment to end our lives. Many such murderers have I sent to their peace," he often said to me. "I am an old man now, but I hope Allah in His mercy will permit me to kris ten more before He gathers me up into His paradise. Just ten more, Rajah Ranee, and then I shall consider my work is done." Poor old Subu, in spite of his bloodthirsty words he possessed a tender heart. He was gentle and kind to children and animals, indeed, to all who were desolate and oppressed.

The people of Sarawak recognize the justice of capital sentences in the most wonderful way. I remember one case in point. The Rajah has a battalion of drilled men, some five hundred in number, recruited from the Dyaks and Malays of Sarawak, together with a few Sikhs, who voluntarily come forward to join this paid force. The Commandant in charge of this battalion—called the Sarawak Rangers—is nearly always a retired officer from the British army, and the Rajah usually engages a retired Gunner from one of His Majesty's ships, as Instructor, to teach the men the use of guns. The men are very apt at drill, and are as active as cats in the manipulation of guns. They all take great pride in their work, and particularly enjoy the management of field pieces. Their uniform is of white drill with black facings; they wear forage caps, and are armed with Snider carbines. Whenever the Rajah goes on expeditions, and sometimes on his journeys up the rivers, a certain number of these drilled men form his bodyguard. They also act as sentries in the Palace and other Government buildings in Kuching.

One day, one of these Sarawak Rangers, with a gang of his friends, all young men, went on a holiday excursion to some fruit gardens in the suburb of Kuching. They came to a tempting-looking fruit orchard, full of ripe oranges, mangosteens, custard apples, pine-apples, etc., fenced in by rotten railings and owned by an old Chinaman. All fruit is dear to native hearts, for they are essentially a fruit-eating people. The youths, seeing these tempting morsels, demolished the palings, entered the garden, and began eating the fruit. The noise they made hacking at the trees brought the old man out of his house built in the orchard. He remonstrated with the thieves, who took no notice, so he raised his voice in order to elicit the help of passers-by on the road. This so exasperated the youths, who were bent on carrying off some of the old man's fruit, that in a fit of anger the Ranger drew his parang[1] (he was in mufti), and killed the Chinaman. Realizing what he had done, he took to his heels, followed by his friends, leaving the Chinaman in a pool of blood under the fruit trees, where he was found by the Rajah's police—an efficient body of Malays under the command of an English officer. The crime was brought home to the Ranger, who was brought to justice and condemned to death.

On the morning of the man's execution, the Rajah had arranged to go for a visit to the Batang Lupar River. I was to go with him, and the guard chosen to accompany him happened to include the brother of the man who was to be executed that day. The Instructor in charge of the men informed the Rajah that the prisoner's brother was in a very excited state, and had been

---

[1] A sword.

heard by the natives speaking rather wildly in the
barracks.   I believe he even expressed himself as
ready to take vengeance on the Government which
had condemned his brother to death.   The Instructor
suggested to the Rajah that it might not be quite
safe to have this man included in his personal
bodyguard.   "On the contrary," said the Rajah,
"for that very reason let him come with us."
Needless to say, the man did accompany us and
behaved himself perfectly, and by the time we
returned to Kuching he had proved himself to
be one of the most exemplary members of the
Rajah's bodyguard.

Now with regard to the police.   It has often been
a matter of wonder to me how efficient this body of
Malays and Dyaks becomes under the charge of young
Englishmen.   The Sarawak officers are chosen in a very
original way.   Many of them fresh from some university
have somehow heard of the methods of the Rajah and
his Government, and very likely feeling an admiration
for the romantic story which has led to the present state
of affairs in Sarawak, feel they would like to join the
Rajah's service.   Often these men have had no particular
training for the work they are called upon to undertake, and yet they grow into it, as it were.   The
heads of the Rajah's police (in the person of the
officers whom he has chosen) have been, and are,
capable of unravelling the most intricate and delicate
affairs.   I cannot imagine what their methods may be,
but plots have been found out, organized by Chinese

Secret Societies against the Government, which, if they had been carried into execution, would have set the capital in flames and killed every white person living in Kuching. Thanks to the intelligence, zeal, and unceasing vigilance of these officers, such calamities have been averted. This efficiency says a good deal for the loyalty and devotion of the Rajah's Englishmen who, in spite of the drawbacks of a tropical climate, of frequent illnesses, lack of amusement, dullness consequent upon no English society to fall back upon in moments of depression, and despite of their very modest salaries, have entered so wholeheartedly into their work. If only their exploits were known and related as they deserve to be in all their details, these English officers would stand in the first rank of heroes, even of those who have won the Victoria Cross. Owing to the little attention given to Sarawak and its affairs, their deeds will never become known to the British public, and although they themselves will not reap the benefit of their unselfishness and loyalty to the Rajah's country, the seed they have sown in Sarawak has borne fruit in the growing security and contentment of its people.

CHAPTER XIV

WE had hardly settled down to our ordinary life at Kuching, when the news came of a tribe of Dyaks giving trouble in the Batang Lupar district. Mr. Frank Maxwell was in charge of the place, and was living at Fort Alice at Simanggang. It happened that the Rajah's yacht was then being docked in Singapore, so the Rajah decided to make his journey to Simanggang in a war-boat. As I was rather anxious for the Rajah's safety on this occasion, I thought I would like to accompany him and to stay at Simanggang while he went up country to quell the rebellion. The Rajah did not like the idea of taking me, on account of the long boat journey, but I insisted and, as usual, got my own way.

We started at midday, and had to spend the first night of the journey anchored in our boat at the mouth of the Sarawak River. I never shall forget the sand-flies that tormented us on this occasion; if possible, these insects are more trying than mosquitoes. They attack one in swarms, and are almost invisible, so that the meshes of a mosquito net are useless in keeping these pests from one's face and hands. The heat was stifling, the tempera-

ture being from 90° to 95°. I wrapped myself up—
face and hands included—in the folds of a silk sarong,
and in that manner passed the night in the boat. A
good deal of discomfort was obviated by my wearing
Malay dress. I need not say that my beautiful
garments, made by the chiefs' wives, were discarded
on this occasion. Over a shift of white silk, I folded
a cotton sarong, and wore a long Malay cotton
jacket over that. In countries hot as is Sarawak,
perpetual changes of garments are necessary, and I
took with me dozens of cotton sarongs, cotton
jackets, and one silk scarf (not forgetting Datu
Isa's injunctions that only the right eye should
be visible). A large conical straw hat effectually
shaded my face from the sun, and served as an
umbrella.

After spending a somewhat disturbed night, in the
morning I had to think about getting a bath. Ima, my
maid, was with me, and proved a valuable assistant
on my journey. Our boatmen, numbering some thirty,
were well acquainted with the banks of the Sarawak
River, and knew of several pools of fresh water not far
from the place where we had anchored. Our boat,
being of great size, could not be pulled level with the
bank, so a very small canoe was brought alongside,
into which Ima and I established ourselves. Ima
took the paddle and we wobbled to the shore. I held
desperately to the sides of the boat, and luckily only
a few strokes were required to bring us to land.
Ima brought my changes of clothes, and directed

me to a pool in the jungle. It was a slimy-looking place, screened in by trees, and here we had our morning dip. I had brought with me a piece of soap, and tying a sarong under my armpits stepped into the pool, and with the help of a dipper made of palm leaves poured the water over my head repeatedly, and in this manner managed to obtain a fairly enjoyable bath. I dressed myself in a fresh sarong and jacket and made my way back to the boat, where the Rajah, who had also found a pool to bathe in, was awaiting me.

We crossed the narrow strip of sea dividing us from the Batang Lupar River, and slept the next night at Lingga Fort. Our paraphernalia when travelling was very simple—the mattresses, which were stretched across the boat for the Rajah's and my comfort during the voyage, were carried on shore and laid on the floor in the Fort, the mosquito curtains were then hung up, and thus we were provided with a comfortable shelter for the night.

The next day, after 45 miles of paddling, we arrived at Fort Alice, taking Mr. Maxwell by surprise, for although he knew that the Rajah would make his way to Simanggang immediately on receipt of his dispatch, he had not expected to see me as well. There, however, as elsewhere, I met with nothing but kindness. Mr. Maxwell cheerfully gave me his rooms, and disappeared—goodness knows where—in some dim portion of the Fort. He would have none of my apologies, and pretended he thought it a pleasure to have the benefit of my company.

The next day great animation prevailed all over the place. The loyal and friendly tribes, who were to accompany the Rajah in his expedition, had been summoned to Simanggang by messengers to the various districts bearing calling-out spears, together with knotted strings. Each morning a knot is taken out by the chief of the tribe to whom the string has been sent, marking off the number of days that are to elapse before the Rajah requires his trusty subjects to follow him. It might be as well to mention that, with the exception of the Rangers (the drilled force from which the Rajah chooses his fort-men, sentries, and bodyguard), the remainder of the force might be compared to the English Reserves, for although the taxes of the people are very light—Dyaks paying one dollar per annum for their whole family— this does not exempt them from military service. Those Malays who pay an exemption tax of two dollars per annum per family are exempted from military service. As a matter of fact, whenever the services of Malays or Dyaks were required on expeditions, the Rajah usually found himself at the head of a far too numerous body of men, every man and boy being always eager for a fight, and whenever the fight was a lawful one, engaged under the leadership of the Rajah himself, hardly any of the Dyak male population could be persuaded to remain in their homes.

A large number of chiefs assembled in the great hall of the Fort, where were stacked the rifles and arms. When any serious matter required to be discussed, these chiefs were bidden into Mr. Maxwell's private sitting-room, capable of holding fifty or sixty people squatting comfortably on the floor. I have often been present at such meetings. The Rajah and Mr. Maxwell sat on cane chairs, and the chiefs squatted in rows on the floor giving vent to long-winded and extraordinarily fluent speeches. I do not know the Dyak language, and it is impossible to imagine the torrent of words that can pour out for hours together from the lips of these warriors. Their language resembles Malay in a disconcerting way; knowing Malay, I supposed I might understand what they said, but I could only catch a word here and there. Sea Dyaks speak in a jerky manner, and in councils of war sit perfectly motionless, their eyes fixed on the ground, and talk interminably, until the Rajah, sifting the important matter from the flow of rhetoric, stops the speaker and orders another man present to give his views on the subject. Dyaks are born orators, and think a great deal of anyone who can hold forth for hours without pausing for a word. They talk about such men in eulogistic terms : " He is good," " He is brave," " His mouth is beautiful," etc. I used to think such councils of war, from the lengthy speeches made, must prove trying to the

8

Rajah and his officers, but living amongst primitive people seems to change the temper, and make patience an ordinary accompaniment to life in those regions.

I well remember the morning of this particular conclave. After the council of war, the Rajah, Mr. Maxwell, the chiefs, and I, went into the hall where the arms were kept. Many obsolete weapons are to be found in nearly all Sarawak Forts. Some of the blunderbusses in Simanggang Fort were more than a hundred years old, having been taken in punitive expeditions from the houses of head-hunters. A Dyak present on this occasion took from a rack an old blunderbuss, and was handling the weapon unobserved by the authorities present. |Suddenly, a sharp report rang out, and we saw smoke issuing from the funnel of the blunderbuss and a Dyak in the crowd holding his head. The man smiled, " Medicine gone from that gun," he said, "and hit my head-handkerchief." He took the handkerchief off and held it up, when we could see it had been pierced by the charge that had so unexpectedly gone off. By a happy chance no person was wounded in the crowded room. I felt disturbed and looked at the Rajah, who was pulling his moustache as he does when anything out of the way takes place. " Strange ! " he said, looking at the man ; but Mr. Maxwell was very angry. " Why do you touch those things ? " he said ; " I always tell you not to meddle with the arms." The man gave a grunt,

but showed no other signs of disturbance, and the
conversation went on as though nothing unusual had
happened. When the Rajah, Mr. Maxwell, and I
met at breakfast, the matter was discussed at length,
and it was thought extraordinary that the powder
should be sufficiently dry to ignite a charge after so
many years. The mystery was never solved, but
the incident had served to bring out sharply a
curious trait in the native mind.

In a few days, arrangements were completed, and
the force started from Simanggang under the command of the Rajah. It was a picturesque sight, the
Dyaks in their war dress, their shields and war caps
bristling with horn-bills' plumes, their flowing waist-
cloths of bright colours, their swords and spears
rattling as they carried them proudly to the landing-
place and stacked them in their boats. A regular
flotilla of large war canoes followed the Rajah's boat,
the paddles making a thundering and rhythmic noise
as they churned up the waters of the river. It was
very splendid, exhilarating, and picturesque. All the
able-bodied Malay men in the place followed the
Rajah, so that the Malay village of Simanggang,
lying beyond the Chinese Bazaar, was almost deserted
of its male population. A prince of Brunei, called
Pangiran Matali, who once had been a subject of
the Sultan of that country but who had become a
Sarawak subject, a chief called Abang Aing, and
two other Malay chiefs from neighbouring rivers,
brothers, called Abang Chek and Abang Tek (whose

names and curious personalities reminded me of Tweedledum and Tweedledee, for they seemed inseparable friends), also accompanied the Rajah. Pangiran Matali and Abang Aing always took their share in expeditions against head-hunters. They invariably stood by the present Rajah through thick and thin, and had on many occasions risked their lives for him. The Rajah has often spoken to me of their loyalty, their courage, and also of their extraordinary aptitude in helping him with advice in political matters referring to the Sarawak Government. Daiang Kota, Abang Aing's wife, was a famous woman, a worthy helpmeet to her husband and a loyal subject of the Rajah's. I knew all these people well, and their memory can never fade from my heart.

A wonderful being, called Tunku Ismael, was left to guard the Fort and me. He was a Serip, a descendant of the Prophet ; he was thin and taller than most Malays, and had beautiful ascetic features, dark piercing eyes, and a hooked nose. He was always dressed in white, and wore the white skull cap that followers of the Prophet often wear, instead of the more cumbrous turban. This charming old gentleman and I were friends, for I always met him during my many visits to Simanggang. Mr. Maxwell's little dog, called Fury, a half-breed Yorkshire terrier, a valiant little creature, old and toothless, brave as a lion and helpless as a mouse, was also left in the Fort, and an old Malay, called Sunok, bent double with age, appointed himself my bodyguard. He slept at my door, and accompanied me in my daily walks round the Malay village and through plantations of sugar-cane and fruit orchards that lay around this settlement. Of course, Ima was with me, and she sent to the village for an old lady of her acquaintance, whose name was Dalima (meaning pomegranate), to come and help her wait on me. My days went by as regularly as clock-work. I got up at 5.30 a.m., sat on the terrace outside the Fort to watch the sunrise, and with Sunok went round and round the paths and through sugar-cane plantations, etc. Then I came in to bathe, have a cup of tea, and receive the Malay women of the place. After this I had my solitary breakfast, served by one of our Malay servants, who had been left behind to attend on me. From 12 to 2 I had my siesta, then more visits from the natives until 5, when it was cool enough to go out again with Sunok until 6.30.—the hour of sunset more or less all the year round. Then, after a hasty meal spent in fighting with mosquitoes which fell in clouds on to my food, I made a hurried exit inside my mosquito curtains to escape from these pests. Here, as elsewhere, the rats were numerous. They almost nightly stole the wick of my night-light from out the tumbler of cocoa-nut oil. They ran away with the candles placed on chairs by my bed-side, and were to be seen in companies scurrying in and out of the guns placed in the port-holes of my bedroom. Sometimes, as I was preparing for the night, the rats would sit upon the guns, their heads on one side, and brush their whiskers, as though they were taking stock of my toilet. Fury used to lie at my feet, inside the mosquito curtains, and it required all my persuasion to prevent him from sallying forth on the war-path against the rats, some of which were almost as big as himself. I dreaded the poor little animal meeting some horrible fate in an encounter with these formidable visitors. The rats, attracted by the candles and cocoa-nut oil, came in such numbers after a few days, that I asked Ima and Dalima to put their mattresses in my room and keep me company during the night. When first this measure was broached to Dalima, she said, "I quite understand your being frightened, because the enemy might attack the Fort and take us unawares during the night!" to which remark I replied—what was really very true—that the rats frightened me much more than could any Dyaks in the country.

Although my stay in Simanggang was rather lonely, I had certain compensations which did not entirely come from human companionship. I fancy every one must have heard of those beautiful birds— now being exterminated all over the world to satisfy the stupid vanity of ignorant and frivolous women—the egrets, or, as Sarawak people call them, paddy birds. From a terrace overlooking the river I used to watch, a little before sunrise and at sunset, for the daily migration of these birds to and from their roosting-places to the fishing grounds on the coast. Simang

gang is divided by about sixty miles from the sea, and
every morning and evening I could be certain, almost
to the minute, of seeing this company of white wings
in triangular battalions flying across the river. The
shafts of light breaking against their bodies in tints
of orange and rose made symphonies of colour
as they formed and re-formed with the movements
of the birds. I fancied the beautiful things understood the pleasure they gave me as they flapped
their great white wings over my head, across the
river, across miles of forest, finally disappearing like
dots of glittering light in the morning and evening
mists.

Another wonderful sight on the shores of that
Batang Lupar River was the Bore, a fort-
nightly phenomenon. Now the Batang Lupar, as
I have said before, is four miles in breadth at its
mouth. This vast volume of water progresses undis-
turbed for fifteen miles from the mouth of the river,
when the channel narrows until at Simanggang there
are only five hundred yards from bank to bank. At
each flood-tide, the water is forced, as it were, into a
funnel, through which it rushes, beating against sandbanks, rocks, snags, and other impediments existing
in this shallow river, hurling itself against such
obstructions with a noise like thunder which can be
heard for miles away. For some minutes the noise of
its advent was noticeable from the Fort, when in great
walls of white foam it rounded the last reach before
it passed Simanggang. Sometimes tiny boats, in

which were seated Malay children, were borne along
the swiftly-moving backs of the waves, the little
canoes looking like flies on the surface of a whirlpool.
The children seem to have charmed lives on such
occasions, for they can apparently play with the Bore
with impunity, although men and women have often
been known to find their death in the flood. As it
pounded up the banks, tossed itself against snags, and
fell back in huge cataracts of water, the spray, touched
by the sunlight, looked like a rain of precious stones.
Then on it went in its furious course, shaking the
boats moored to the banks near the Bazaar, tossing
them hither and thither, sometimes tearing one or
two away from their moorings, until growling, fighting,
and wrestling, it was lost to sight. For the first weeks
of my stay in Simanggang, the flocks of egrets and
the Bore were the two great attractions of the place.

As I was seated at breakfast one morning, a per-
spiring Dyak, frightened and incoherent, found his
way to my room and fell at my feet. Ima and
Dalima were with me, and Dalima, understanding
the Dyak language, translated the man's words to
me. "The Rajah is killed," he said. "All are dead,
and I go home." I looked at the man and saw his
complexion was of a pale greenish brown, like that of
some people when terrified or ill, and I imagined he
must be of an hysterical nature. I sent for Tunku
Ismael, who was then having his breakfast at his
home in the village. The refugee sat on the floor,
dressed in a bark waist-cloth and wearing a dirty

cotton handkerchief round his head. I told him not
to move, when he gave vent to sighs and grunts, and
remained speechless. When Tunku Ismael arrived,
he shook hands with me, and took his seat cross-
legged on a sofa opposite me near the wall. He did
not speak, but sat with his eyes cast down and his
hands palms downwards on his knees. "Tell me,
Tunku," I said, "what is the meaning of this? This
man says the Rajah and his followers are killed. He
is a liar, is he not?" "Bohong benar" (truly a liar),
the Tunku replied. "It is impossible such a thing
could have happened and he the only survivor."
"You are a liar," said Tunku Ismael, turning to the
man, who had become greener than ever. "You
have left the force because you are afraid." Another
grunt and contraction of the throat from the man on
the floor. "Dead, all dead," he repeated, "the Rajah
too, and the enemy will be here to-morrow." "All
lies," Tunku Ismael assured me, and once more turning to the man, he said, "Get out of this, and never
let me see you again." With that the man slowly
departed, left the Fort, and to my knowledge was
never again seen or heard of. I asked Tunku Ismael
why the man should have told this story. The
Tunku thought he must have become terrified and
run away from the force. "Let him go in peace," he
added, "a coward like that is better out of the Rajah's
bala" (force). No more attention was paid to this
rumour than to the buzzing of a mosquito, and we
soon forgot all about it.

Shortly after this incident, Tunku Ismael came to me one morning with a grave face and said, "Rajah Ranee, you are under my care, you go out for long walks all round the settlement, and seem to have no idea of danger, or that there might be bad spirits about. Sunok is exceedingly old, and if anything should happen to you during your long walks, what could I do to protect you?" I inquired what danger there was, for I knew of none. "Oh yes," he said, "there are many dangers. There are people we call *Peniamuns* who dress in black, cover their faces with black cloth, and sit in trees waiting to pounce on passers-by. Now, Rajah Ranee, should one of these *Peniamuns* get hold of you, we could never get you back again, so will you kindly walk up and down the terrace of the Fort, and not go any farther, for the *Peniamuns* are a real danger." I listened politely to Tunku Ismael, but continued to take my customary walks down to the Bazaar, across a plank of wood thrown over a ditch, separating the Chinese Bazaar from the Malay settlement, along the row of Malay houses, where the women and children were always on the look-out for me, and then home by the more lonely orchards and sugar plantations, so feared by Tunku Ismael.

One morning, I saw through the lattice-work of the Fort a flotilla of some fifteen war-boats coming up the river. I hastily sent for Tunku Ismael to inquire what these boats were. Tunku Ismael could not quite make them out, because, he said, they

looked like war-boats. We watched the boats as
they were paddled past the Fort, anchoring along
the banks near the Bazaar, and we stepped outside
to see what was happening. We saw a group of
Kayans from the boats, carrying spears and swords,
rushing up to the Fort, headed by a small man
recognized by Tunku Ismael as being a chief named
Tama Paran, who did not bear a very good character
in the Rejang district. This chief came up to me,
brandishing his spear, and carrying a basket which,
he said, the tribe had made for me. I asked him
where they had come from, and tried to look very
stern. "We hear the Rajah has gone on the war-
path, and we have come to accompany him," said
Tama Paran. "But," I replied: "the Rajah has been
gone on the war-path this last month, and you do not
know exactly where he has gone. You cannot accompany him now to the scene of action." "Yes," he
said; "we are going on to-morrow, because we wish
to fight for the Rajah." I realized that this was a
serious state of things. If I allowed this force to
go after the Rajah, with no responsible European
or Malay leader to keep it in check, the Kayans
might attack some unprotected village up the higher
reaches of the Batang Lupar River, take some heads,
and pretend it was done on the Rajah's behalf. I
said to the chief, "You must not move from here
until the Rajah comes back, unless you return to
your village." The man did not look pleased. He
could not wait in Simanggang, he said, neither could

he return home, but at any rate he consented to remain at Simanggang that evening. Tunku Ismael and I, with Sunok present, then held a council of war. We agreed it would never do to allow these Kayans to follow the Rajah, as they would probably endanger the safety of the country up river and frighten its inhabitants. We could see the fleet from the Fort, anchored near the Bazaar, and the Tunku estimated that the force numbered some six hundred men. He owned it would be somewhat difficult to keep them in order if the Rajah's return was long delayed, but, at the same time, we intended to do our best.

Tunku Ismael warned me not to walk out that evening along the Bazaar, because he feared that these Kayans, not being accustomed to white Ranees, might be disagreeable. I also felt a little apprehensive as to what my reception would be, but after thinking the matter well over, I came to the conclusion that if I did not take my usual walk, the women and children of the settlement would feel nervous, for, after all, it was unlikely the Kayans would do me any harm, for fear of the consequences when the Rajah returned. I therefore sallied forth that evening feeling a bit nervous, accompanied by the trembling octogenarian, Sunok, and the small dog Fury. I went along the Bazaar, and found the Chinamen standing outside their shops, who told me, in Malay, as I passed, that they wished very much those men would go away. The Kayans were cooking their rice, and were not at all friendly. They

made no attempt to shake hands with me, and say
" How do you do," as they would have done under ordinary circumstances. They looked rather impertinently,
I thought, at my humble procession. When I reached
the end of the Bazaar and was about to cross the
narrow plank of wood leading to the Malay settlement,
I saw a big burly Kayan standing the other side of the
plank with his legs straddled, almost daring me to pass.
His arms and legs were tattooed, his ears were ornamented with wild boar's tusks, his hair hung over his
neck, cut square in the front, and he wore a little straw
crown and a waist-cloth of bark.   I got within two feet
of the man, who gave a not very pleasant smile as
Fury barked loudly.   There he stood motionless.   I
turned to Sunok. " Remove that man," I said, but
Sunok weakly replied : " He is too strong, I can't ! "
The situation was ludicrous.   Had I turned back, it
would have shown fear on my part, so I asked the man,
in Malay, to get out of my way, but he remained as
though he had not heard me.   There was nothing left
for me but to press forward.   I walked slowly across
the plank until my chin (I was taller than the Kayan)
nearly touched his forehead.   Still he did not move,
so I stood as immovable as he, and waited.   After a
few seconds the man skulked off, and I went on my
way.   The Malay women had witnessed this incident
from their gardens, and they rushed up to me saying :
" Do take care, Rajah Ranee, and do not go out by
yourself like this.   The Kayans are a terrible people,
and might cut off all our heads before we know where

we are." I laughed lightly, although feeling somewhat upset, and finished my evening walk.

The next day, two or three Kayan chiefs came and asked for a sum of money which they knew was kept at the Fort, in order, as they said, that they might buy provisions and follow the Rajah. I again told them they were not to follow the Rajah and that I should not give them any money. Every day the chiefs came on the same errand, requesting money and permission to move. Personally, I was surprised they did not move, because nothing I could do would have prevented them. Tunku Ismael said they feared me, and he was sure the course we were taking was the only one to prevent disturbances in the country.

These Kayans were a great nuisance in Simanggang. They went about flourishing their spears and swords, frightening the shop-keepers and agriculturists into providing them with food. Indeed, the situation was daily becoming more alarming, and the interviews between the intruders and myself became more and more stormy, until one afternoon, when they had been in the neighbourhood for ten or twelve days, they became almost unmanageable. "We must have money," they said, "and we must follow the Rajah, and we do not care what anyone says." Tunku Ismael and I hardly knew what to do, when a bright thought struck me. I knew these people liked long speeches, discussions, councils of war, etc., and attached great importance to dreams; so putting on a very grave expression, I said, "Tama Paran and you

all who are his followers, listen to my words. You are
not to go up river, and you are not to have money,
because the Rajah would not wish it. But as I see
there is a strong will among you to do what you should
not do, at any rate, stay here over to-morrow; for to-
morrow is a particular date I have fixed within myself,
having last night had a dream. To-morrow I will tell
you about that dream, and I will make you understand
my reasons for wishing you to do as I tell you." "And
if we go to-day, what will you do?" inquired Tama
Paran. I pointed to the guns—with, I hope, a magnificent gesture. "If you disobey my orders, the
medicine from those guns will swamp every boat of
yours in the river." With those words, I got up and
dismissed them, after they had promised to come and
hear my speech the next day. Tunku Ismael gently
remarked: "But we do not know how to fire the
guns." "No," I said; "that does not matter; they
think we know, and after all that is the chief thing!"

That evening I went for my walk unmolested, and
retired to bed earlier than usual. I felt anxious. I
should have been so disgusted had the Kayans gone
away, in spite of my orders to the contrary. I should
have lost prestige with the women and even the children of Simanggang, so that I think had I seen any
signs of their boats leaving the place, I should somehow have found means to fire the guns into their midst.
All that night I could not sleep. I was wondering
what on earth I could say to the intruders to make
them realize the force of my arguments.

The question, however, settled itself. The very next morning I heard the yells of victorious Dyaks in the distance, then their paddles, and I knew all would be safe because the Rajah was returning. The Rajah soon sent the Kayans back to their homes, and, when all was said and done, I had quite enjoyed the novel experience.

CHAPTER XV

THE Rajah's expedition had been successful. The enemy's villages and rice farms were destroyed so as to compel the people to move farther down the river and form settlements under the supervision of the Lobok Antu Fort officials, about fifty miles above Simanggang.

Two or three days after the Rajah's return we took leave of Mr. Maxwell, and embarked in our travelling boat to return to Kuching. We spent the night at Lingga, and started off again the next day, intending to break our journey at a place on the coast called Sibuyow. We arrived late in the evening at Sibuyow village, where a messenger, sent by the Rajah the day before, had informed the people that we wished to spend the night at the chief's house. It had been exceedingly hot during the journey, and when we arrived at our destination I was almost dead with fatigue. Serip Bagus, another descendant of the Prophet, chief of Sibuyow, accompanied by the whole village, men, women, and children, was awaiting our arrival on the bank, with gongs and all sorts of musical instruments, making a weird and

9

rhythmic noise. The moon had risen and the palms
and mangroves lining the banks looked jet-black
against the pale, starlit sky. The mangroves
all down the river were one mass of fire-flies,
reminding me of Christmas trees magnificently
illuminated.

My passage on shore was made with the
customary difficulty. The ladder, laid across the
mud, was not at all easy for me to negotiate,
for the rungs were from two to two and a half
feet apart. There were so many people to help
me, however, that I managed the ascent without
mishap.

Serip Bagus and his wife, the Seripa, had taken
great pains to put their house in order for our arrival.
Following the Rajah, the chief's wife took me by the
hand and led me into a room, at one end of which
was a large raised platform, on which were laid mats
and embroidered cloths for the Rajah and myself to
sit on. This audience-room, similar to those built in
almost all Malay chiefs' houses, was filled with the
village people, who had come to see the Rajah and
listen to what he had to say. I was very tired and
longed for rest, but did not like to say anything for
fear of disappointing the people who had so kindly
prepared this reception for us. The Rajah and I sat
side by side on the platform, whilst the chiefs made
interminable speeches. I got more and more tired,
and at last said to the Rajah : " I must go away ; I
am so tired." The Rajah begged me to try and

keep up a little longer on account of the people. At length, however, people or no people, I could stand it no longer, and going behind the Rajah on the platform, laid full length on the floor, and fell fast asleep, regardless of any kind of etiquette. I must have woke owing to the conversation ceasing, and found the chief's wife bending over me. She told me she would lead me to a room where a bed was prepared for me, and taking my right hand, followed by her daughter, a young girl, dressed in silks, satins, and gold ornaments, together with four of the most aged females it has ever been my lot to see alive, she led me into the women's apartment, where, occupying about a quarter of the room, was a huge mosquito house. This was hung with valances of red-and-gold embroidery. Lifting up a corner of the curtain, the chief's wife took me, as she called it, to bed. Seven pillows, like hard bolsters, stiff and gorgeous with gold embroidery, were piled one over the other at the head of the bed—these being the seven pillows used on all Muhammadan couches, and below them was a hard, knobbly gold-embroidered bolster for me to rest my head on. The chief's wife took her position at my feet, with a fan, whilst the four old ladies, who grunted a good deal, each occupied a corner of the curtains, two of them holding sirih boxes and two paper fans, in order that I should not want for anything in the night. When daybreak came, I knew I should have to tell them I was awake and wanted to get up, seeing they would not dare to speak. All over Sarawak, whether amongst Malays or Dyaks, it is thought dangerous to awaken anyone from sleep, in case their souls should be absent from their bodies and never return again. Ima was not permitted inside my mosquito curtains, nor was she allowed to accompany me to my morning bath. The chief's wife, his daughter, his female cousins, his aunts, and the four old cronies with their sirih boxes and paper fans, came with me into the garden, where there was a pool of water. I stepped into this, and was handed a leaf bucket by the chief's wife, with great ceremony; this I filled repeatedly with water from a jar at the side of the pool and poured over my head. Dressed, as I was, in Malay costume, and bathing in a sarong, my change of clothes was easily effected. After my bath I joined the Rajah, who was having his tea. We partook of this meal in public, the villagers bringing us baskets of mangosteens, oranges, limes, eggs, ancient and modern, and many other things, too numerous to mention, considered delicacies by these people.

On this occasion we were without either guards or police, and if I remember rightly, the Rajah's crew consisted of men from the village of Simanggang.

As I was in the throes of negotiating the slippery ladder at the landing-place, on my way to the boat, a very shabby and not overclean old lady, who, I believe, was one of the chief's servants, rushed up to me and deposited in my hand a solitary egg. I carried this touching little present to the boat in fear and trembling, lest it should break or fall out of my hand, and thus disappoint the old dame.

Our journey across the sea was not without incident. We were in a shallow canoe, manned by some thirty men, and as we hugged the shore (it would not have been safe to go very far out to sea) a storm came on, and the boat began to rock badly. It was lucky that at critical moments our crew could jump out along that shallow part of the coast and keep the boat from turning turtle. Curiously enough, I am never sea-sick in a small boat. The danger on this occasion lay in the fact that to get into the Sarawak River we had to cross the mouths of the Sadong and Samarahan Rivers, and although I was perfectly unaware of the danger, the Rajah was a little anxious once or twice when, in crossing the bar, great rollers dashed themselves against our palm-leaf awnings and threatened to overwhelm us. I think the journey took about six hours, and by the time we entered the Sarawak River we were drenched. It was difficult to change one's clothing in the boat, as we were exposed to view, so we had to make the best of it. It is often said that sea water never gives one cold, and I suppose this must be true, for in spite of our wetting we were none of us the worse for the experience. Ima was very amusing; she kept whispering to me that if the Rajah liked he could make the sea behave better, but as he did not seem to worry, she supposed it did not matter very much. I was very glad when we arrived at our comfortable Astana, and could sleep between linen sheets once more.

CHAPTER XVI

A WEEK after our return to Kuching, the Rajah and I had the great pleasure of welcoming to Sarawak our eldest son. An experienced English nurse had brought him out, and I remember so well the mail-boat arriving late in the afternoon, when from the verandah I saw through my glasses a short European lady, in white, carrying in her arms a baby in a blue sash. I am sorry to say that the salute from the guns of the Fort annoyed him exceedingly, and he was brought yelling and screaming to the landing-place, and it took some time before we could soothe his shattered nerves, unaccustomed as he was to such honours. The next day, all the chiefs' wives, Datu Isa heading the contingent, and nearly all the women in Kuching, came to see the boy. He was very good with them, and appeared to understand that they were his true friends. It is a real happiness to me to know that the affection which he showed these people at the beginning of his life has lasted all through these years.

I was not destined to remain long in peace at Kuching, for the Rajah was always full of work in his schemes for the advancement of his country.

Many requests came to him from chiefs of rivers beyond our territory, begging to be allowed to become his subjects, in order to be placed under the protection of his Government. It would perhaps be as well just now to refer to the map of Sarawak. When the first Rajah began to reign, Sarawak consisted of the territory stretching between Cape Datu to the Sadong River. The maladministration of the Sultan of Brunei's agents in the rivers of the Rejang, Muka, and Bintulu forced the people of these districts to seek for better government. This, they found, so to speak, at their very doors. In the space of fifteen years, these rivers were annexed to the Sarawak Government, at the request of the inhabitants, so that when the present Rajah first inherited the country from his uncle it extended as far as the Bintulu River. Turning again to the map, it will be seen that the rivers of Baram, Trusan, Lawas, and Limbang now also form part of the Rajah's territory, but in the days of which I write the Baram River still belonged to the Sultan of Brunei, although the people were discontented under his rule.

The Baram River possesses a considerable Kayan population, and these people were anxious the Rajah should visit them in order to establish commerce and trade with Sarawak. The Sultan of Brunei was averse to the idea, and did all he could to prevent the Rajah's influence extending to this district. At that time, Her Majesty's Government had a Representative in the little island of Labuan, off the coast

THE AUTHOR AND IMA, MORNING ROOM AT ASTANA, KUCHING

of Borneo. Sometimes these Representatives were hostile to the Rajah's policy, taking the Sultan's side, without perhaps knowing the intricacies of the case. The Rajah was eager to go to Baram to ascertain for himself the position of affairs in the neighbourhood, and in order not to appear as though he were embarking on a hostile expedition against the Sultan's Government, he thought it advisable to take me with him on this trip.

We stayed two days at Muka Fort on our way up the coast. Muka was then in charge of the late Mr. Claude Champion de Crespigny, a man whose name must be beloved for all time in Sarawak. He was sympathetic, wide-minded, intelligent, and the Muka people loved him. The people of Muka are Milanoes : they work the sago, which flourishes in this district and forms a very important article of commerce in Sarawak. Some one told me that more than one-half of the whole of the sago exported to England comes from Muka and its neighbourhood. I do not know if this is so, but it is certain that a great deal of sago does find its way from this place to the English markets. The Borneo Company, Ltd., had then a sago factory at Muka.

I remember our tour in a boat round the Muka township : it was like most Malay settlements—the houses are built on the river-banks on piles. I thought a sago manufactory the most evil-smelling thing in existence. Here I observed how my rings, chains, etc., made of almost unalloyed Sarawak gold, turned black, and it was impossible to restore them to their original colour so long as I remained in the atmosphere of this busy but unsavoury town. The Milanoe women flocked to the Fort to see me, but they were not very talkative, and were rather shy, as hitherto they had had no experience of Englishwomen. Their features are square, and they have the slanting eyes, the squat noses, and thick lips of the Mongolian race, but their complexion is fairer than that of the other natives in Sarawak. They flatten their children's heads when they are tiny babies; oddly enough, the same custom exists amongst the American Indians inhabiting the Mosquito River. I have been told that the religion of the Milanoes resembles that of the Cochin Chinese, and this fact reminds me of the opinion expressed by Mr. Wallace as to these people originally coming to Borneo from the north. Milanoes are not so refined in their diet as are the Sea Dyaks. For instance, Sea Dyaks would never dream of eating oysters as we do, for they consider them living things. Milanoes prefer to eat uncooked fish cut up very fine, and are very fond of grubs; they also eat monkeys, sharks, snakes, and other reptiles. A great delicacy with them is a sort of transparent white-wood worm, which they rear with as much care as do English people oysters. They soak a large raft made of soft wood in the river for some weeks, when it is supposed to have fulfilled its purpose. It is then fished up, laden with the wriggling bodies of the worms.

After leaving Muka, we sailed for the Baram River, and about thirty-six hours' steaming brought us to its mouth. This river has an evil reputation; it is very broad, and a sandbank lying across its mouth only permits of the passage of shallow ships. The *Heartsease* drew seven feet of water, and as we could not find any channel deep enough to float her across, we embarked in the Borneo Company's vessel, called *Siri Sarawak*, which was accompanying us on this trip. The scenery is very different in this more northern part of Borneo. Instead of mangroves and nipa palms lining the banks, we saw great plains of coarse lalang grass and stretches of sand.

It was ticklish work proceeding up this river, there being no chart, for we were the only white people who had as yet entered its inhospitable borders in a vessel of any size. Mr. de Crespigny, who had been an officer in the English Navy, undertook to make a chart, and sat on the bridge the whole day, paper and pencil in hand, as we steamed carefully by snags and sandbanks, under the direction of a Kayan, who had been induced to leave his canoe at the mouth of the river to pilot our vessel to a place called Batu Gading, our destination. As we passed the Kayan houses, built on high poles near the banks, the people crowded on their verandahs to see the passage of the "fire ship." It was very exciting, and we all pulled out white handkerchiefs and waved them at the people to make them understand we were peaceful visitors. I did not like to ask indiscreet questions, but it did occur to me at the time whether these natives understood our signs. I have since found out that they did.

I think it took us about ten days to reach the settlement of Batu Gading (meaning rock of ivory, so called from a white rock embedded in the bank, shining like a beacon up one of the reaches of the river). Batu Gading was then the most populous Kayan settlement up this waterway, and it was here that the Rajah intended to land. We anchored in front of the longest Kayan house I had yet come across, but we could see no signs of life in the village. The Rajah sent his interpreter on shore to parley with the chief, Abang Nipa, but the answer returned was that the house was under what they called "pamale" (under a ban, spiritual or otherwise), and that the people of the village could not allow us to land because, under the circumstances, it was impossible for them to receive visitors. The Rajah, Mr. de Crespigny, and a gentleman belonging to the Borneo Company, Ltd., talked the matter over, and came to the conclusion (afterwards proved to be correct) that emissaries of the Sultan of Brunei, fearing a visit from the Rajah, were in the village and were preventing the people from receiving us inside their houses. Notwithstanding this drawback, our ship remained anchored in the middle of the stream, and a messenger was sent daily from the Rajah, always returning with the same answer. After the fourth or fifth day, the Rajah made it understood that if the pamale were to last a year, he would wait a year also, and that he was determined to see the chief in spite of all pamales. At length the princes of Brunei saw the futility of preventing the Rajah from carrying out his intention, and one morning Abang Nipa's son, accompanied by four or five stalwart Kayans, was seen on his way to our steamer. They brought with them an invitation to the Rajah from the chief, asking him to pay them a visit, and the interview was fixed for that very afternoon. A discussion then followed as to whether I should accompany the party on shore or not. The Rajah and Mr. de Crespigny, who knew the working of primitive people's minds better perhaps than any Europeans alive, thought it would be a good thing if I went also.

I remember the visit as though it were yesterday. A dinghy was prepared, and the Rajah, Mr. de Crespigny, the Borneo Company's agent, the English officers who had escorted the Rajah (my brother being amongst them), and I, entered the boat and were rowed to shore. The Rajah was followed by four or five of his guard, carrying muskets, but as they were about to step into a second boat the Rajah waved them back. "There must be no armed man in our party," he said; "for the slightest appearance of suspicion on our part might put the Kayans' backs up, and perhaps make them dangerous." As the guards disappeared, I wondered how it would be, but was not seriously apprehensive.

I never shall forget getting up the pole into this

house. As usual, the house was built on stilts, but these were higher than those of any house I had previously seen, and the notched pole, serving as a ladder, slanted at an angle of one in ten for about forty feet! It was no use worrying—up this ladder I had to go. The Rajah hopped up it like a bird. The chief's son and two or three other Kayans, seeing my hesitation, came forward and helped me up the perilous way. I must say, my helpers were most gentle and charming, and they took me up as though I were as brittle as egg shells. The other Europeans present found it quite easy to mount this interminable pole. I dare say it was my petticoats that made my ascent difficult, for women's clothes are much in the way on such occasions. The entrance into the broad verandah was a wonderful sight. All the way down, as far as I could see, it was lined with rows of fighting men, holding their lances in one hand, in all their war dress, tattooed from head to foot, with boar's tusks sticking out from their ears, grass crowns round their flowing locks, and holding themselves as though they were Greek gods. We walked as far as the centre of the house, where the chief's apartments were situated. There we found two stools, covered with yellow calico, and fine mats laid on the floor in readiness for our reception. The interior was divided by curtains made of mats or of Kayan stuffs of wonderful designs, similar to Celtic patterns, brown, white, blue, and very deep red. The Rajah and I seated ourselves on the

little stools, whilst the other Englishmen took their
places on the floor. We were quite silent, and the
presence of two of the Sultan's emissaries moving
in and out of the crowd, whispering to the people, did
not look very promising for the success of our
mission. The Rajah pulled his moustache, but said
nothing, and we sat on, all silent, looking at one
another. At last Mr. de Crespigny said to me :
" There are no women or children here. We must
get them in." I believe it is a fact that amongst
uncivilized or barbaric tribes the absence of women
and children is one of the signs of intended treachery.
Mr. de Crespigny suggested I should ask the chief
if I might make the acquaintance of his wife and the
other women of the tribe. I turned to the chief and
asked the question in Malay, which our interpreter
translated into Kayan. The Sultan's emissaries did
not look pleasant, but the chief seemed pleased, and
made a sign to one of the men standing near him,
who at once disappeared behind the curtains. In a
few moments the man came back and held the
curtains aside, when, through the opening, came a
procession of women. It was a pretty sight. The
chief's wife, a remarkable lady, much feared and
respected by her tribe, headed the procession. Her
black hair flowed over her shoulders, falling almost
to her knees, and on her head she wore a fillet of
straw. Her garment of white cotton hung in folds
from the waist to her right ankle, leaving her left
side bare, excepting at the hips, where it was

fastened with strings of beads.   Her left arm and leg
were bare but tattooed, and looked as though they
were encased in sheaths of dark blue velvet.   All the
women following her, young and old, wore the same
costume.   They might have been Greek priestesses
paying tribute to some god.   They shook hands
first with the Rajah, then with me, and seated themselves in a group at my feet.   The usual conversation
followed as to the number of their children, how their
farms were progressing, etc., and I then asked to
see some of the mats and cloths they had made.
After these had been duly admired, we became
quite friendly.   My sleeves were pushed up to see
whether my arms were white all the way up.   From
the ejaculations which followed, I cannot be certain
whether they were those of admiration or not!

I had round my neck a gold chain from which
was suspended a red coral charm, much in vogue
amongst Neapolitans to ward against the evil eye.
Mr. de Crespigny suggested I should give this to
the chief's wife, and I at once took the chain of gold
off my neck and put it round hers.   I remember how
the little narrow gold chain looked as it lay against
her mass of black hair, and the blood-red coral charm
appeared extraordinarily strange, yet picturesque,
as it hung amongst the folds of her white cotton
garment.   She was delighted with the ornament,
and when we parted the Rajah and the people
had become good friends.   I said good-bye to the
chief's wife, and experienced a strange pang of

regret, as I always did when parting, perhaps after a few minutes' conversation only, from a newly made friend, a member of a tribe whom I might never see again.

It is extraordinary what important parts several of these Kayan women have played in the history of those far-off countries. This particular chief's wife became, on the death of her husband, a great force for good in the Baram River, whilst another chieftainess, Balu Lahai (meaning widow of Lahai), had a powerful influence for good over a tribe of some thirty thousand people, who acknowledged her as their Queen. She undertook the management of the whole tribe, and until the day of her death (which occurred not so long ago) her word was law to every man, woman, and child in the village.

To make a long story short, the Rajah's visit to the Baram River produced great results. The Sultan of Brunei, powerless to stem the will of the Kayans, ceded the river to the Rajah. Forts and trading settlements sprang up as though by magic all along its banks, and it is now one of the richest and most populous rivers of the country. Mr. de Crespigny was the first of the Rajah's officers to take charge of the Baram district, and he did very valuable work out there before Dr. Charles Hose became Resident there some years later, at Mr. de Crespigny's death. Mr. de Crespigny was true to the Rajah's policy, and notwithstanding ill-health he most unselfishly and courageously remained at his post, and by so doing gave additional impetus to the trade and commerce of Sarawak, and security to the life of its inhabitants. Dr. Hose became his worthy successor, and by his zeal, hard work, and true sympathy with the natives has managed to crown Mr. de Crespigny's work by the magnificent results he has achieved in the true civilization of the Baram people.

On our return journey to Kuching, we stayed for a few days at Bintulu Fort. The dress of the women of Bintulu differs slightly from that of the Kuching Malays, as regards the texture of their sarongs and jackets, and as regards their gold ornaments. These people appear to prefer sombre tints to the bright colours worn by their Kuching sisters. A sarong much favoured by the Bintulu women is made of cotton with fine black threads running through, forming a check pattern all over the skirt, without the dog-tooth stripe so conspicuous in Javanese, Sumatran, and Malayan designs. This cotton material is so fine in texture that it is as costly to buy as some of the gold and silken brocades. The Bintulu women manage to obtain a gloss on the material making it shiny like satin. One has to pay as much as £6 or £7 for one of these sarongs. Over this black-and-white sheath, these women wear a jacket of either black or dark blue satin, imported from China. It fastens in front with three huge knobs of gold, and small gold knobs are sewn all up the slashed sleeves. Large round ear-rings, some-

times very exquisite in design, shaped like open
lotus flowers, are thrust through the lobes of their
ears. Their scarfs are of quiet colours, devoid of
gold thread, but their hats are marvellous. Sometimes they are as much as a yard across, so that no
two women can walk near one another. They are
made of straw, conical in shape, and are ornamented
with huge pointed rays of red, black, and yellow,
meeting towards the centre. Mr. de Crespigny,
who knew of the dresses and habits of these people,
told me to look out for the ladies as they wound
their way up the path leading to the Fort, and
it was indeed a curious sight to see two or three
hundred of these discs, one after the other, apparently
unsupported, winding slowly up the steep ascent.
When the women reached the Fort, they left their
hats somewhere—I never fathomed where—before
they came into the reception-room.

They are pleasant-looking people, these Milanoes
of Bintulu, with their square, pale faces and quantities
of jet-black hair. Their ankles and wrists are not
perhaps quite so delicate as are those of the more
southern people, for Milanoes are sturdier in build.
They belong to the same tribe as the sago workers
of Muka, but, owing to their more sedentary habits,
their complexion is paler. Europeans who know them
well have many interesting stories to relate regarding
their superstitions and incantations, particularly in
the case of illness, when the beautiful blossom of the
areca-nut palm plays an important part.

On the night of our arrival at the Fort, native dances were the programme for the evening. A few Kayans from the far interior were present, and we were promised some new and original performances. A large space was cleared in the middle of the reception-room, when a small, rather plump individual, a Kayan, active as a cat, was ushered in, brandishing his parang. At first he crouched down and bounded about the room like an animated frog. After a while he gradually straightened himself, and bounded from one side of the space to the other, jumping with the most wonderful agility, spinning round on one leg, and screaming out his war-cry. His parang, in his rapid movements, became multiplied and appeared like flashes of lightning. Once or twice he came so near to where we were sitting that I fancied the blade caused a draught over my head. I said nothing and sat on unmoved, but, before one could realize what was happening, three Kayans squatting on the floor sprang to their feet, and taking hold of the man, led him out of the hall. The Rajah pulled his moustache. "What is it?" he said. "Why has the man been taken away?" We were then informed that this Kayan, who was a famous dancer, had previously, in a country outside the Rajah's jurisdiction, become so excited in his dancing, that he had actually swept the head off one of his interested spectators. The three Kayans who had taken hold of the dancer had witnessed the gruesome scene, and they realized that on this occasion he was becoming over-excited. Other dances followed, some sedate and slow, others frenzied and untamed. The evening ended very pleasantly, and at a somewhat late hour the Rajah dismissed his guests and we retired to bed. I thought a good deal about the little dancing man, and came to the conclusion that he must have been an artist in his way!

CHAPTER XVII

ONE morning, as I was watching the arrival of
the mail-steamer from my verandah at Kuching,
I noticed the figure of a tall European lady
standing on deck. A few moments after, a messenger
brought me a letter from Singapore from the
Governor's wife, Lady Jervois, introducing a
traveller to Sarawak, whose name was Marianne
North. The Rajah was away, so I sent his Secretary
on board with a pressing invitation to the lady, of
whom I had heard so much, but had not had the
pleasure of meeting. Miss North's arrival in
Sarawak is a great and happy landmark in my life.
Many of my English friends were devoted to her,
and I was delighted at the idea of her coming to stay
with me. I watched our small river-boat fetching
her from the steamer, and went to meet her. She
was not young then, but I thought she looked
delightful. We shook hands, and the first words she
said to me were : "How do you know if you will
like me well enough to ask me to stay with
you?" From that moment began a friendship
which lasted until her death. Many people know
the great work of her life, and must have seen the

SUN SETTING BEHIND THE MOUNTAIN OF MATANG

gallery of her pictures which she gave to Kew Gardens. Many of these pictures were painted in Sarawak.

The first evening of her stay in Kuching we went for a row on the river, and the sunset behind Matang was, as she said, a revelation. That land of forests, mountains, and water, the wonderful effect of sunshine and cloud, the sudden storms, the soft mists at evening, the perfumed air brought through miles and miles of forest by the night breezes, were an endless source of delight to her. Sometimes as we sat on our verandah in the evening after dinner, a sweet, strange perfume wafted from forest lands beyond, across the river, floated through our house—" The scent of unknown flowers," Miss North would say.

Our boat-boys were sent on botanical expeditions for jungle plants, and every morning and evening a great variety of things arrived at the Astana, many of which I had never seen or even heard of. In the morning I would take my work into Miss North's room and sit with her whilst she painted, for I loved her companionship. She it was who first made me realize the beauty, solace, and delight found in trees, plants, and flowers. But sometimes she was very stern ; she thought me young and stupid. She would look at me through her spectacles, very kindly, I must say. " Why, you know nothing," she said, "although you are so late from school ! " She once asked me where pitcher-plants were to be found.

"Pitcher-plants," I said; "I have never heard of them. I don't think there are any in the country." "But this is the land of pitcher-plants," Miss North replied, "and if you like we will try and find them together." I sent for the boat-boy. I remember distinctly the picture she was painting at the time— a clump of sago palms growing in our garden. She told me how I could describe pitcher-plants to the faithful Kong Kong, one of our boat-boys, a Sarawak Malay, an odd and uncouth individual, with long hair flowing over his shoulders. He had been with the Rajah for many years. "Oh yes," said Kong Kong, "I know. They grow where earth is marshy. I can show you where they grow." One morning Miss North and I got up early and crossed the river almost before sunrise, and with Kong Kong as our guide, went in search of the pitcher-plants. We walked for a little way along the Rock Road, and turned into a path leading through a kind of moor, where the sensitive plant lay like a carpet covering the ground. That curse of agriculturists always delighted me. I felt a certain enjoyment in walking through the great patches of this shrinking stuff with its myriads of leaves closing at the slightest touch. We left a pathway behind us of apparently dying vegetation, but a minute or two after our passage it resumed its normal shape. Malays call it the "Shy" plant. Kong Kong then led the way over a swamp, where logs of wood were laid to keep passers-by off the mud. Our progress across these logs was not an easy matter. We went through a grove of trees, and suddenly, in a clearing, we came to the spot. I do not think anyone who has only seen pitcher-plants growing in the sedate way they do at Kew can have any idea of the beautiful madness of their growth when in a wild state. Here they were, cups long, round, wide, and narrow, some shaped like Etruscan vases, others like small earthenware cooking-pots, the terminations of long, narrow, glossy green leaves. Their colour, too, was perfectly exquisite — a pale green ground, splashed over with rose, carmine, yellow, and brown, the little lids to the cups daintily poised just above each pitcher. I suppose there must have been thousands of these plants, twisting, creeping, and flinging themselves over dead trunks of trees, falling in cascades of colour above our heads, forming a perfect bower. We all stood still, silently looking at them. At length Miss North remarked: "And you said yesterday there were no such things in the country!"

Miss North remained with us about six weeks, and when I very sorrowfully accompanied her on board the steamer on her return to England, I felt that something new and delightful had come into my life, for she had not only introduced me to pitcher-plants, but to orchids, palms, ferns, and many other things of whose existence I had never dreamed. Miss North was the one person who made me realize the beauties of the world. She was noble, intelligent, and kind, and her friendship and the time we spent together are amongst my happiest memories. She used to paint all day, and, thinking this must be bad for her, I sometimes tried to get her away early in the afternoon for excursions, but she would never leave her work until waning daylight made painting impossible. I remember how she painted a sunset behind Matang, which painting she gave to me. She sat on a hill overlooking the river until the sun went behind the mountain. The world grew dark, and the palms in the neighbourhood looked black against the sky as she put her last stroke into the picture. She put up her palette, folded her easel, and was preparing to walk home with me to the Astana, when for some moments she stood quite still, staring at the thread of red light disappearing behind the shoulder of the mountain. "I cannot speak or move," she said. "I am drunk with beauty!"

But there was one thing that Miss North and I did not agree upon. She did not approve of the view I took of our Dyak and Kayan people. She liked to meet Malay ladies, because, as we all know, they have better manners than most Europeans, but she could not bear the thought of either Dyaks or Kayans. I could never eradicate from her mind the idea that they were savages. I used to try and interest her in these people, for I longed that she should accompany us in some of our journeys into the interior, but this she would never do. "Don't talk to me of savages," she would say; "I hate

them." " But they are not savages," I would reply.
" They are just like we are, only circumstances have
made them different." " They take heads : that is
enough for me," she would add severely, and would
listen to no defence for that curious custom of theirs,
for which I could find so many excuses.

CHAPTER XVIII

A FEW months after Miss North's departure, my second son Bertram was born. His arrival gave pleasure to the people of the country, for they think a great deal of a Rajah's son who is born on their soil. It may be on this account they look upon him as their particular property. My Malay friends poured into my room as he lay in his cradle, and made various remarks as to his future: "A Sarawak boy," "A son of our Rajah," "He will be great some day," "Look at his nose," and they tenderly took this feature between their thumb and forefinger (even in those days Bertram's nose was rather prominent), and then felt their own flat noses. The many toys and jingling ornaments that hung over his cradle made a forest of glittering things above his head and caused him much enjoyment. He is called "Tuan Muda" (young lord), a title given in Sarawak to the second brother in succession to the Raj. Malay children were brought to play with him, and his arrival strengthened even more the bonds of friendship already existing between the people and the Rajah's family. "How good it will be, Rajah Ranee," Daiang Sahada would say, "when he grows up and marries and has children, and you and I will be here to take care of him and his family. It will make Sarawak still more beautiful than it is now, for it will ensure our future happiness." It is sad to think that nearly everything we most look forward to in life does not come to pass, and instead of my now being with my sons, their wives, and their children, happily settled in Sarawak amongst the best friends we have in the world, I should be writing this book and wasting my life here in this city called London.

Bertram's arrival on the scene prevented me from taking as many expeditions with the Rajah as before. I now spent months together in Kuching, and day by day added to my knowledge of the people, of their beliefs and their aspirations, and made me love them more than ever. It was during this period the idea came to me that it was a pity Malay women could not read or write their own language. They were fond of ancient lore and enjoyed hearing the legends and romantic tales relating to their race, handed down to them through traditional sources. In all the suburbs of Kuching curious old women were to be found, many of whom had acquired in some mysterious manner these tales from those of past generations. Such old women were called reciters, and Malay ladies when giving parties often hired their services to entertain their friends. Having learnt of this amusement, I started parties of recitation at the Astana,

which generally took place in the evening. Clad
in our best silks and satins, and stiff with gold
brocade, we sat together in my private room with
the reciter, poorly dressed in dark cotton clothes,
pouring out wonderful stories of kings, queens, and
princesses ; of royal gardens, monkey-gods, peacocks,
flowers, perfumes, and such-like things. I could not
follow these stories very well, because these old
ladies sang every word. Sometimes the voice was
low, sometimes very shrill, and when embarrassed
for a word, they trilled and quavered, remaining on
a very high note until they remembered how the story
went, when they gleefully descended the scale, began
again, and poured forth further torrents of words.
Sometimes they paused, walked rapidly across the
room, and spat through the window. "She is full
of understanding," Datu Isa would say after one of
these journeys to the window. "She knows her
work !" "Her words come from ancient times !"
"It is beautiful exceedingly !" Meanwhile, the
reciter, holding her draperies firmly round her, left
the window, and bending double as she passed us
as a sign of respect, took her place once more in
the centre of her admiring circle and began afresh,
until stopped again in the same way, when the same
ejaculations of admiration came from us all.

After one of these evening parties, as Datu Isa
and her satellites were sitting talking to me in my
room, I suggested that we should all learn to read
and write Malay, which language is written in Arabic

DAIANG SAHADA, DAIANG LEHUT, MRS. MAXWELL, THE AUTHOR AND ATTENDANTS

characters. I asked Datu Isa how we had best set
to work, for I thought it would be good for the
Malay women and myself to be able to read and
write Malay for ourselves. "No," said Datu Isa;
"that would never do. Writing amongst women is
a bad habit, a pernicious custom. Malay girls would
be writing love letters to clandestine lovers, and
undesirable men might come into contact with the
daughters of our house. I do not agree, Rajah
Ranee, with the idea, and I hope it will never come
to pass." This was rather crushing, because Datu
Isa was a tremendous force in our social life in
Kuching, but I was not altogether dismayed, and
being anxious for this additional pleasure to come
into my friends' lives, I pondered on the subject.

A good many months went by before I could
put my suggestion into execution. Meanwhile I
began to study on my own account, and sent for
Inchi Sawal, a celebrity in the Kuching circles of
those days. He was called a "Guru" (master of
arts). He knew Arabic, was a good Malay scholar,
and had taught a great many of the Rajah's officers
in the intricacies of the language. Formerly he had
been Malay writer to the late Rajah. Malay is easy
enough to talk ungrammatically, and one can make
oneself understood by stringing together nouns and
adjectives, regardless of verbs, prepositions, etc. The
natives of Sarawak, although learning the language
by ear, speak very good Malay, but it was deplorable,
in those days, to hear it spoken by some of the

English people residing in Kuching. The Rajah, however, is one of the best Malay scholars in Malaya, and it is a real pleasure to hear his Malay speeches to his people.

Inchi Sawal was a great stickler for grammar. He was a Sumatran Malay, and his face was rounder, his features rather thicker and his complexion darker than our Malays; moreover, his hair was curly, and his whole appearance was cheerful, genial, and kindly. His functions were numerous. He was, of course, a Muhammadan, and had friendly relations with all the Malay chiefs of Kuching, by whom he was looked upon as a cultured man : in fact, they considered him the arbiter of Malay literature. He was a butcher, and knew exactly what was required in the killing of bullocks for Muhammadan consumption. He was a wonderful confectioner, and made delicious preserves with little half-ripe oranges growing in orchards round Malay houses in the town. He sent me some of this preserve as a present for New Year's Day, and as I liked it so much, I wanted to know how it was made. Accordingly, Inchi Sawal came to the Astana to give me a lesson. It would take too long to tell of the methods he employed in the preparation of the fruit, but it seemed to me that a good deal of religion was mixed up with the cooking of those small, bobbing green balls, as they simmered in the boiling syrup. A number of invocations to Allah secured a good result to his labours. Inchi Sawal had a different appearance during each of his occupations.

When cooking oranges, a grave, religious aspect seemed *de rigueur* as he leant over the pot. When talking of bullocks, his victims, a devil-me-care expression spread over his countenance, as though in the slaughter of each beast he had to wrestle with a sanguinary foe. At lessons he became urbane, courtier-like, and mild.

When his teachings began, Inchi Sawal brought with him pens made from the mid-ribs of palm leaves, used by most Arabic scholars in Malaya. I am afraid I did not prove a very apt pupil. My tutor pronounced a word, which I said after him. I found great difficulty in giving an adequate sound to the Arabic letter ع (*aing*), awkward for Europeans to pronounce. I read Malay in these characters with him, and it annoyed him very much whenever I let a vowel pass without pronouncing it properly. "The beauty of reading," he would say, " is to look at a word well before you give vent to its sound. Think over the letters, Tuan, and although it should take a year to master one word, when you have mastered it, it will give your heart relief and comfort."

One morning Inchi Sawal was more solemn than usual. "I have spoken to the Datu Imaum about our lessons," he said, as he came into the room, "and he quite agrees that we should together study the Koran. I will bring the book wrapped in many cloths, and, if you do not object, we will wash our hands before we handle its leaves. We might do a little of the Koran before we begin our Malay lessons, which will put us in the proper frame of mind for the things we have to learn. The Datu Imaum also approves of your learning to read and write, as he thinks it will be a great incentive to the Malay women to improve their minds and strengthen their hearts."

Very gravely he unfolded the wrappings in which the Koran lay, and reverently handled the pages of this marvellous book of wisdom, as we read together the first chapter :—

" Praise be to God, the Lord of all creatures ; the most merciful, the king of the day of judgment. Thee do we worship, and of thee do we beg assistance. Direct us in the right way, in the way of those to whom thou hast been gracious ; not of those against whom thou art incensed, nor of those who have gone astray. . . ."

As time went on and Datu Isa found I could read and write Malay, she relented so far as to allow her married daughters and daughters-in-law to join me in my studies. We had great fun over our lessons, and, after some time, Daiang Sahada (Datu Isa's daughter-in-law) began to write almost better than the great Inchi Sawal himself. She commenced to describe the history of Sarawak, from the advent of the first white Rajah, in poetry, and played a prominent part in the education of her sisters. In her comfortable house, she and her husband, Abang Kasim (now the Datu Bandar), helped me in my efforts by institut-

ing a school for women and young boys. In a short
time the pupils were too numerous for the size of her
house, and the Rajah, being interested in this new
impetus given to education by the women of Kuching,
built a school where Malay reading and writing were
taught, and installed Inchi Sawal as master.[1]

One must mention that even in those days the
Mission schools, organized by the Protestant Bishops
of Sarawak, their chaplains, and missionaries, had
attained considerable proportions, and were doing
immense good amongst the Rajah's Chinese and
Dyak subjects, but for very good reasons the Muhammadans were never approached by Christian teachers.
As the country developed, the Muhammadans (Malays)
also longed for educational facilities on their own
lines, so the Rajah instituted a school where Arabic
was taught.

Writing of these educational matters recalls many
happy hours I spent in Inchi Sawal's company. I
regret to say that some years ago he was gathered
to his fathers, and buried in the little Muhammadan
cemetery I know so well. I can fancy his weeping
women wrapping him in a sheet, according to the
Muhammadan custom. I can also picture the little
procession of boats, accompanying the canoe in
which his body was placed covered with a white
umbrella, paddling to the shores of his last resting-
place, where his grave had been dug by members of

[1] This school became known as Abang Kasim's school, and now has
a large attendance.

the Faith — that shallow grave about three feet
deep, allotted to followers of the Faithful, from
whence, at the resurrection, at the bidding of the
Angel Azraïl, together with other good Muhammadans, Inchi Sawal shall rise up and be folded
in the bosom of Allah—the Merciful, the Com-
passionate.

Another Malay school, on the opposite side of the
river, was founded by Inchi Bakar, the son of old
Inchi Buyong, also a Sumatran Malay. Inchi Bakar
succeeded his father as Court Interpreter, and was
also the Head of the Customs. He and his family are
great friends of mine, and I often paid them visits.
He is, perhaps, more a man of the world than was
Inchi Sawal. The profession of butcher fell into
other hands, nor do I think that Inchi Bakar is an
adept at cooking the little oranges of which I was so
fond. He is, however, a great light in his way, and
his house is a meeting-place for the more educated
Malays of Kuching. Whilst retaining his Arabic
culture, one can talk to him almost on any subject,
for he reads and writes English as well as most
Englishmen. He was partial to Chinese society, for
amongst the Chinese merchants of Kuching are to be
found enlightened and cultured gentlemen. Many a
time I have sat on the broad and comfortable verandah
of Inchi Bakar's house and witnessed Chinese plays
enacted on narrow wooden tables, with their feast of
colour, curious costumes, Chinese music, and clashing
of cymbals. Although the stage was narrow and there

VERANDA IN DAIANG SAHADA'S HOUSE AT KUCHING

was no scenery beyond curtains of scarlet and gold, on which were embroidered rampant dragons, we could understand the intricacies of the drama better, perhaps, from the fact that so much was left to our imagination. Chinese players often came to Sarawak, and are now permanently established in the Chinese Bazaar, but as it is not customary for Malay women to mingle with a crowd, private parties, at which these dramas were acted for their benefit, were frequent amongst the aristocrats in Kuching.

I am happy to say that Inchi Bakar is still living, and I often hear from him. Although he and I may be parted, sometimes for years together, the friendship that exists between us is as strong as it was in the early days of our acquaintance, when he was a young lad visiting me at the Astana with his mother and grandmother. Malays are faithful friends, nor does absence blunt their friendship. I derive great consolation from that fact, when, as often happens, a sort of home-sickness comes over me, and I feel as though I must take the next ship back to the land I love so well, never, never to leave it again.

In those days Inchi Bakar's wife was also included in our educational group. She was a relation of Datu Isa, and she and Daiang Sahada were friends. I should like to draw special attention to the part played by these two Malay ladies in the education of the women in Kuching, who were much impressed by their kind interest and sympathy. Those were pleasant days for us all, groping about the letters of the Arabic alphabet, and trying to obtain calligraphic perfection. After what we considered our hours of hard work, we thought recreation was necessary, so that on most days, as it got cooler and the sun began to sink behind Matang, we would go into the Astana garden in order to " eat the air," as they said. Those walks in our garden were a great delight to them. They loved the roses, the jasmine, the honeysuckle, the tuberoses, and many other tropical plants which grew in beds on the closely mown lawns round our house. They often asked permission to take some of the flowers home, and their methods of picking the flowers were so refined, gentle, and economical, that they might pick as many as they liked without any devastation being noticeable in the beds after their passage. Malays never pick flowers with their stems ; they only take the heads of flowers which they set floating in saucers filled with water. They used to ask me why we ordered our gardeners to break off great branches of blossoms to put in water in our drawing-room. " They are so high up," they would say, "their perfume can never be thoroughly enjoyed. Besides it destroys the plant." So that in my rooms I always had great basins full of sweet-smelling stemless flowers floating on the surface of the water to please my friends. If only we could free ourselves from the conventional ideas, we must realize it is entirely erroneous to imagine that in order to make a room beautiful we must decorate it with long stems of flowers and buds.

DAIANG LEHUT—DAIANG SAHADA'S DAUGHTER

I think Malays have much better taste in such matters, because flowers smell quite as sweet and last just as long under the methods they employ of perfuming their houses.

Our evening strolls through the Astana grounds reminded my friends of the legends related by the old lady reciters. "Here we are," they often exclaimed, "in the Rajah's gardens, playing, smelling sweet perfumes, and looking at ponds over which floats the lotus—just like the old stories." Beyond the miles and miles of forest land stretching to the north between Kuching and the sea, the mountain of Santubong could be seen from our garden towering on the horizon. Viewed from Kuching, the outline of the mountain as it lies against the sky, has the appearance of a human profile, bearing an extraordinary resemblance to the first white Rajah of Sarawak. The Malays are aware of this fact, and the women have frequently said to me as we stood looking at the mountain, "The gods knew what they were about, they fashioned Santubong so that the image of the first white Rajah should never fade from the country."

Another source of joy on these occasions was the presence of a peahen we kept roaming about at liberty in our garden. The naked feet of the women pattering up and down the paths was, for some mysterious reason, more than the bird could stand. The appearance of my Malay friends was the signal for it to single from out the group one unfortunate member, when it would rush at her toes and follow her in and out the bushes on the lawn. The victim, half-amused and half-frightened at the pecks, would move quicker than is customary amongst Malay aristocrats. Sometimes the bird got so violent in its attacks, that I had to call the sentry on guard at the door of the Astana. The sentry (either a Malay or a Dyak), in his white uniform with black facings, musket in hand, appeared very courageously at first to protect the woman from her feathered persecutor, until the peahen turned her attention to his toes, whereupon his musket was dropped, and the little figure of the sentry rushing hither and thither in his frantic attempts to escape from the bird caused us much merriment. This was a frequent occurrence, and my Malay friends called it "playing with the peahen"! I was glad I wore shoes, for I do not think I should have enjoyed the bird's antics quite so much as they did.

Sometimes the party stayed until 6 p.m., when, on fine evenings, more punctual than any clock, we heard a shrill trumpeting noise issuing from the woods near the Astana. I believe this came from a kind of cricket. "It is the six o'clock fly telling us to go home," they said, and, at the first sound of this musical alarum, my friends bade me good-night, stepped into their boats, and were paddled to their homes. I often watched them as they went away in their covered boats, the paddles churning up the golden or flame-coloured waters of the river

tinted by the sunset, and thought how absurd it is that
different coloured skins should be a bar to friendship
between white and dark people, seeing that kindness and sympathy are not confined to any region of
the earth, or to any race of men.

CHAPTER XIX

MALAY people have a great reverence for age, and Datu Isa's many years apparently endeared her still more to the younger generation at Kuching. Her children, grandchildren, and I, were delighted when she would tell us about her early life, and also about the superstitions and legends of her country. Her conversation was always interesting, and I wish I could give an impression of her manner when relating these tales. When sixteen years of age, she, together with several Malay women of Kuching, had been liberated from captivity by the menacing guns of James Brooke's yacht, turned on to the Palace of her captor, Rajah Muda Hassim, who had intended to carry her off to Brunei for the Sultan's harem. This personal reminiscence invariably served as the prelude to other interesting tales. The story of the Pontianak ghost, for instance, was the one which perhaps thrilled us most. Malays almost sing as they talk, and their voices quaver, become loud or soft, or die off in a whisper, the words being interspersed with funny little nasal noises, together with frowns, sighs, or smiles. When about to relate a dramatic incident, Datu Isa became silent for a moment, looked at us with knitted brows, although she did not see us, so intent was she on her story.

This is the story of the Pontianak. When a baby is about to be born, the father walking under the flooring of his house hears a low chuckle behind him. He turns round, and sees a beautiful woman looking at him. Her face is like the moon, her eyes are like stars, her mouth is like a half-open pomegranate, her complexion is white, her hair intensely red. She wears a sarong round her waist, and no jacket covers her shoulders. Should the husband have neglected to set fire to the bunch of onions, tuba roots, and other ingredients, the smoke of which keeps evil spirits away, the woman stands there for some moments without uttering a sound. Then she opens her mouth, giving vent to peals of laughter. By this time the husband is so frightened that he can think of no spell by which to combat her evil intentions. After a while, her feet rise an inch or two from the ground, and as she flies swiftly past him, her hair flows straight behind her like a comet's tail, when he sees between her shoulder blades the large gaping wound, signifying that she is a Pontianak. After this apparition, there is no hope for the woman or the babe about to be born, they are doomed to die, so that the Pontianak is one of the most dreaded ghosts haunting Malay houses.

As Datu Isa finished the Pontianak story, we all clamoured for more. The old lady loved to see

our interest, and went on telling us many other
superstitions : Unless you cover the heads of sleep-
ing children with black cloth, and put a torn fishing
net on the top of their mosquito curtains, the birds,
Geruda, Dogan, and Konieh (supposed to be eagles),
will come close to them and cause convulsions.   You
must put knives or pinang cutters near your babies,
and when walking out with them you must take these
instruments with you, until your babies can walk
alone.   Then turning to me, Datu Isa would say : " I
hope you will never see the sun set under the fragment
of a rainbow, Rajah Ranee, for that is a certain
portent that the Rajah's wife must die, although
rainbows in other portions of the sky do not matter
if you know how to address them.   When my children
and grandchildren are out in the garden, and a rainbow arches over the sky, we pluck the heads off the
more gaily coloured flowers and place them on the
children's heads, and say : ' Hail, King of the Sky,
we have come out to meet you in our finest
clothes.' "

It is unlucky for a child to lie on its face and
kick up its legs, this being a sure sign the father or
mother will fall sick.   When a woman expects a
baby, the roof of her house must not be mended, nor
must her husband cut his hair or his nails.   During
this time a guest must not be entertained for one
night only ; they must stay two.   When a woman
dies in childbirth, during the fasting month of the
Muhammadans, she becomes an "orang alim" (a

good spirit), and all the sins she may have committed are forgiven her.

Datu Isa had great faith in a bangle I possessed, made of a kind of black seaweed found on the Sarawak coast, and she was anxious I should take care not to break it. It was given me in this way : During the first years of my stay in Sarawak, an old gardener employed at the Palace, having in some way misbehaved himself, was dismissed. Shortly afterwards, I met the old man in a state of great depression during one of my walks the other side of the river, and he begged me to use my influence with the Rajah and get him taken back again, promising he would behave better in the future. He was a lazy old man, but as I felt sorry for him, I asked the Rajah to give him another trial. The Rajah agreed, and the man resumed work in the Astana garden in his own desultory way. I often used to watch him pulling up the weeds from the paths; he would sit on his haunches, stare at the river, and take some minutes' rest after every weed he extracted. Notwithstanding these drawbacks, he was a grateful soul, and on the morning of his reinstalment amongst the Rajah's gardeners he brought me a bangle made of this black seaweed. It was very small and I had difficulty in getting it over my hand, so the old man put it into boiling water to make it more elastic, and, after some little trouble, it was forced over my hand. "Lightning, snake bites, and antus can never harm you," he said, "as long as you keep the bangle round your wrist, but should it ever break, it would bring you bad luck!" The bangle is on my wrist now, and I dread lest anything should happen to it, for should it ever get broken, I should feel just as nervous of the result as would any of my Malay women friends.

Some of the Malays in Sarawak use somewhat disconcerting methods to frighten away evil spirits on the occasion of very bad storms. After a frightful gale, accompanied by incessant lightning and thunder, that occurred in Kuching, two or three owners of plantations in the suburbs of the town came to the Rajah and complained that some of their Malay neighbours had cut down all their fruit trees during the hurricane, in order to propitiate the spirit of the storm. Nowadays these drastic measures to other people's property are seldom heard of, because the Rajah has his own methods of dealing with such superstitious and undesirable proceedings. It took some time to eradicate these curious and unneighbourly customs, but I believe they are now a thing of the past.

I must tell one more curious belief existing amongst Malays. Just before I left for England, a Malay woman from one of our out-stations brought me a cocoa-nut, very much larger than the ordinary fruit of the Archipelago. I believe these huge cocoanuts are only to be found growing in the Seychelles Islands, and the natives call them "cocoa de mer." The woman told me she had brought me this fruit on account of the luck it brought its possessor; at the

INCHI BAKAR—SCHOOL MASTER, KUCHING

same time assuring me it came from fairyland.   I
asked her to tell me its story, when she informed me
that, as every one knows, in the middle of the world
is a place called "The navel of the sea."   In this
spot, guarded by two dragons, is a tree on which
these large cocoa-nuts grow, known as Pau Jinggeh.
The dragons feed on the fruit, and when they have
partaken too freely of it, have fits of indigestion,
causing them to be sea-sick; thus the fruit finds its
way into the ocean, and is borne by the current into
all parts of the world.   These enormous nuts are
occasionally met with by passing vessels, and in this
manner some are brought to the different settlements
in the Malayan Archipelago.   The fruit brought for my
acceptance had been given to the woman by a captain
of a Malay schooner, who had rescued it as it was
bobbing up and down in the water under the keel of
his boat.   " I thought you would like to have it,
Rajah Ranee," she said, "because it cannot be
bought for love nor money."   The fruit now occupies
a prominent position in our drawing-room at Kuching,
and is a source of great interest to the natives.

With our ideas of European wisdom, we may be
inclined to smile superciliously at these beliefs, but
we should not forget that a great many of us do not
like seeing *one* magpie, we avoid dining thirteen at
table, we hate to see the new moon through glass,
we never walk under a ladder, or sit in a room where
three candles are burning; and how about people
one meets who assure us they have heard the scream

of a Banshee, foretelling the death of some human
being? Putting all these things together, I do not
think either Malays or Dyaks show much more
superstition than we Europeans do; after all, we are
not so very superior to primitive races, although
we imagine that on account of our superior culture
we are fit to govern the world.

CHAPTER XX

DURING my residence in Sarawak, I witnessed several epidemics of cholera, and to any who have nervous temperaments, its advent is alarming. On one of its visitations, some curious incidents occurred, on account of the superstitious practices of the Chinese residing in Kuching.

In order to allay panic as much as possible, the Rajah and I drove or rode every morning through the Bazaar, where cholera was rife and where the atmosphere was impregnated with the smell of incense and joss-sticks, set burning by the Chinese in order to mitigate the plague. Many devices were resorted to by these people, superstitious and otherwise. I remember one magnificent junk, built regardless of expense, the Chinese merchants and their humbler and poorer brethren giving their dollars and cents ungrudgingly to make this vessel glorious, as a sop to stay the ravages of the infuriated god. The junk was placed on wheels and dragged for three miles down a bad road to a place called Pinding, where it was launched on the waters of the river, to be borne by the tide—it was hoped—to the sea. The procession accompanying this vessel was extremely picturesque. Great banners, scarlet, green, and blue, on which were embroidered golden dragons, etc., were carried by Chinamen, and the clashing of cymbals made a most frightful noise.

Nor was this the only procession organized whilst the cholera was at its height. One morning, after I had been riding round the settlement, and had got off my pony at the door of our stables across the river, I saw in the distance a crowd of people coming along the road, shouting, clashing cymbals, and bearing something aloft. This "something," on coming nearer, turned out to be a man seated on a chair looking like an arm-chair, but formed entirely of swords, their sharp edges forming the back, the seat, and the arms. The man was naked, with the exception of a loincloth and a head-handkerchief. His head rolled from side to side, his tongue protruded, and only the whites of his eyes could be seen. I thought he must be mad or in a fit, but one of our Syces told me the man was trying to allay the cholera. The mob following him was screeching, yelling, bounding about, beating gongs, and making a terrific noise. As it swept close to where I stood, I could see that no one in the crowd took notice of anybody or anything in their way. The procession went round the Chinese quarters of the town, and, meanwhile, the man in the chair was apparently immune from wounds. Our English doctor subsequently examined the chair, and having realized for himself the sharpness of its blades, he could not understand how the man could have escaped cutting himself to pieces.

This gruesome procession took place morning and evening during the first weeks of the epidemic, but instead of allaying the scourge it appeared to have the effect of increasing it. Moreover, the minds of the people were in danger of becoming unhinged by this daily spectacle, and the man who sat in the chair was beginning to exercise an undesirable influence over the people in the Bazaar. This senseless proceeding also became a serious obstacle to the more intelligent attempts to stamp out the disease. The Rajah therefore ordered the procession to be suppressed. The day after the order was given, the Rajah and I were driving in one of the roads near the town, when we met the forbidden procession with a still more numerous following of Chinamen than hitherto. The Rajah said nothing at the time, but when we reached the Palace he sent a force of police under an English officer to arrest the sword-chair man and imprison him. The following morning, before daylight, a band of Chinamen encircled the gaol, and somehow managed to liberate the fanatic. The Rajah, hearing of this matter, sent for the principal shopkeepers in the Bazaar, and informed them that if the man was not restored to the prison before six o'clock that evening he would turn the guns of the *Aline* on to their houses in the Bazaar, and batter them down over their heads. It was an exciting time. I remember seeing the *Aline* heave anchor and slowly take its position immediately in front of the Bazaar. At five o'clock that evening a deputation of Chinamen asked to see the Rajah. " The man is back in gaol," they said; "he will not trouble the town any more." The Rajah smiled genially at the news, shook hands with each member of the deputation, and I realized again, as in so many other cases, the Rajah's wisdom in dealing with his people. The man who was the cause of the trouble was subsequently sent out of the country.

There are many mysteries regarding these curious Eastern people which Europeans are not able to fathom. Another practice of the Chinese, when in any straits or when about to embark on some new commercial enterprise, is to lay down burning charcoal for the space of several yards, over which two or three initiated individuals are paid to walk barefooted. If they come through the ordeal un-scathed, which I am given to understand is nearly always the result, the enterprise is considered a favourable one. This practice was once resorted to in Kuching, when a company of Chinese merchants, anxious to open up pepper and gambier gardens in Sarawak, set certain Chinamen to gambol up and down the fiery path unscathed. The pepper and gambier gardens were established, and proved a great success. One can only wonder how it is that these people's bare skins appear to be impervious to fire and to sharp instruments.

The outbreak of cholera did not confine itself entirely to the Chinese quarter. It began picking out victims here and there, and the Kampong of my friends, Datu Isa and her relations, also suffered

severely. Every morning, notwithstanding, my Malay
friends found their way to the Astana, and during one
of these visits, whilst we were talking quite happily and
trying to keep our minds free from the all-absorbing
topic of the sickness that was laying so many low
and bringing mourning to so many houses in
Kuching, I saw the Datu Tumanggong's wife, a
buxom lady of forty years, fat and jolly in appearance, suddenly turn the ashy-green colour that reveals
sickness amongst these people. She rubbed her chest
round and round, and then exclaimed : " Wallahi, I
feel very ill." Good heavens ! I thought, she is
seized with cholera. Datu Isa said to me, " Wallahi,
perhaps the sickness ! " I had recourse to heroic
methods. I sent for a bottle of brandy, some hot
water, and chlorodyne. I gave the poor lady a strong
dose of the spirit (which certainly, being a Muhammadan, she had never tasted before), mixed with
about twenty drops of chlorodyne. The mixture filled
half a tumbler, and I told her to drink it and she
would feel all right. She was trembling and
frightened, but did not demur for one instant, and
swallowed the draught, making an extraordinary gulp
in her throat. She gave me back the tumbler, and
immediately sank back on the floor and lay inanimate
on the rugs in my room. For one moment I thought
I had killed her, and looked at Datu Isa and my
other friends to see how they would take it. " You
have cured her, Rajah Ranee," they said. " We will
go home and leave her to finish her sleep." I

pretended to feel no anxiety, although I must say I did not feel very comfortable.

I sent for Ima, and we two stayed in the room to await developments. The lady lay like a log, and her pulse beat very fast. After some time, I saw her colour becoming restored, and in the space of two hours she sat up and appeared to be perfectly well again. "Wallah, Rajah Ranee," she said. "You do understand. You white people have secrets that no one else can know." Personally, I was not so sure, but I was delighted when I realized she was none the worse, and saw her escorted down the path to her boat by Ima and the boat-boys. Her attack and my remedy did not appear to do her any harm, for, from that day, she always came to me for help in any ailment.

The Rajah was called away from Kuching during the epidemic, and I was alone with the children at the Astana. One morning, a chief, whom I knew very well, paid me a friendly call. We sat and talked on the verandah, and I thought he had never been so talkative or seemed so full of life as on that particular morning. About eleven o'clock we shook hands, and he went back to his house. That same day, as I was getting up after my afternoon nap, Talip came to my room and asked whether Datu Mohammed's wife could have some flowers from our garden. "Certainly," I said; "tell them to pick what flowers they like. But I did not know Datu Mohammed was having a feast to-day." "He is not,"

Talip replied; "he died of cholera at three o'clock." This was said with a smile, for Malays, whenever they have sorrowful or tragic news to impart, always smile, in order, I suppose, to mask their feelings. The death of a favourite cat would elicit sighs and groans, but in any sorrow they hide their true feelings, even from their nearest relations.

Some of the Malays had curious methods in trying to combat the disease. There was an old lady living in Kampong Grisek, called Daiang Kho, who was beloved by the Malays of Kuching on account of her blameless life, her rigorous attention to religious duties, and above all, because she had achieved the great pilgrimage to Mecca. Daiang Kho had brought with her from Mecca a Muhammadan rosary, and this was made great use of in cases of illness in Kuching. The rosary was placed in a tumbler of cold water over night, and the liquid poured into various bottles the next morning, to be used as medicine. Daiang Kho informed me that the cures performed by the rosary were wonderful, but, as we all know, in some cases mind triumphs over the body, and I was not therefore surprised at hearing that this innocuous drink had sometimes been successful in curing sufferers when attacked by the first symptoms of disease.

CHAPTER XXI

DURING one of my visits to England our youngest son Harry was born. He is called Tuan Bungsu (the youngest of a family), a title given to the youngest son of the Rajahs of Sarawak. As time went on and our boys were growing up, it became incumbent on me, for obvious reasons, to spend more time away from our country. I had to make my home in England, on account of the education of our sons, but, whenever possible, I hurried over to pay visits to what is, after all, my own land. I think one of the happiest periods of my life occurred just before Bertram went to Cambridge, when he accompanied me to Sarawak. We then stayed there some months, part of which time the Rajah was obliged to be in England.

Bertram and I gave many receptions to our Malay friends, and it did not take us long to pick up again the threads of our life in Sarawak. I should like to give an account of some journeys which Bertram and I took to some of the out-stations. For instance, I was anxious we should visit the Rejang district together, and the Rajah, agreeing with these plans, gave us his yacht for our journeys.

We started one morning from Kuching, accompanied by our great friend Mr. C. A. Bampfylde, then administering the Government in the Rajah's absence, and Dr. Langmore, who had come with us from Europe, for a round of visits to our Dyak and Kayan friends.

We stayed a day or two at the little village of Santubong, at the mouth of the Sarawak River, where the Rajah had built a bungalow for the use of Europeans requiring change of air to the sea. The chief of this village is a kindly, well-educated Malay, named Hadji Ahmad. This gentleman has been to Mecca, and is thought a great deal of both by Europeans and natives. At any of these small settlements in the Rajah's country, Malay gentlemen of the standing of Hadji Ahmad occupy the office of magistrate, and are entitled to inquire into, and try, all the petty cases that may occur even in such simple out-of-the-way and almost sinless communities. As I think I have remarked before, the more serious criminal cases are under the control of the Rajah and his Council at Kuching.

When we arrived at the bungalow, we found Hadji Ahmad's wife, sisters, aunts, and female cousins sitting on the floor arrayed in silks and satins with gold bangles, waiting for us. Hadji Ahmad was anxious we should be amused during our stay, and, being an enthusiastic fisherman, he was eager to show us a good day's sport. He offered to erect a fishing-shed for us, with as thick a roof as possible, to protect us from the sun, on the shallow, shelving bank of sand which at low tide lies uncovered for miles on the Santubong shore. When the hut was built, some twenty fathoms from the shore, Hadji Ahmad asked permission to bring his family to join in the expedition. We started off at ebbtide in a long, narrow canoe, covered with white awnings. The Malay ladies had taken their position in the boat for about an hour and a half before our arrival, and as I stepped into the canoe they almost sent us overboard in their tender attempts to settle me down in the most comfortable corner. Hadji Ahmad's wife was a buxom dame of thirty years. She and her five companions talked incessantly, and one of the elder women kept us amused and the Malay women in a perpetual giggle, at the manner in which she chaffed her brother, who was our helmsman. She was most personal in her remarks, drawing attention to his swarthy complexion, his beard and moustache that sparsely covered his chin and lips (Malay men are seldom adorned with either beard or moustache), but he took his sister's witticisms good-humouredly.

The fishing-hut looked like a bathing machine, standing on stilts in the middle of the risen tide. It had been decorated with the beautiful blossom of the areca-nut palm, and mats and all kinds of draperies embroidered in gold (the work of the Malay women of the village) were hung round the hut. We made our way up the wide-rung ladder, some ten feet high, through which the water shone and glistened in the most alarming manner. A salvo of Chinese crackers were let off as we entered the hut, causing great delight to my female escort, who highly approved of the din. The hut groaned and creaked as our party, some fourteen in number, took their seats on a small platform jutting out from it over the sea. The construction of these sheds was very ingenious. They were erected upon a series of stout timber poles disposed at the back of the leaf building in the shape of a boat's keel. A number of canoes, which had conveyed ten or fifteen of the most experienced fishermen in the village, were tied to these poles. Four great poles, acting as levers, swung horizontally each side of the hut, jutting out twenty feet in front, between which the nets were hung.

As the tide came in, the excitement of the party grew intense, and the fishermen sang a dirge-like melody, inviting the fish into the net, telling them the Rajah's wife and son were expecting their arrival, and that, therefore, it would only be good manners and loyalty on their part to pay their respects by being caught and eaten by them ! When sufficient time had elapsed, according to Hadji Ahmad's idea, for the net to be full of fish, the fishermen hung on to the poles at the back of the hut, their weight swinging the ends on which the nets were tied out of the water, when we saw a number of fish wriggling in their meshes. Amongst the fish were two or three octopuses, those poisonous masses of white, jelly-like substances which all fishermen in the Straits dread like the evil one himself, on account of their poisonous stings; these, when captured, were tossed back again into the sea.

After an enjoyable day, we went back to the house for tea, and started off again in the cool of the evening to visit a creek in the neighbourhood, where lies a great boulder of sandstone, upon which the figure of a woman is carved. On this occasion, we travelled in one of the *Aline's* boats, our crew having provided themselves with paddles in order to make their way through the aquatic vegetation which abounds in the small streams. Bertram took his place at the helm, and, without asking any questions, proceeded to steer us through a maze of nipa palms and mangroves, twisting in and out of these numerous channels for an hour or so. Dr. Langmore and I, thinking the way rather long, at last inquired whether we were on the right track, when Hadji Ahmad informed us that we were drifting in quite the wrong direction. "But why did you not say so?" I said to Hadji Ahmad. "We could not set the Rajah's son right until he asked us to do so," he replied. Therefore, had we not inquired the way, I suppose we might even now be wandering about the maze of water, with Bertram at the helm. The Hadji soon put us right, and Bertram was as amused as we were at the extreme politeness of our Malay entourage. At length the stone was reached, and it was indeed a curious object. One had better explain that at the foot of this mountain

of Santubong, in the alluvial soil washed down by
the frequent rain of those tropical countries, traces
of a former settlement, in the shape of beads, golden
ornaments, and broken pottery have been found
lying here and there with the pebbles, gravel, and
mud, rolled down from the mountain.   Experts who
have visited this spot are confident that a considerable
number of people once lived here, and, owing to some
unknown cause, deserted the spot.   Amongst some
of the debris, the remains of a glass factory and
golden ornaments of Hindoo workmanship have been
discovered.   This race of people has faded completely from the memory of the present inhabitants
of Santubong.   The sandstone boulder with its
effigy was only discovered during quite late years
by a gardener who was clearing the soil in preparation for a vegetable garden.

We landed in the midst of mud and fallen trees.
Narrow planks of wood, raised on trestles, led us
through a morass to the figure.   It rests under a
roof of iron-wood shingles, erected by the Rajah's
orders to protect the carving from the effects of the
weather.   The carved figure is about life-size, and
apparently represents a naked woman flung face
downwards, with arms and legs extended, clinging to
the surface of the rock ; a knot of hair stands some
inches from her head, and all round the figure the
stone is weather-beaten and worn.   Lower down, on
the right of the larger carving, Bertram and I discovered the outline of a smaller figure in the same

position.   A triangular mark, with three loops on its upper bar, is to be seen near by on the stone, looking like the head of an animal rudely scratched.   The natives of Santubong have turned the place into a sort of shrine for pilgrimage.   Hadji Ahmad told me that the men and women of his village imagine the figure to have been that of a real woman, given to torturing animals for her amusement, and turned to stone by an avenging Deity.   The people of Sarawak, at least all those with whom I have come in contact, are under the impression that anyone guilty of injuring, ill-treating, or laughing at animals is liable to be turned into stone by an offended god, and nearly all the stones or rocks to be met with in the beds of rivers, and elsewhere, are thought by the people to be the remnants of a human race, guilty of such crimes.   They call these stones Batu Kudi (the stones of curses), but how these legends took root and became so firmly implanted in the minds of Sarawak people remains a mystery to this day.

This mysterious Santubong figure puzzles and interests me greatly.   There is no one nowadays in Kuching capable of fashioning such a thing.   Moreover, the tops of carved pillars, and other fretted fragments of stone, have been found in these gravel beds, so that I imagine somewhere on the mountain must be hidden more vestiges of a long-departed people, in the shape of temples and maybe of other buildings.   When one remembers Angkor Wat and the manner in which that stupendous work of men's

hands lay buried for centuries, under its shroud of
leaves, which more completely than desert sand ob-
literated the works of humanity for a long while,
one can almost be certain that Santubong and its
mysteries will be unveiled some day.   I only wish I
could live long enough to see it.   Musing over the
past history of semi-deserted countries, such as these,
entrances and terrifies one.   Under the shade of innumerable generations of trees, men and women have
come and gone, struggled to live their lives, raised
altars and temples to their gods, with perhaps the
quietude of endless previous centuries lulling them into
factitious security.   Then that "something" happens,
when, helpless as thistledown blown about by puffs of
wind, such people are destroyed, driven forth or killed,
when the relentless growth of the tropics takes possession of their deserted homes, and the trace of their existence is blotted out by leaves.   Those great forests
of the tropics must hold many secrets, and when staying near the Santubong mountain, its mystery weighed
on me, and I longed to know the fate of those who
had gone before.   For reasons such as these, it is a pity
that some of the Europeans who come into touch
with natives should do all they can to wipe out
from their minds legends and tales bearing on the
origin of their race—yarns they call them.   Hadji
Ahmad was a proof of the manner in which these
methods affected him.   I was anxious to know what
was thought by the Santubong people about this stone.
The Hadji said some obvious things, but when I

pressed him further, he begged me not to do so, for he was afraid Englishmen in Sarawak might accuse him of telling lies; therefore he preferred to keep what he thought about the stone to himself. I cannot repeat too often that such criticisms made by Europeans to imaginative Eastern peoples amongst whom they live are helping to suppress secrets which, if unveiled, might prove of inestimable value to science.

Before closing this chapter, I must recount a conversation I had with one of my Santubong friends the evening before our departure to the Rejang. It was a beautiful moonlight night, and the mountain of Santubong looked black against the sky. Within a few yards of the house a grove of casuarina trees were swaying in the evening breeze. The murmur of their frail branches made an exquisite sound in the stillness of the night. As we stood on the verandah, my Malay friend said : " If you like to go out by yourself, Rajah Ranee, and stand under those trees at midnight, you will hear voices of unknown people telling you the secrets of the earth." I wish now I had gone out and listened, for I am foolish enough to believe that the secrets told by those musical branches might have been worth listening to, but afraid of the night, of the solitude, and, above all, of the criticisms of my European friends, I refrained. I have since come to the conclusion that I have lost a wonderful and beautiful experience which may never occur again.

" I know a story about the mountain of Santubong.

Would Rajah Ranee like to hear it?" said my friend, as we stood looking at the mountain. "Say on," I replied; "I should well like to hear." "In the days of long ago," she began, "a holy man, whose name was Hassan, lived in a house at the foot of this mountain. He was a Haji, for he had been to Mecca, and wore a green turban and long flowing robes. He read the Koran day and night, his prayers were incessant, and the name of Allah was ever on his lips. His soul was white and exceedingly clean, and whenever he cut himself with his parang whilst hewing down the trees to make into canoes, the blood flowed from the wound white as milk.[1] He occasionally visited his brothers and sisters living in Kuching, taking about half a day to accomplish the journey, but he was never away from his solitary home by the sea-shore for very long. He never suspected that a beautiful lady, the Spirit of Santubong and the daughter of the moon, lived on its highest peak, and from thence had watched him admiringly on account of his blameless life. One day she flew down into the valley, entered his house, and made friends with him. Their intercourse ripened into love, they were married, and the daughter of the moon waited her Haji husband to her home beyond the clouds. Haji Hassan and his spirit-wife lived for some years in this lofty region. They were such good people that it seemed as though nothing could ever happen

---

[1] An idea entertained by some Sarawak Malays that the blood of those who lead holy lives is white instead of red.

to mar their happiness. But as time went on, the good man grew weary of this unalloyed happiness, and sighed for a change. From his home on the mountain-top he could see the roof of his little palm-thatched house, where he had lived alone for so many years, and he could see the lights of the village near it twinkling in the darkness of nights. He thought of his brothers and sisters in Kuching, and of his other friends living there, and a great longing came over him to return, if only for a short space of time, to the grosser pleasures of earth.

"One day he spoke these words to his wife : ' Delight of my life and light of my eyes, forgive me for what I am about to say. I want to go to Kuching to see my brothers and sisters, and to stay with them a while.' A great sickness of heart seized the daughter of the moon ; nevertheless, she let him go, pledging him to return to her when a month had gone by. She called her servants and ordered them to prepare a boat to carry her husband to Kuching. So the Haji departed, and the days seemed long to the daughter of the moon. At length the Haji's time had expired, but week after week went by and his wife sat alone on her mountain peak, longing for his return.

"Meanwhile, Haji Hassan was enjoying himself with his friends at Kuching. He was made a great deal of ; bullocks were killed for his consumption at great banquets in the houses of his friends, where he was the honoured guest, and always the one chosen to admonish his friends and give them lessons in good conduct before the meal began.   In fact, he was so lionized that he forgot his wife waiting for him amongst the clouds at the top of Santubong.

"Some months had elapsed, when one morning, as the Haji was returning from the river-bank where he had bathed and prayed before beginning the day, he looked towards the north and saw a great black cloud forming over the peak of the mountain ; then he suddenly remembered his wife.   He hastily summoned his servants, and, when the boat was made ready, the tide and strenuous paddling of his crew bore him speedily to the foot of Santubong.   He clambered its steep sides and reached his home—only to find it empty and desolate, for the daughter of the moon had flown.   At this the Haji's heart grew sick and he shed bitter tears.   He went back to his relations at Kuching, and there became gloomy and silent, constantly sighing for the presence of his wife.

"One evening, a man in a canoe passed by the Haji's landing-place, where he was sitting, staring at the river.   'Eh, Tuan Haji,' the man called out, 'your wife has been seen on the top of Mount Sipang,' and quickly paddled off.   The Haji sprang into his canoe tied to the landing-place, unloosed its moorings, and paddled himself to the foot of Mount Sipang.   He rushed up to its highest peak, but his wife was not there.   Subsequently he heard news of her on Mount Serapi, the highest peak of the Matang range, but on reaching the mountain-top he was again disappointed. Thus from mountain peak to mountain peak the disconsolate husband sought his wife all over Borneo, but the daughter of the moon had vanished out of his life for ever. He went back to Kuching, and soon after died of a broken heart."

This was the end of the story, but my friend went on to explain that whenever the peak of the Santubong mountain is bathed in moonlight the people imagine the daughter of the moon is revisiting her old home.

It was almost midnight. "I ask your leave to go, Rajah Ranee," my Malay companion said. "I hope you will sleep well." She walked away in the moonlight to her home in the village below, and I went to bed and dreamed about the Haji and his moonshine, whilst the talking trees outside told their secrets to the stars.

CHAPTER XXII

ONE of my places of predilection in the country is called Lundu. It differs from most of the other settlements in Sarawak by the fact that a good deal of agriculture goes on in the neighbourhood, and that the country is flat near the Government Bungalow. We embarked for this place in the *Aline*, and although the water is shallow on the bar we managed to time our arrival at high tide, when the nine feet necessary to float our yacht enabled us to steer our way comfortably into the river, the banks of which are sandy at the mouth. Groves of talking trees grew close to the sea, and tufts of coarse grass were dotted over the sands. As we proceeded farther the soil became muddy and nipa palm forests appeared. We could see the mountain of Poe, three thousand feet in height, towering inland. It is one of the frontiers between the Dutch country and Sarawak, so that the Rajah and the Dutch Government each possess half of this mountain. It is not so precipitous as is Santubong, and has forest trees growing thickly right up to the top. Fishing stakes were stretched across some of the sandbanks at the mouth, but not a living soul was to be seen on the sea-shore. We steamed through a broad morass, crossed in every direction by little streams travelling down to the main river. Farther on we noticed, about twenty or thirty yards from the banks, a tree full of yellow blossoms, like a flaming torch in the green gloom of the jungle. No one could tell me what these blossoms were, and I was deeply disappointed at our inability to reach the tree and obtain some of its branches, which might as yet be unknown to science. It would have taken our sailors many hours to hew their way to it, so we contented ourselves with looking through opera glasses, across a jungle of vegetation, at the gorgeous blossoms, although that did not help us to discover what the tree was.[1] A little farther on were huts built near the river, and we could see men sitting on the rungs of ladders leading from their open doors to the water.

When we arrived at Lundu, our friend Mr. Bloomfield Douglas, Resident of the place and living in the comfortable Government bungalow situated a few yards from the river, came to meet us at the wharf, accompanied by a number of Dyaks. A Dyak chief styled the Orang Kaya Stia Rajah, with his wife and relations, came on board with Mr. Douglas

[1] This tree, which no one could tell me the name of at the time, was the only one of its kind I had seen ; therefore, it was not strange I formed the idea it might be unknown to science. Its leafy image persisted in my mind, and the thought of it haunted me. I have now been informed that it is not unknown, and is a creeper, called Bauhinea, and not a tree at all. Seen at a distance, its appearance is like that of a tree in blossom, for it completely covers—and perhaps smothers—the tree upon which it fastens itself.

to take us on shore. Both men and women wore the conical hats of the country, made of the finest straw. A piece of light wood delicately carved to a point ornamented their tops, which were made splendid with bright colours. My old friends, the Dyak women, were affectionate and kind. They took hold of my hand, sniffed at it, and laid it gently back by my side; some of the Dyak men followed suit. These people never kiss in European fashion, but smell at the object of their affection or reverence. I always felt on such occasions as though two little holes were placed on the back of my hand.

On the day of our arrival, the sun was blazing overhead and it was fearfully hot. Our shadows were very short as we moved along, and the people lined the way right up to the Resident's door. We had to touch everybody individually as we marched along, even babies in arms had their little hands held out to touch our fingers. These greetings took some time in the overpowering heat of midday, and it was a great relief when at last we reached Mr. Douglas's pretty room, which he had been wise enough to leave unpainted and unpapered. The walls were made of the brown wood of the country, and were decorated with hanging baskets of orchids in full flower, vandalowis, philaenopsis, etc.—a mass of brown, yellow, pink, white, and mauve blooms, hanging in fragile and delicate cascades of colour against the dark background. Rare and wonderful pots of ferns were placed in my bedroom, and quantities of roses, gardenias, jasmine, and chimpakas scented the whole place.

In the evening we took a walk round the settlement. The many plantations of Liberian coffee trees looked beautiful weighed down with green and scarlet berries, some branches still retaining their snowy blossoms. The contrast of berries and flowers, with the glossy dark green of the leaves, made them a charming picture in the landscape. We went through fields planted with tapioca and sugar-cane, and across plantations of pepper vines. These latter are graceful things, trained up poles, with small green bunches hanging down like miniature clusters of green and red grapes. In every corner or twist of the road we met little groups of men and women waiting for us. They stood in the ditches by the side of the paths until we came up to them, when they jumped out, rushed at us, sniffed at the backs of our hands, and retired once more to the ditches without saying a word.

During the night I heard the Argus pheasant crying in the woods, in response to distant thunder. These beautiful birds roam about the hill of Gading, which is close by the bungalow and thickly covered with virgin forest. The sound they make is uncanny and sorrowful, like the cry of lost souls wandering in the sombre wilderness of innumerable trees, seeking to fathom the secrets of an implacable world. Any sudden loud sound, as of a dead tree falling or the rumble of thunder, however remote, apparently calls forth an echo of terror from these birds.

MALAY STRIKING FIRE FROM DRY TINDER

The next evening the chief of the village invited us to a reception at his house, situated a short distance from the bungalow. It was a fine starlight night, and we walked there after dinner. The house was built much in the same way as are other Sea Dyak houses, the flooring being propped on innumerable poles about thirty feet from the ground. A broad verandah led into the living-rooms, but, as usual, we had to climb a slender pole with notches all the way up, leaning at a steep angle against the verandah. The chief, with an air of pomp and majesty, helped me up the narrow way as though it were the stairway of a palace. His manner was courtly and his costume magnificent. His jacket and trousers were braided with gold, and the sarong round his waist was fastened with a belt of beaten gold.

The house was full of people : Dyaks who had come from far and near, Chinamen resident in the place, Malays from over the Dutch border, and even a few Hindoos, or Klings, were to be seen. The chief took us to the place prepared for us at the end of the verandah, where was hung a canopy of golden embroideries and stiff brocades. Branches of sugar-canes and the fronds of betel-nut palms decorated the poles of the verandah. A great many lighted lamps hung from the roof, and the floor was covered with fine white mats. Bertram, Mr. Douglas, Dr. Langmore, and I sat on chairs, whilst the rest of the guests squatted on mats laid on the floor.

The women and young girls sat near me, one of

the latter, whose name was Madu (meaning honey), being very pretty indeed. Her petticoat of coarse dark cotton was narrow and hardly reached her knees, and over this she wore a dark blue cotton jacket, fastened at the neck with gold buttons as big as small saucers. Her eyes were dark, beautiful and keenly intelligent, and her straight eyebrows drooped a little at the outer corners. The high cheek-bones, characteristic of her race, gave her a certain air of refinement and delicacy, in spite of her nose being flat, her nostrils broad, and her lips wide and somewhat thick. Her hair was pulled tightly off her forehead, and lay in a coil at the nape of her neck; it seemed too heavy for her, and as she carried her head very high, the great mass looked as though it dragged it backwards. Her hair, however, had one peculiarity (a peculiarity I had never seen in Sarawak before); it was streaked with red, and this made Madu unhappy, for Malays and Dyaks do not like the slightest appearance of red hair, some of the tribes shaving their children's heads from early infancy until they are seven years old, in order to avoid the possibility of such an occurrence. The little creature looked pathetic, as she sat nursing her sister's baby, around whose wrist was tied a black wooden rattle, like a small cannon-ball. The baby was about two months old, and appeared to be healthy, but a sudden kick on its part removed a piece of calico, its only article of clothing, when I saw that the child's stomach had been rubbed over with turmeric, to prevent it from being seized by the demon of disease. The chief told his daughter to leave the child to its nurse, when a very old lady rushed forward and took it away.

Refreshments were then handed round. We had glasses of cocoa-nut milk, cakes made of grated cocoa-nut and of rice flour, intensely sweet. There were large trays of pumeloes, cut in quarters, together with oranges, bananas, and mangosteens. Glasses of gin, much diluted with water, were handed to the male guests, and after refreshments a place was cleared right down the room, the chief's native friends sitting on mats on the floor, leaning against the walls.

The orchestra was placed on one side of the hall. It consisted of a set of gongs, called the Kromang, seven or eight in number, decreasing in size, fixed in a wooden frame, each gong sounding a different note —a scale, in fact. These gongs are beaten by one individual, and when skilfully played they sound like running water. Other members of the orchestra played gongs hung singly on poles, and there were also drums beaten at both ends with the musician's fingers. These instruments played in concert and with remarkable rhythm were pleasant to listen to. When the band had finished the overture, two young men got up after an immense amount of persuasion, and walked shyly to the middle of the cleared space. They were dressed in Malay clothes — trousers, jackets, and sarongs—and smoking-caps, ornamented with tassels, were placed on one side of their heads. They fell down suddenly in front of us, their hands clasped above their heads, and bowed till their foreheads touched the floor. Then they got up slowly, looked at one another, giggled, and walked away. The master of the house explained that they were shy, and thought their conduct quite natural. It was evidently the thing to do, for several other couples went through this same pantomime. At last the first couple were induced to come back, when their shyness vanished, and the performance began.

One of the dancers held two flat pieces of wood in each hand, clicking them together like castanets. The other man danced with china saucers held in each hand, keeping time to the orchestra by hitting the saucers with rings of gold which he wore on each forefinger. He was as skilful as any juggler I had seen, for he twisted the saucers round and round, his rings hitting against them in time to the music with wonderful accuracy. The dancers were never still for a second. Their arms waved about, their bodies swayed to and fro, they knelt first on one knee with the other leg outstretched before them, then on the other, sometimes bending their bodies in a line with the floor—the castanets and the saucers being kept going the whole time. Although the movements looked stiff, it was impossible for them to be ungraceful, and at every new pose they managed to fall into a delightful arrangement of lines. The dances were evidently inspired by Malay artists, although performed by Dyaks, for they were full of restraint.

Other dances followed, all interesting and pretty.

Sometimes empty cocoa-nut shells, cut in two, were placed in patterns on the floor. The dancers picked up one in each hand, clashing them together like cymbals, whilst hopping in and out of the other cocoa-nuts, this performance being called by the people "the mouse-deer dance," for they imagine that the noise made by clashing the cocoa-nut shells resembles the cry of plandoks (mouse-deer) in the forests.

After the men had finished, the women's turn came. These wore stiff petticoats of gold brocade, hanging from under their armpits and reaching almost to the floor, under which were dark blue cotton draperies hiding their feet. The pretty Madu, with the red-streaked hair, headed a procession of about thirty young women and girls, who emerged from the open doorway at the other end of the room, in single file. They stretched out their arms in a line with their shoulders, and waved their hands slowly from the wrists. Their sleeves were open and hung from the elbow weighted with rows upon rows of golden knobs. With their heads on one side and their eyes cast down, they looked as though they were crucified against invisible crosses, and wafted down the middle of the hall. When they approached us, they swayed their bodies to right and left and extended their arms, beating the air gently with their hands, keeping exactly in line, and followed Madu's gestures so accurately that from where I stood I could only see Madu as she headed the dancers. It would be interesting to know the origin of such dances. I imagine the Hindoo element pervades them all. How surprised these so-called savages would be if they were present at some ballet, with women in tights and short stiff skirts, kicking their legs about, or pirouetting on one toe, for these natives are innately artistic, if kept away from the influence of European art and its execrable taste. Each time a movement more graceful than the last was accomplished by these young women, the men evinced their approbation by opening their mouths and yelling, without showing any other signs of excitement on their immovable faces.

The dances went on for some time, after which wrestling matches took place between little boys of the tribe, about eleven or twelve years of age. When one of these small wrestlers was defeated he never showed bad temper or appeared maliciously disposed towards his conqueror.

We all enjoyed ourselves, and it was late when we left this hospitable house. The chief and his daughters offered us more cocoa-nut milk, cakes, and bananas, and the leave-taking took some time. One old Sea Dyak, who had been very conspicuous during the evening, for he had bounded about and joined in the dances, took my hand and put it into the hand of a friend of his, another Sea Dyak, whom he particularly wished me to notice. "You make friends," he said, "for my friends are your friends." I hope I responded sympathetically, and after a while we managed to drag ourselves away.

Our hosts escorted us back to Mr. Douglas's

bungalow. I led the way, hand in hand with the chief, and Bertram followed, hand in hand with the chief's son, who kept assuring Bertram that he felt very happy, because they had become brothers, for was not Rajah Ranee, his mother, walking home hand in hand with his father, and as he was doing the same with her son, that quite settled the relationship. The orchestra followed us the whole way home, and the people sang choruses to impromptu words, composed in our honour by the poet of the tribe. The chief told me the song was "manah" (beautiful), as its words were in honour of Bertram and me.

A recent shower had left the night fine and the air cool, as we went through avenues of betel-nut palms and over carpets of lemon grass, whose long spikes beaten over the path by the rain gave a delightful fragrance crushed by so many feet. We crossed a little bridge over a bubbling stream, and passed by Chinese houses, whose inhabitants opened their windows to look at our midnight procession. When we reached the bungalow, the arbor tristis or night-flowering jasmine was in bloom all over the garden, and white moon-flower bells hung wide open over the verandah. Half an hour later, as I leaned out of the window of my bedroom, I could still hear the people singing on their way back to the village. The trees in the garden were full of fireflies looking like stars entangled in the branches.

We left Lundu the next day with regret. We were sorry to say good-bye to our kind host, Mr.

Douglas, and to the Dyaks of the place, and as we steamed away I felt almost inclined to cry. Although I may be accused of being unduly emotional, I am not ashamed to own that after a visit in any of the Sarawak settlements I always left a piece of my heart behind.

CHAPTER XXIII

WHEN Bertram and I stopped at Sibu for a few days on our way up the Rejang to Kanowit, he was much interested in all the things I had to tell him about Sibu. The early days of my life were lived over again, and I was delighted to see the interest he took in the smallest details of my first and most interesting stay in these regions so many years before. During this later visit, Mr. Bampfylde told me of a Haji who had experienced an interesting and somewhat alarming adventure with a sea-serpent. As I wished to hear the tale from the man's own lips, Mr. Bampfylde sent for him the next morning. Haji Matahim was a typical Malay from Sambas. He lived at Sibu with his relations. He possessed a small trading schooner of about 200 tons, and made voyages to the Dutch Settlements, to Rhio, and to Singapore. His face was round and short; he had a receding chin and a protruding upper lip, shaded by a black and bristly moustache. He was flat between the eyes, and his complexion was rather darker than most Malays, being tanned by exposure and sea air.

He told me that about two or three months

before the time of which I write he was sailing from Pontianak, a place in Dutch Borneo, with a cargo for Singapore. One day he was becalmed not far from an island called Rhio, when his ship was suddenly surrounded by an extraordinary shoal of fishes. As the fish swarmed round the ship, the crew managed to haul them up with buckets and baskets, capturing them in enormous quantities. Having no salt on board, with which to preserve the fish, the crew, eight in number, cleaned them there and then on the vessel's deck, and threw the offal into the sea. Haji Matahim was standing in the bows looking at this extraordinary capture, when suddenly the rudder chain snapped. This was nothing out of the way, for it had previously been broken and mended with a piece of wire. The Haji and his crew were busily discussing how best they could remedy the accident, when a man in the stern saw a floating mass of "something," striped white and green, lying motionless under the clear surface of the water. He rushed up to the Haji and told him what he had seen, whereupon the Haji ordered the lead to be thrown over to ascertain the depth at which this unlooked-for object was lying. The lead gave only six fathoms, whereas it is well known that in that particular region the sea is about fifty fathoms deep. Then the Haji saw a flat, monstrous head rising out of the water, some ten or twelve yards from the vessel, the schooner's bows floating between its eyes. The head was like that of a fish, and, according to the Haji's account, the eyes looked like two round balls stuck at the end of spikes, seven or eight inches long : the time for observation was sufficient, as the monster remained motionless for about half an hour. The Haji and his crew were too terrified to move or speak, but after a time they collected their wits together sufficiently to procure some tuba and garlic (stowed on board for cases of emergency), which they hung over the side of the ship, whereupon the beast slowly sank and disappeared. I could not find out from the Haji how much the water was troubled when the monstrous head plunged back again into the sea, for if the beast had been of such extraordinary dimensions, it must have caused some motion to their vessel, however slowly it went under. The Haji was not very coherent on the subject, and he told me at the time that he intended giving up trading voyages for the rest of his life. Subsequently he changed his mind and continued his trading excursions in the same schooner for some years afterwards.

Personally I am inclined to think that the creature, whatever it was, could not very well have remained motionless for the length of time as stated by the Haji, but I give his tale as I took it from his own lips. Mr. Bampfylde told me that he had taken the trouble to question some of the members of the crew separately, and the tale told by the Haji tallied in every respect with theirs. I have related this story because it struck me as interesting, but am not prepared to enter into the old controversy as to whether the sea-serpent exists or not. It has been said that even the scientists are now keeping an open mind on the question. Well, I am going to do the same. It is perhaps necessary to say that garlic plays a great part in the superstitious rites of some Malays, and I believe the Haji was firmly convinced that the tuba and garlic together were quite sufficient to make the monster disappear.

A day or two afterwards we embarked on the *Lucille*, a small steamer of forty tons kept for the use of the Rajah's officers at Sibu, and started in the cold mists of morning for Kapit. As we forced our way round a somewhat difficult point, through a mass of driftwood borne down by a freshet, after heavy rains during the night, our vessel bumped against and heeled over a snag. Great trunks of trees swirled and eddied round the ship at this spot, and the Malay at the wheel changed from one leg to the other, cleared his throat perpetually, frowned, and stared vacantly ahead until the corner was rounded, the mass of driftwood passed, and the danger over. Although the steersman handled the ropes very gently, as though fearful of breaking them, he got over the difficulties with the greatest ease and with little waste of energy. After this trifling incident, we went on our solitary way, our steam-launch the only living thing in this wilderness of wood and water. Farther up the river the years that had passed by since my first visit to the district had brought peace, comfort, trade, and commerce

MAKLUMAT PENTING

PERINTAH PANDU ARAH UDARA MALAYSIA PERKARA 40 (1) memaktubkan bahawa, "Seseorang itu tidak dibenarkan memasuki atau berada di dalam mana-mana pesawat udara ketika berkeadaan mabuk".

SEMENTARA

AKTA KESALAHAN-KESALAHAN PENERBANGAN MALAYSIA 1984 memperuntukkan bahawa mana-mana orang itu:-

a) Ditegah daripada melakukan apa-apa tindakan keganasan terhadap penumpang-penumpang atau kru mana-mana pesawat udara sedang dalam penerbangan.

b) Dilarang melakukan dalam pesawat udara sedang dalam penerbangan apa-apa tindakan keganasan yang mungkin membahayakan keselamatan pesawat udara itu.

Adalah dimaklumkan bahawa mana-mana orang yang melakukan suatu kesalahan di bawah Akta ini boleh, apabila disabitkan, dikenakan hukuman penjara seumur hidup.

IMPORTANT INFORMATION

THE MALAYSIAN AIR NAVIGATION ORDER ARTICLE 40 (1) states, that "No person shall enter or be in any aircraft while in a state of intoxication".

AND

THE MALAYSIAN AVIATION OFFENCES ACT 1984 provides that a person should not, whilst in an aircraft:-

a) commit any act of violence against other passengers or crew;

b) commit any act which is likely to endanger the safety of the aircraft.

Please be informed that:

A person may be arrested for an offence under the said Act and shall be liable **ON CONVICTION** to imprisonment for life.

Pas Masuk
Boarding Pass
KELAS GOLDEN CLUB

Golden Club CLASS

malaysia AIRLINES

Pintu / Gate	Penerb. / Flight	Destinasi / Destination
NSST 13	MH 0002	LHR

Nama / Name
CORTIS HMR

Kelas / Class	Tarikh / Date	Tempat duduk / Seat
350 C	16MAR-KUL	9H

Sila laporkan diri di Pintu Masuk 30 minit
sebelum waktu berlepas
Please report at Boarding Gate 30 mins

IMPORTANT INFORMATION

THE MALAYSIAN AIR NAVIGATION ORDER ARTICLE 40 (1) states, that, "No person shall enter or be in any aircraft while in a state of intoxication".

AND

THE MALAYSIAN AVIATION OFFENCES ACT 1984 provides that a person should not, whilst in an aircraft:-

a) commit any act of violence against other passengers or crew;

b) commit any act which is likely to endanger the safety of the aircraft.

Please be informed that:

A person may be arrested for an offence under the said Act and shall be liable **ON CONVICTION** to imprisonment for life.

MAKLUMAT PENTING

PERINTAH PANDU ARAH UDARA MALAYSIA PERKARA 40 (1) memaktubkan bahawa, "Seseorang itu tidak dibenarkan memasuki atau berada di dalam mana-mana pesawat udara ketika berkeadaan mabuk".

SEMENTARA

AKTA KESALAHAN-KESALAHAN PENERBANGAN MALAYSIA 1984 memperuntukkan bahawa mana-mana orang itu:-

a) Ditegah daripada melakukan apa-apa tindakan keganasan terhadap penumpang-penumpang atau kru mana-mana pesawat udara sedang dalam penerbangan.

b) Dilarang melakukan dalam pesawat udara sedang dalam penerbangan apa-apa tindakan keganasan yang mungkin membahayakan keselamatan pesawat udara itu.

Adalah dimaklumkan bahawa mana-mana orang yang melakukan suatu kesalahan di bawah Akta ini boleh, apabila disabitkan, dikenakan hukuman penjara seumur hidup.

Pintu / Gate	NSST 13
Penerb. / Flight	MH 0002
Destinasi / Destination	LHR

Nama / Name	CORTIS AMRS

Kelas / Class	Tarikh / Date	Tempat duduk / Seat
351 C	16MAR–KUL	9K

Sila laporkan diri di Pintu Masuk 30 minit sebelum waktu berlepas
Please report at Boarding Gate 30 mins before departure time

to the river-side, and one or two new settlements. It was interesting to notice at Kanowit that the beneficent efforts of our Roman Catholic missionaries were bearing splendid fruit. The missionary fathers have built there a substantial and handsome church; their school, also, is remarkable for the efficiency of their Dyak and Chinese scholars. A group of nuns have set up a school for girls, near by, which is being well attended and productive of good results in the civilization of the people. The Roman Catholic methods of teaching these native children are excellent. It would take too long to describe them in full, but the blameless lives of these men and women, who have cast away all thoughts of comfort in the world and elected to throw in their lots for ever amongst the aborigines, cannot fail to impress the people amongst whom they live. Spiritually and materially their beneficent influence is felt throughout the land, and when we are gathered to our ancestors and the tales of these rivers are told, I believe it will be known that one of the principal factors in the spiritual advancement of Sarawak is largely due to the work of Roman Catholic missionaries.

Farther up the river, we passed another small settlement of recent growth, called Song, where a small Fort stands on the top of one of the little hills shelving into the river. Along the road, lining the bank, stood a row of Chinese houses, and a footpath, made of wooden planks and supported on poles, was crowded with Dyaks and Chinamen. The banks were covered with bundles of rattans, brought from the interior. Mats, baskets, cordage for ships, flooring for houses, etc., are usually made of rattans. The Tanjong people are about the best basket-makers of the country, and the wild Punans make the best mats. At this spot, where the trade in rattans is active, we saw up-river Dyaks hurrying up the steep banks with loads of rattan and gutta-percha, on their way to sell them to Chinamen. A great many boats, full of produce, were anchored to the banks, waiting their turn to be unloaded. The little Bazaar was crowded with almost naked people, for they only wore waistcloths. Even the Chinamen, with their pigtails twisted round their heads, had nothing on but cotton drawers. No women were to be seen, and the men looked like long brown-legged spiders, jumping or clambering in and out of the water.

Having passed this spot of activity in a desert of leaves and water, reach after reach was rounded, where we met with no other company but that of hawks flying rather low overhead, of brown moths so large that I mistook them for birds, and of butterflies, blue, yellow, and white, appearing here and there over the mud-banks in clusters of delicate colours.

About six in the evening we reached Kapit. The Fort stands on a hill, and steps cut out in the sharp, steep banks lead up to its front door. It stands some forty feet above the level of ordinary tides, but in the rainy season, when heavier freshets than those in the

fine season collect up river, the water has been known
to reach several feet above the flooring of the Fort.
As the anchor was dropped near the wooden wharf, a
crowd of Chinamen, Dyaks, Tanjongs, and Kayans,
rushed from the Bazaar and helped to carry our
luggage. We had brought our Chinese cook with
us, and he struggled up the bank with cages full of
cocks and hens which he had brought from Sibu.
Some of the people carried my dressing-bag and rugs,
Mr. Bampfylde's, Dr. Langmore's, and Bertram's
portmanteaux were seized and borne to the Fort
by Kayans with their hair streaming over their
shoulders. All these people talked at once, ordered
one another about, exclaiming, screaming, and hustling
in the most good-humoured and merry fashion.

Suddenly the crowd fell back, as a rather stout,
dark, middle-aged man came down the path to
meet us. This was F. Domingo de Rosario (called
"Mingo" by his friends), Commandant of Kapit Fort.
His father was a Portuguese from Malacca, and
Mingo had come to Sarawak during the reign of
the first Rajah Brooke, to whom he was butler.
Mingo was born in Sarawak, and was educated
at the Protestant Mission at Kuching, and when
old enough to join the Rajah's service he was sent to
the Rejang district, where he has remained ever
since. Mingo is well acquainted with the wild
inhabitants in his district, and is much beloved by
them. With his burly figure, his dark, kindly face,
his utter disregard to personal danger, and, above all,

for the way he has of looking at life as a huge joke, the Dyaks often compare him to "Simpurei," one of their jolly war-gods.

Mingo has been through strange adventures, fought many battles, and on one occasion, many years ago, was attacked in a place called Ngmah, where a Fort had been erected, but which has long since been pulled down and dismantled. In these quieter days, when life on the banks of the Rejang is comparatively free from danger, Mingo is sometimes heard to regret the fine old times when his time was spent in perpetual excitement. Notwithstanding these drawbacks, he takes the change philosophically enough. He is married to a Tanjong woman, who takes great care of him, and they have a daughter named Madu (meaning honey), to whom he is much attached.

We settled down comfortably in Kapit Fort, and the days passed quickly by. A constant stream of Dyaks and Kayans came from the countryside to see us, for Mr. Bampfylde had made them aware of our intention to visit Belaga, a place some three weeks' journey by boat, situated at the head-waters of the Rejang — Belaga being the real object of our journey up this river. Knowing my intense wish to visit all the places I possibly could, Mr. Bampfylde had suggested this trip to Bertram and myself. The great charm of the undertaking lay in the fact that to get to Belaga innumerable rapids had to be surmounted, and we had to go through an interesting stretch of country lying between Kapit and this distant Fort, for it is essentially the land of Kayan people, and here and there along the banks of those higher reaches of the Rejang are to be seen interesting and wonderful monuments of Kayan industry, in the shape of tombs carved by the people containing the remains of their most famous chiefs.   On such expeditions, it is customary for the people of the country to paddle the boats in which the Rajah or his family make excursions up these difficult and sometimes dangerous cataracts, like giant stairways, which lead into the interior.

Many of the chiefs and people who came to Kapit were old friends of mine, whilst others were strangers, for only the year before a head-hunting craze had broken out in the neighbourhood, and one of the most smiling chiefs, named Rawieng, who came to greet us on this occasion, had been attacked by the Government, his house burned down, and his possessions taken from him, owing to members of his tribe taking heads of innocent people living in the remote interior.   Rawieng took his punishment well, for he bore no malice, and stretched his hand out to us all with the utmost cordiality.

Although the greetings I received at the hands of these chiefs were usually hearty and affectionate, I thought on this occasion their manner was more friendly than usual, and the reason came out before long. Having been summoned by Mr. Bampfylde to paddle my boat and accompany me to Belaga, they imagined I intended going on the warpath.

This idea pleased them much, and great was their disappointment when Mr. Bampfylde informed them that my journey was quite a peaceful one.

But our cherished plans were doomed to failure. When all preparations were completed for our great voyage, the weather behaved in an unexpected manner for that time of the year ; for we were then in July, at which period, in the ordinary course of things, heavy storms of rain are rare. However, the day after our arrival and for many days and nights, heavy storms of rain thundered on the roof of the Fort, and the water of the river almost flooded the banks on which it stood. Tree-trunks, leafy branches, fruits, berries, and even blossoms, were torn from the banks and swept along in the angry stream, and it seemed as though the bad weather would never come to an end. The rapids in the neighbourhood were insurmountable, and day after day the chiefs, Mr. Bampfylde, Mingo, and ourselves discussed the situation, wondering whether or no it would be safe to face such torrents. The Sea Dyaks, who thickly populate this district, were present at these discussions and gave vent to their opinions in endless streams of words. The near inhabitants of Kapit, who were Tanjongs, with Tubam and Salleh, their chief men, whose houses were built on the banks opposite the Fort, were annoyed at the Dyaks from neighbouring rivers laying down the law about matters in which they thought themselves more competent to give an opinion, owing to their closer acquaintance with the rapids.

Therefore, in these discussions, Tubam, who had frequently been to Belaga, thought he had every right to assert himself.

Tubam's appearance was not prepossessing. He was old, shrunken, and wrinkled. His black hair, untouched with white, hung in oily corkscrew ringlets from under his little Kayan crown of plaited straw. Three lines of tattoo simulated a beard round his chin. He had plucked out his eyebrows and eyelashes, and his eyes looked like two little slits framed in pink lids, the pupils being almost invisible. One day he made a speech. He said he felt anxious about our going up the rapids with the river in its present state. Only that morning he had seen on its surface flecks of foam from the great cataracts miles away, borne past his house just above the Fort. "It would not matter much to Rajah Ranee, or to Tuan Muda, if either of them was drowned," he said, but it mattered much to him. "Think of the shame," he went on, "which would fall on me and my tribe if such a thing were to happen in our river." Then he got excited, clenched his fists, his thumbs pointing in the direction of the river. "And I forbid you to go, for are you not my grandmother, and as old as the world?"

These words of his would have clinched the argument with his own people, for they elicited nods and murmurs of approbation from Salleh and other members of his tribe. Salleh was second in importance in the village, and had offered to steer our boat on the occasion of our journey up the rapids. He was the most skilful steersman in the district, and he now confessed that he did not like the job unless the water were in a better condition. But the Sea Dyaks were persistent. They insisted on having the last word, and Hovering Hawk (a title given him by his tribe on account of his exploits in war) came up to me, picking his steps across the room, and moving his legs with high, birdlike action. He squatted himself by me, sniffed, cleared his throat once or twice, and whispered, "Don't mind what Tubam says; he knows nothing about it. He talks too much, his mouth is very large, and he is a bumptious fellow!"

Seeing that the Dyaks and the Tanjongs were of different opinions, I asked Hovering Hawk news of his wife and family, and a vexed subject was dropped. Then Hovering Hawk, purring with contentment, imagining he had got the best of the argument, un-fastened a small basket hanging at his side and emptied its contents on to a piece of rather dirty white calico he laid on the floor for the purpose. Bits of betel-nut, shreds of tobacco, a little brass box filled with lime, and a piece of sirih leaf fell out one after the other. He smeared the leaf over with lime, collected the other ingredients together, wrapped them in the leaf, and, with this large pill swelling one side of his face, sat contentedly at my feet for the remainder of the interview.

As day after day went by, and still the rain

showed no signs of abatement, we realized that it would be impossible for us to undertake the journey in the time at our disposal. Mr. Bampfylde, seeing my disappointment, suggested the better plan would be to stay on at Kapit until the weather improved, when we could at least take a shorter journey to a rapid, called Pelagus, the first cataract of a series up the Rejang River. This comforted us somewhat, and we thought of ways and means of diverting ourselves and our company whilst being kept prisoners in the Fort by the flood.

Many of the boats that had brought Dyaks from all parts of the neighbourhood were anchored in the river below. Tubam, Salleh, and the Tanjong women could easily reach the Fort from their houses close by, so Mr. Bampfylde and I arranged an evening reception for our friends, and invited them to the Fort after dinner. Some of the Tanjong women and other warriors, competent in such arts, having expressed their willingness to give us a performance of the dances of their tribes on the occasion, we were able in spite of the bad weather and delay to pass the time very agreeably.

CHAPTER XXIV

ON the evening fixed for the party a storm was raging; the rain poured on the roof with the noise of a hundred cataracts, making conversation impossible. Vivid flashes of lightning revealed patches of the surrounding country through the lattice-work of the room; we could see little bits of the river-bank opposite, the rank vegetation, an intricate entanglement of creepers and parasites, palms tossed about by the wind and rain, blazing into view, exuberant in detail, like over-exposed photographic plates. A thick grey veil of water streaked the landscape with silver bars, and each vivid flash was succeeded by terrific peals of thunder almost overhead. It was a weird scene. The walls and ceiling of our rooms were of wood, the mats on the floor were dark, a lighted lamp hung from the centre of the ceiling, and here and there were placed tumblers of cocoa-nut oil in which floated lighted wicks, giving out a flickering light.

Tubam had come at the head of the men and women of his village. Kayans from the far interior were easily recognizable by their hair cut in a fringe over their foreheads, flowing behind, and covered with crowns of plaited straw. Their bodies were tattooed,

and two great fangs from some wild beast's jaw
were thrust through their elongated ears. The Sea
Dyaks were very picturesque; their young warriors
wore a mass of fringes and beads, of silver bangles,
of waving plumes, of ivory and brass armlets, and of
silver waistbands. Their women shone resplendent
in innumerable rows of brass rings twined under their
armpits, reaching far below their waists, over very
short petticoats of beadwork, that glistened at every
movement.

All natives seem to love the ceremony of touching
hands. Dyaks and Kayans turn the palms of their
hands upwards, and bend their fingers in the shape
of claws; into these cavities you dip your finger-
tips, when the slightest touch on your part appears
to give satisfaction. It is extraordinary how cool
and dry the hands of Sarawak natives are at night,
or when a storm is in progress. On this tempestuous
evening, none of the hands I touched felt either warm
or clammy.

Our guests were very affectionate to Bertram and
me, and seemed glad to see us again. The Tanjong
women were the first to come forward; their silken
draperies rustled, their armlets tinkled, but their
naked feet moved noiselessly across the matted floor;
they swept along as though wafted by an invisible
wind, and in the semi-darkness looked like groups
of brightly draped ghosts. After them came the
Dyak women, noisier and heavier of tread, with
their Amazon-like cuirasses, and their very short

petticoats. When the women had passed, Kayan warriors swaggered up. Then came the Dyaks, and the long procession finished with the flower of ci-devant piratical contingents—thin, spare old men, still known and addressed by glorified titles won in exploits during their youthful days—Bald-Headed Hawk, Torrent of Blood, Face of Day, the Cobra, and many other titles, equally terrifying and appropriate. These old gentlemen were full of swagger, with a tremendous sense of their own importance.

The greetings having taken place, we called for the dances to begin. On such occasions the arrangement of the programme is a matter of difficulty, as none of the performers appear to like figuring in a *lever de rideau.* I inquired in Malay who should begin the performance, Mingo translating my remarks in a loud voice, so that all should hear; but the women sat sullenly in their corner, the men squatted motionless in various parts of the room, and no one seemed inclined to respond to the invitation. We waited a considerable time, and I began to despair. There was nothing for it—Mingo must come to the rescue. I told him to ask the Tanjong ladies to open the ball. Mingo looked at me sternly, nodded his head, glared round him for a second or so, and then marched up to one of the corners of the room, where the girls were sitting in a group. He laid hold of two shrinking figures and dragged them resolutely under the lamp swinging from the centre of the ceiling. For a minute or two the girls remained where he placed them, giggling, shrugging their shoulders, and pulling the hem of their jackets over their mouths. They pretended to be shy, sliding their feet in and out of their trailing petticoats, and suddenly rushed back to their former places and flopped down in the midst of their friends. Quick as lightning, Mingo was after them. He got hold of their hair, their arms, their draperies, anything that came to hand, and pulled them back under the lamp.

Meanwhile the music had started. A clear space was left in the centre of the room, and three young Tanjong girls were sitting there in preparation. They were a pretty group, huddled close together, their eyes cast down and their features expressionless. Two of them pinched the strings of bamboo guitars, thereby producing the mildest, meekest little tinkles imaginable. The third damsel beat the ends of a bamboo drum, thus bending her fingers back almost to her elbows. The music continued through the pantomime of refusal, the musicians taking no notice of what was going on.

We began to think we should not see any dancing that night, and even Mingo seemed about to lose his temper. He stood in the middle of the room, storming at the girls, threatening them with fines, with imprisonment, and with all manner of punishments, unless they commenced to dance. I must say Mingo's threats did not appear to have much effect on them, for they stood obstinate and immov-

15

able. But by and by, for no apparent reason, their bodies began to sway to and fro, and we understood that at last the performance had begun.

The change that came over these girls was wonderful. Their nervous giggling came to an end, an expression of scorn appeared on their faces, their eyebrows were lifted higher than usual, and their heavy eyelids were half-drawn over their eyes. They looked like tiny sphinxes, ancient and inscrutable, as though moving in a dream, obedient to an occult power. They might have been Hindoo goddesses, torn from off the wall of a Brahmin temple, practising strange rites in the midst of ordinary mortals. They were slim, young, and fragile-looking, with pale yellow skins, made yellower by a liberal amount of turmeric rubbed over their faces, necks, and arms. Their mouths were large, their noses flat and broad, but we scarcely noticed their departure from our European standards of beauty, so charmingly did the girls fit into their surroundings. We could almost admire the lobes of their ears, hanging down to their collar-bones, weighted with pieces of lead. We remembered Sakhya Mouni's descendants who are always depicted with very long ear-lobes. Some people will tell you this ear fashion is a sign of princely descent amongst Buddhist believers. The girls stood and moved so well, a straight line might have been drawn from the crown of their heads to their heels. Their costumes were pretty, their black satin jackets, fringed round with little bells,

reaching half-way to their knees, and their long petticoats of fine dark red and blue tints sweeping over
their feet.   Their straight black hair hung as far as
their shoulder-blades, from whence it was gathered
up in sweeps of darkness and tucked inside little
crowns of plaited straw, brightened with beads,
cowrie shells and all manner of glistening things.
Knobs of beaten gold fastened their collars, and the
sleeves of their jackets were pushed above their elbows,
revealing masses of shell, ivory, and silver armlets
encircling their arms ; I thought this a pity, since the
ornaments hid the symmetry of their slender wrists.

The dance is difficult to describe.   It was slow,
undulating, seductive, tender.   As the dancers stood
motionless before us, their draperies hung straight
from their chins to their toes, their feet being
hidden in the folds of their petticoats.   When they
slowly lifted their arms, an undulation wrinkled
up the folds of their garments, as though a sigh,
beginning at their heels, ran upwards and lost
itself in the air above their heads.   Then putting
their heels together, they slid along the floor, their
toes, peeping in and out the trailing folds, beating
the ground in time to the music.   Sometimes the
figures were drawn up to their full height, when
they looked like empresses in the regal pose of their
heads.   Sometimes they hung their heads, stretched
out their arms and flapped their hands, like the
wings of a bird, when, in the sudden transition from
an appearance of haughtiness to one of humility,

they looked charming, unhappy, and meek. I turned my head to listen to a remark Bertram made, and when I looked again the dance was finished. The proud and mysterious goddesses had vanished, and the giggling girls had reappeared. They moved awkwardly, I thought, as they waddled back to their corner in the midst of their friends, where they were lost in the shadows of the room.

Meanwhile the storm continued and increased in fury. A vivid flash of lightning was followed by a terrific crash, and a gust of wind blew the rain through the lattice-work across the room. Mingo rushed to the shutters, pulled them to, and barred out the storm. This unexpected douche appeared to silence the party; conversation flagged, and I am not sure that we were not becoming a little bored. Suddenly a luminous idea struck Mingo, and he rushed off for refreshments! Although these were of the simplest description, our guests were mightily pleased when Mingo reappeared with a great black bottle of gin under his arm, followed by a satellite bearing some water and two tumblers. The spirit was measured out in the tumblers by Mingo with the most punctilious care, and diluted with a fair amount of water, when the tumblers went the round of the hall, each warrior drinking his share and passing the tumblers back to Mingo, who, bottle in hand, refilled them. There were cocoa-nut cakes, cocoa-nut milk, coffee, biscuits made of sago, and other delicacies for the ladies, some of whom glanced wistfully at the black bottle, and perhaps regretted that the spirit should be kept entirely for the men. This diversion infused new life into the party, and the hum of voices was soon heard all over the hall.

At this juncture, a strongly built and very brown old gentleman left his seat and moved towards me with ponderous dignity. A handkerchief was twisted round his head, and he wore a cotton scarf held tightly across his bony shoulders. We had already greeted one another in the general "shake-hands" earlier in the evening, but it all had to be gone over again. "Long I have not seen you," he said, as his hand shaped itself into the customary claw in which I dipped my fingers. He fairly beamed on me; his smile was patronizing and friendly, and although I knew his face I could not remember his name. I turned to Mingo, who was standing at my elbow, and a whisper from him soon put matters straight between us. I was glad to see that Rawieng, who only the year before had kept the district in a state of terror owing to the head-hunting propensities of his tribe, had mended his ways; his presence at the party being an irrefutable proof of the purity of his future intentions. It was interesting to notice how friendly were the relations existing between Rawieng and Mr. Bampfylde. Only two or three years previously, owing to an atrocious murder committed on the main river by some of Rawieng's followers whom the old chief refused to give up to justice, Mr. Bampfylde (then Governor of the Rejang) was compelled to lead a fleet of boats into Rawieng's country, attack his village, and burn his paddy. Nor was this result obtained without a good deal of risk and difficulty to the attacking party, for owing to Rawieng's conservative ideas he had pitched his house on a precipitous hill, only to be reached after scaling innumerable rapids and marching a considerable way inland. Rawieng was a rich old man, and was heavily fined for the atrocious murders his tribe had committed. The long line of jars ranged along the walls of his house (the chief glory of the village, as they were supposed to have been made by spirits and given by them to Rawieng's ancestors) were taken by Mr. Bampfylde and stored in the Fort as pledges and hostages for Rawieng's future good behaviour.

There we were, that evening, the recent enemy and I, sitting over the spot where the precious jars were stored. Rawieng's conduct at our party showed that he did not bear malice, though it was but a few weeks since he and his people had tendered their submission to the Rajah's Government. His tribe had become weary of wandering as outcasts in the forests, and the only food they could obtain—wild fruits, game, and anything they might pick up— was not sufficient. Although there were many warriors present who had followed Mr. Bampfylde's expedition and lent a helping hand in punishing Rawieng's tribe, it was amusing to hear the old man holding forth before these people as to the completeness of his defeat. "Tuan Bampy (for so he pronounced Mr. Bampfylde's name) was a very pandi (clever) Tuan. He could fight for the Rajah and punish evil-doers, and, above all, he knew not what fear was." Imbued as all these people are with a veneration for courage, Rawieng expatiated at length as to the risks run by the white man's attacking force, and how thoroughly he and his people had been vanquished. Then, The Bald-Headed Hawk, The Cobra, The Torrent of Blood, and other old chiefs seeing that Rawieng and I were holding an animated conversation, and disliking being left out in the cold, joined us, and thus turned the channel of our talk into other directions.

The refreshments having again been handed round, and other dances being in the programme, Mingo decided that some of the Dyaks should now entertain us.

Three warriors came into the cleared space in the centre of the room, dressed in bark waistcloths, their black hair streaming down their backs. One man played the keluri, a Kayan instrument, made of bamboos of different lengths and sizes, fixed on a gourd, and in sound resembling bagpipes, although softer and more musical. To the tune of the keluri these men danced the deer dance, the monkey dance, and the mouse-deer dance, winding up with the head dance, this being considered the "clou" of the evening. Two performers wore their war dress for the occasion. Their arms were thrust into sleeveless jackets, covered with rows upon rows of hornbill's feathers, which stood out like the quills of a porcupine at every movement of the dancers. In one hand they grasped long, narrow-pointed shields, ornamented with a monstrous human face—two round staring eyes, a stroke that served for the nose, and a wide mouth with teeth sticking out—painted in red and black, over which hung patches of human hair. In the other hand they held sharp swords, which play a great part in such performances.

This principal item, the head dance, contains a shadowy kind of plot. Two men are supposed to meet in a forest; they are unacquainted with one another, therefore they are enemies. From the first moment they are supposed to catch sight of one another through the entanglement of tropical vegetation, they crouch and jump about like frogs, looking first to one side and then to the other, from behind their shields. One of the dancers suddenly springs to his full height, and rushes at his opponent, who is ready to receive him. A struggle begins, and they appear to be in deadly earnest. They wave their swords with such rapidity that it looks as though a number of steel Catherine wheels were flying about the room. They hack at one another, but never thrust. After this sort of thing has been going on for some time, one of the performers becomes exhausted, and falls to the ground, when his opponent seizes the advantage, grips him by the throat, kneels on his fallen body, and pretends to saw at the head until it is apparently separated from the body. This part of the play, somewhat disagreeable to me, was received with yells of delight from the warriors present, who made a noise as though a number of dogs were baying at the moon. The victor then takes the cap from the fallen man's head, to represent the real head he is supposed to have cut off. He then takes high jumps and rushes about the room in the exhilaration of his victory. As he is about to hang the trophy to his waist-belt by the lock of hair left for the purpose, he looks at the dead face and discovers the head to belong to his brother. Another dance is gone through, but now the steps denote dejection. The man goes about with bent knees, dragging his feet; he rubs his eyes with his knuckles, and fondles the headless body, imploring it to return to life. But even this tragedy ends happily. A friendly spirit passes by and whispers advice in the bereaved brother's ear. Acting upon the spiritual counsel, the murderer fits the head into its place between the shoulders of the corpse, when in a short time it is supposed to grow again on the body. The brothers are reunited, and another dance of whirling sabres, of leaps and bounds, takes place, after which the head dance is ended. Through it all, the lightness of the dancers is extraordinary, for however high they jump, or however far their stride may be, these Dyak dancers are invariably graceful and noiseless as panthers.

By this time it was getting late, the room was stuffy and hot, so I left the party as quietly as possible and went to the other side of the Fort, fitted, for the time being, as my private room.   The rain had ceased, and the moon in its last quarter was struggling through the clouds.   I lay in a long chair, and could see through one of the port-holes some of our guests returning to their boats, the lighted torches they carried being reflected in the turbid waters of the river.   Only a night-light was burning in my room, and I fancied myself alone, when a nervous cough behind me made me start.   I called for lights, and when they were brought, I saw a row of people sitting on the floor against the wall.   I was surprised, for natives are usually very tactful.   Salleh was the culprit on this occasion ; he had come with his wife Penus, and his daughters Remi and Remit, to ask me if I could see an Ukit woman, who had been too shy to come forward and speak to me before so many people at the party.   Having heard that morning that she was in the neighbourhood, I told Salleh to bring her to me one day when I should be alone, so I suppose he did not see why he should not effect the introduction there and then.   After all, I was anxious to see and talk to an Ukit woman, and as Penus was present and understood her language, this was a good opportunity.

Judging from what I had heard about the wild habits of the Ukit people, I was surprised to find my visitor an engaging little person.   She was curious looking, but not quite ugly. An enormous breadth lay between her high cheek-bones, and there was absolute flatness between her eyes, which were small, narrow, and raised in the outer corners. Her figure was slight, and her wrists and ankles delicate to a degree. She usually wore a short petticoat of bark, but Penus had evidently attempted to improve her appearance for the occasion by lengthening it with a broad piece of red calico falling over her feet. Her hair hung down to her knees, and she wore a little crown of black and yellow beads, a head-dress usually worn by these people. The little thing soon lost her shyness, and talked away quite unreservedly. Her language sounded soft and guttural. She had a pretty voice, and very nice manners. Her weird, fantastic appearance attracted me, and I took a great interest in this creature of the woods. She addressed some remarks to me, and was evidently asking for something. Penus, interpreting her words, told me she wanted some of the "sweet-smelling gutta" that white people rub over their skins when they wash themselves. I sent for a piece of soap (I had brought a good deal of this commodity with me); it was wrapped in mauve paper, made glorious to such eyes as hers with gold letters. I gave the package into her hands, and showed her how to take the paper off. She followed my instructions with great care, folded up its mauve wrapper with its tissue lining, and stuffed both in her hair inside her crown. She sniffed at the soap and handled it as though it were brittle. "Now

I shall sweeten the air for a great space as I walk along," she said, and moved off to crouch near the wall of my room, with the soap at her nose the whole time. But she had a husband, and he had been looking for her. Mingo ushered him into my room. He looked more like her grandfather than her husband, for he was very old, and she almost a child. He was a dirty old man too, and belonged to another branch of this Ukit tribe. He came up to me grumbling, and as I put out my hand, he pinched the tips of my fingers. He then showed me his wrist, round which was tied a piece of mouse-deer's bone to take away his sickness, as he had sprained his arm whilst cutting down trees in the forest a few days previously. He did not remain long with us, but told his wife to come away. She obeyed meekly, and he followed her, scowling, and chewing betel-nut. We wondered whether he were jealous of his attractive wife, and felt sorry for the little creature, whose soft and charming manners had, even in so short a time, won our hearts.

I bade Salleh and his party good-night, but Penus stayed behind, as she wanted to have a parting word. Moreover, she had brought a basket she had made for me, thinking it would be useful in packing some of my things on my boat journeys. The basket was a large cylinder, made of palm-straw, and woven in intricate patterns of black and white, with a dome-shaped cover fitting into its top. These kind of baskets are quite impervious to rain, and the Tanjong

people excel above all other tribes in their manufacture.   I thanked Penus for her kind present.   "It
is good to see you here," she said, "and our hearts
are glad.   I only wish my daughter, who died last
year, had been here too."   Penus was very sad about
the death of this daughter.   She had never spoken
about her to me before, but I suppose the lateness of
the hour, the night, and our parting of the next day,
made her more expansive than usual.   "Do you
think the dead come back, Rajah Ranee?"   I could
not answer her, for I don't suppose I knew more
about the matter than she did.   But I asked her if
she believed in Antus (spirits), or if she had ever
seen one.   "Oh yes," she said; "a spirit often comes
to our house.   When it gets dark, and night is not
yet come, he stays in the rafters of our room, and
the spark from his cigarette comes and goes in the
darkness."   "Do you ever speak to him?" I asked.
"Oh no; because Antus never answer human beings.
If I could speak to him I would ask him the road by
which my dead daughter went, so that I could follow
her."

We touched hands, and Penus left me to join her
friends.   As I fell asleep, I heard the murmur of the
people as they settled themselves for the night in
their boats anchored in the river.

CHAPTER XXV

THE day had not risen when Mr. Bampfylde, Bertram, Dr. Langmore, and I, started from Kapit Fort two days after the floods had ceased and the river had resumed its normal aspect. We were followed down the steep steps leading to the river by a great company of Kayans and Dyaks, our Chinese cook, our Malay servants, and Ima, my inseparable attendant when I lived in Sarawak. Mr. Bampfylde, Ima, and I, occupied one of the war-canoes, and Bertram and Dr Langmore another. Our boat was called *Bujang Naga* (Bachelor Dragon), and was a splendid specimen of a Dyak war-boat. Our crew, amongst whom were the élite of the chiefs staying with us in Kapit Fort, numbered about forty. Salleh was steersman, and stood at the stern with half his body appearing above the roof, his head protected from the sun by a large conical straw hat. The rudders of these boats are like those used by ancient Egyptians, according to the pictures in the British Museum, for they are rigged on the side of the vessel, instead of being fixed on the stern. A covering of palm leaves was stretched from one end of the boat to the other, and I could see from where I sat some twenty-five naked arms paddling as though for dear life. Those seated nearest to us were Unggat, Merum and Grasi, all renowned warriors. Our journey being a peaceful one, the chiefs had discarded their beautiful war accoutrements, and their appearance was homely, not to say dowdy. Hovering Hawk was wrapped in an old tartan petticoat or sarong, The Cobra had a loin-cloth as his only covering, and their companions followed suit. But the younger warriors were very smart; they had stuck alamanda and hibiscus blossoms in their head-handkerchiefs, and their waist-cloths were bewilderingly bright. We paddled on, hour after hour, and I thought it extraordinary that these men could last so long without a break in their fatiguing labour. They appeared as though they enjoyed themselves, and when the rhythmic stroke of the paddles flagged, a shrill scream from the man sitting in the bows, and who directed the speed of the boat, instilled renewed vigour in the crew, especially when the leader plunged his paddle into the water, flung a comet-like spray, reaching beyond the boat's stern, yelling and shouting, "Paddle, paddle," "Do not get slow," "Don't get soft." "Ah-a-a," he would scream again. Sometimes our crew raced Bertram's boat, and when his boat shot on ahead, Hovering Hawk and Flying Snake gave vent to ejaculations of disgust, abusing our crew roundly, and asking them whether they were asleep or awake. I remember passing a little stream, where, near the bank, about twenty or thirty yards away, a crocodile lay motionless flush with the water. Hovering Hawk pointed it out to me, and the man in the bows stopped the boat. My rifle lay loaded by my side—I cannot explain why it was there; I suppose I thought it sporting to carry a gun about. Mr. Bampfylde suggested I should try and shoot the crocodile, which I did, whereupon the beast rose in a mighty cataract of water and flopped down again into the stream. This feat of mine was much approved by the crew, who with grunts and ejaculations congratulated me on my exploit! I do not know whether I killed the beast. I do not think a bullet from my rifle could really have ended its life, for crocodiles are difficult to destroy; yet natives say that if a bullet penetrates their thick hide, it leads to their death, on account of the open wound becoming filled with maggots from the rivers, that kill them in time. Being a lover of all animals, I must explain that I have never, before or since, willingly killed any living creature, but a crocodile, with its hideous habits of killing, wounding, and maiming people—many of whom being people I have known—made me anxious to try and send one of these monsters to another world. I am not sure I was right in doing so, although I may have been the means of ridding the rivers of Sarawak from a dangerous pest.

At mid-day we stopped on a sandbank to lunch, and to give our crew an hour or two's rest. The Dyaks had erected a little palm-leaf house to shelter us during the halt, whilst they themselves, under the

shade of scattered rocks, set their rice boiling in pots
hanging from tripods made from branches of trees
cut down in neighbouring forests. Very soon little
fires began to spring up all over the sandy expanse.
As usual the noonday silence of the tropics reigned,
broken only by that bird whose sweet song rivals
our nightingale. I think this bird's song most
ravishing; its trills are velvety, soft, and yet so
loud that they can be heard for some reaches down
the river. Our famous Sarawak naturalist, Dr. Hose,
who is an expert in the sounds of birds, disagrees
with me; he thinks its note shrill and sometimes
disagreeable. I beg respectfully to differ from such
an authority, and still maintain that the alligator
bird (the name given to the bul-bul by the natives
of the country) is among the sweetest songsters of
the world.

By three o'clock in the afternoon the crew were
ready to proceed. Presently the river became so
shallow that poles had to be used instead of paddles.
Great trees, growing on rocks, overshadowed the
water, where it was difficult to understand how they
could live. The river became quite clear, rippling
over a pebbly bed. I wish I knew what those pebbles
were, for I believe in these river-beds are to be found
amethysts, tourmalines, and even sapphires. Dr.
Hose told me that on one of his travels up these
inland streams, his war-boats floated over the dust
of sapphires. An orchid branch drifted towards us,
rosy, white, and waxy, looking like a smile upon the

16

water. One of our Dyaks tried to get hold of it for me, but I prevented him. I preferred to think of the flower dying in the fresh cool stream, rather than see it fading in my hot hand.

The great stairway of rock was before us, and the crunch of gravel under our boat's keel warned us that the water could float it no longer. Some of the crew jumped overboard and made secure long lengths of rattan, in order to drag the boats up the many barriers that lay in our way. The men bounded over these impediments, and we bumped and creaked as the rattan ropes dragged us up these enormous boulders, the water pouring over them in all directions. Sometimes the torrent was so impetuous, and the rocks of such a height, that our boat was poised on the centre of a great boulder, its keel grating backwards and forwards, whilst the muscles of our crew stood out like cords on their necks and limbs, as they pulled at the rattans with all their might. Whenever our boat was safely lodged on a rock, the crew rested for a while and bathed in the deep pools of quiet water lying between the stones. They might have been bronze tritons escaped from fountains, endowed with life, and disporting themselves in these waters. The agility of an old Bukitan, who must have been at least sixty-five years old, amused me much. His crown of plaited straw lay over snow-white bristles, and a fine crop of snow-white hair ornamented one side of his cheek, whilst his other cheek was bare. He was

proud of his one whisker, and whenever he rested in
his arduous work, he stroked it continually.   A towel
round his waist was his only covering.   The old man
bounded from rock to rock, agile as a tiger cat ; he
frequently held the rattan rope in his teeth in helping
to pull the boats up.   After about an hour's such
toil, we found ourselves above the first ledge of rocks
in this great cataract of Pelagus.   We clambered up
the rocky banks and stood on the edge of a great
forest.   Rhododendrons, scarlet with blossom, wild red
hibiscus, and convolvuli of all colours, hung over the
water, whilst masses of tiny flowers, vaguely reminding us of violets, made a mauve carpet for our feet
as we stepped along, and in so doing, alas, helped
to spoil the picture.   We looked up a great reach of
the torrent mounting straight and closing the horizon.
At our feet the waters were divided by a small, rocky
island, on which grew, in scrappy bits of soil, lofty
trees with leafy branches.   The water frothed and
foamed round this impediment, and Mr. Bampfylde
informed me that at this spot many boats are swamped
and lives lost every year.   Then, beyond the horizon
lay numberless rapids, not so dangerous as is that of
Pelagus, and before reaching Belaga, the water flows
tranquilly along until the upper reaches of the Rejang
are reached.   Belaga is a great centre for rattans,
camphor, and gutta-percha.

As I stood looking at the whirlpool, Hovering
Hawk, who was standing near me, pointed with his
thumb to the swirling water all flecked with foam.

" See there," he said, " who knows how many eyes lie buried beneath that foam ! "

Beyond this foam, on the opposite bank, were quantities of wild sago palms, drooping their metallic green fronds over smaller-leaved forest trees ; then, lower down on the rocky banks, were entanglements of red rhododendrons, of scarlet berries and leaves, sprinkled by the spray. The mystery, the strangeness of the place, so like, and yet so unlike, European waterfalls ; the groups of Dyaks scattered about, grave and silent, perhaps remembering comrades of theirs who had found their deaths in the whirlpool; the perfumes of moss, damp earth and flowers, and the sound of running water, made us thoughtful, until Face of Day, with a pompous air, pulled his sword from out its wooden sheath, cut a branch of leaves and berries from a shrub near by, and handed it to me. " Its leaves are tongues, and its berries flaming hearts—manah (beautiful)," he said. His gift somewhat impeded my progress as I struggled down the slippery rocks to our boat, but I managed to carry the branch in safety, and one of its leaves now rests between the pages of St. Francis of Assisi's *Flowerot* book I always keep by me.

We then embarked for the return—I looking eagerly for a new experience, that of shooting the rapids. It was very great fun. Salleh stood in the bows with a long pole, and two or three of the crew also took poles, whilst the remainder of the Dyaks sat in their places in the boat, no doubt rejoicing in having nothing to do. We bounded like corks over the crest of the waves ; we were carried into pools, from whence we emerged by clever strokes of Salleh's pole against intervening rocks, and rounded great stones which, a moment before, appeared as though nothing could prevent our boats being dashed against them. It was shady, cool, and peaceful ; flowers, leaves, and mosses smelt sweet ; pale blue butterflies hovered over the banks, and a hawk hung motionless in the air above our heads. When we had passed in safety the most dangerous part of the cataract, our crew sang their home-coming song, a sort of dirge sounding something like a Gregorian chant. Mr. Bampfylde told me it was a thanksgiving song to the gods for having floated us safely over the dangers of the great Pelagus rapid.

As I write, it all comes back to me as though it only happened yesterday, for the impression was so intense that at times I fancy myself again in that spot, flying down the rapids like a bird. I think if, at the end of my life, I had to give an account of the happiest time I have ever spent, it would be of those too brief minutes when Salleh and his picked crew steered our boat down those foaming waters.

CHAPTER XXVI

AFTER a short journey, we encamped for the night on a gravel bank, still within sound of the cataract's roar. On our way, we paddled by a jagged rock, about twenty feet high, standing in the middle of the stream. Salleh pointed it out to me, and told me that Kling (a hero of Dyak mythology) had with one blow from his biliong (axe) cut its top in two. On the gravel bed a hut of fresh pale green palm fronds had been run up for me to sleep and bathe in. It was very comfortable, with a bamboo bench, some three feet wide, resting against its leaf walls for me to sleep on. Salleh had hung ferns, flowers, and leafy branches on its walls, and had strewn the floor with sweet-smelling leaves. A large expanse of shingle lay all round the hut, and our two boats were tethered to the shore just below. Camp-fires were soon lit here and there for the crew to boil their evening meal of rice. It was nearly full moon; the water rippled over its gravelly bed and moved the sedges in the river with a musical sound. Some palms in the neighbourhood rustled as though a shower of rain were falling, and the millions of leaves of the forest trees, covering the hills and valleys, gave back to the air in perfumed mists the heat that had beaten on them during the day.

After dinner, rugs were spread on the pebbles for us to sit on. Our friends, the Dyak and Tanjong chiefs, were invited to join us and have their coffee and cigarettes with us. The moon appeared above the trees; mists began to rise, and in the forest near by we heard the little black and white owl crying for the moon. The Sarawak people call it Pung-Gok, and the sound of its two notes, musical and tender, made us feel happy and yet sad. This was the moment for our Dyak and Tanjong friends to tell us some of their legends. " How about the flood?" said Mr. Bampfylde to Salleh. (I think Mr. Bampfylde knew what was to come.) " Oh yes," replied Salleh, " I know all about the flood. It is a true story and I will tell it you.

" When the world was very old and the people very wicked, the heart of the great god Patara grew sick in heaven. He sent two dragons, man and wife, to the earth, which were so large that they could hook their tails in heaven and hang their heads to the earth. They ate up the paddy all over the world, so that many of the people died of starvation, and after doing all this evil, they hoisted themselves back into heaven by their tails. At that time there were seven Rajahs in the world,—Rajahs Sinddit, Niuka, Nugu, Amban, Kagjup, Lubah, and Umbar. Rajah Sinddit, the eldest, said to his brothers, ' We must kill these two dragons, for never in all these years have I been so hungry.' The brothers inquired how he suggested killing these monsters. 'With arrows poisoned with upas,' he said, and they commenced making preparations so as to be in readiness for the dragons' next visit.

" In a short time they saw from their hiding-place the two dragons letting themselves down from heaven, and beginning again their work of devastation. So the brothers sent showers of poisoned arrows, hitting the dragons every time. The dragons felt rather sick, and hoisted themselves back to heaven: the poison soon began to take effect, and the beasts shook all over and fell to earth. Then the seven Rajahs came forward, followed by the population from their respective countries, and cut the dragons to pieces. Some took pieces of flesh, others portions from their breasts, whilst others filled gourds with blood, each according to his fancy. Some of the Rajahs cooked their portions in bamboos, others in earthenware saucepans. When the flesh began to boil, the fat bubbled over and went into the rivers of the seven countries. The waters immediately began to rise, and the people flew to the hills.

" As the waters of the rivers were not sufficient to flood the world, Patara sent rain which lasted for three years, so that the waters covered the mountains and high places of the earth, and all the people in the world perished, with the exception of one woman, named Suki, who survived in a boat. After a long time, the flood subsided, and Suki was alone in the world, but there were a few animals that had also escaped destruction, these being a dog, a deer, a fowl, a pig, and a cat. These remained with Suki during her peril, but when the waters retreated, they all ran away and she was left sorrowing, for she had not even the animals to speak to.

" Patara, seeing her loneliness, took pity on her, and sent the god of the storms, Antu Ribut, who made her his wife. They had a son, named Sinpang Tinpang, and a daughter. In time the brother and sister married, so as to increase and replenish the world. After many years the people began to get wicked again, and a Rajah of this new population, whose name was Gading, collected an army and went to fight to the edge of the sky. He led his army through forests and valleys, up and down great mountains, until he arrived at a land of fields, where the army slept for the night. The next morning the people saw an enormous mushroom, called Kulat Liman ; it was so big that it took seven days to walk round it. The Rajah's army, who had finished their provisions during their march, waxed hungry at the sight and hacked at the mushroom, cooking and eating the pieces they managed to obtain. When they had eaten their fill, they became very drunk and began to speak in different languages. The Hindoos rolled about in charcoal and thus became black, the Kayans pierced their ears in all directions, the Chinese shaved their heads, the Malays shaved off their every hair, and the Bukitans and Ukits tattooed themselves. Then Kling, the god of war, came down at Patara's command to confuse them, and all the people commenced to speak in strange languages, so that the army could not be led further, and they all separated into different countries and the world became what it is now."

Salleh finished his tale quite abruptly. We all thanked him, and his friend Merum told us that he knew a good story about the Rejang, so we lit fresh cigarettes and composed ourselves to listen. He cleared his throat and began—

"The giant Goa is the root of the Rejang tribe. He lived up the river, as far as the Pelagus Sukat rapid, and made the tribe by killing his daughter and a lot of animals and pounding them all up together. When he had finished making the tribe he moved down to the sea-coast to live near the river Igan; as he walked down the Rejang river, he was such a big man that the water only came up to his knees.

"Goa had a son-in-law, named Bessiong, and as his rice farm was much troubled with pigs, he gave Bessiong a valuable spear and told him to kill the animals. Bessiong accordingly went up the river in a canoe to the farming ground, and, seeing a white pig rooting up the paddy, he flung the spear, which struck the pig and broke in two, the animal running away with the spear-head still sticking in its neck. Bessiong could not follow the pig up, and went home to tell his father-in-law. Goa was exceedingly wroth and sent him back to find the spear-head.

" Bessiong returned to the rice farm and managed
to track the pig some way by the spots of blood.
When these came to an end he looked up and found
he had wandered into an unknown country. He
roamed about, and at last came to a great village
inhabited by a strange people, living in very large
houses. Looking into one of the houses, he saw
that the people were holding incantations over one
of the inmates. When the people, from inside the
house, saw the stranger, they called out to him and
asked him where he had come from. Bessiong told
them, and asked permission to enter the house.
This they said he might do if he could doctor, as
the Rajah's daughter was dying and none of their
medicine men could save her. Bessiong, agreeing
to try and make her well again, was taken to see
the patient, who, he was told, was suffering from
a wound in the neck. On looking at the wound,
he saw the end of his father-in-law's spear sticking
into it. Bessiong said he could cure her, but that he
must first go outside to obtain remedies ; accordingly
he went, and returned in a short time with a piece of
bamboo and a cloth. He covered the girl's head and
neck over with the cloth, extracted the spear-head,
and slipped it in the bamboo. He then instructed
the people to give her certain remedies, and in a short
time the wound healed and the girl recovered.

" The Rajah, grateful to Bessiong, gave him
his daughter in marriage. They lived together for
a year or two, and one day she took her husband

down to bathe. She showed him two wells, and confessed that she and her people were a pig tribe. She told him that if they bathed in one of these wells, they were turned into pigs, and were restored to their human form by bathing in the other well. She asked him to dip his leg into the pig well, and when Bessiong did so, it was changed into a pig's leg. He then dipped it into the other well, when his leg was immediately restored to its original shape. After a time, Bessiong became rather weary of the company of his pig wife, and wished to return to his father-in-law's village. His wife then warned him that if ever he met a herd of pigs swimming across a river, he must be careful not to kill the middle one, for it would be herself. At the same time, she informed him that she intended to swallow all her jewels and turn into a pig. She cautioned him that if he did happen to kill her, he would die himself.

"After these admonitions, he went back to Goa. One day, when he was on a hunting expedition with his two dogs, he saw a herd of pigs swimming across the river. The ci-devant husband at once recognized his wife, and a longing for wealth took possession of him. He thereupon threw a spear at the middle pig and killed her just as she reached the shore. He ran to the place where she lay, ripped her pig body open, and found all her jewels. But no sooner had he the wealth within his grasp than he died himself as the proper punishment for his treachery. Thus it happens that his tribe is scattered all over the country, and the tribe which Goa manufactured fell to pieces, the remnant being made up by Tanjongs, Kanowits, Bliens, Kejamans, Sekarrangs, etc., all reduced in number."

This story of the pig lady was evidently a favourite one, for the chiefs listened to every word of the legend as if they had never heard it before, although they appeared to know it so well that, whenever the reciter paused for a second, one or other of the warriors seated round immediately prompted him.

It grew cold. The mists were making themselves felt, they wreathed themselves round the tree-tops and formed into walls over the waters of the river, so that the distant hills became invisible. But the little owl's voice was still heard crying for the moon. He had flown farther away in his search for higher branches of trees whence he could see his lady love. By and by, the moon itself was lost in the mist, and the little bird lover's cry was silenced, when the ripple of the water over the pebbles, and the roar of the distant cataract, were the only sounds we heard. I said good-night to my friends and walked off to the hut with Ima, whilst Bertram, Dr. Langmore, and Mr. Bampfylde went to sleep in the boats moored by the river's side. Salleh accompanied us to the hut, and when I said good-night to him and hoped he would sleep well, he said, " Oh no, Rajah Ranee, I shall not sleep to-night. I shall just doze like a

Kijang,[1] with one eye open, so as to be on guard near your hut, ready for any emergency." A quarter of an hour had not elapsed before I heard Salleh's snores behind the thin walls of my leafy shelter! Then I fell asleep, and was awakened by wild and very sweet sounds. They were like the silvery tones of a flute, pouring forth triplets of notes, some long, some short, in the minor key. I got up and opened the leafy door. The half-light of dawn lay over the mists, enwrapping the trees and still hiding the river. As they lifted and rent themselves away from the branches of a bush growing near, I saw Salleh standing there, flute in hand. "Is that you, Salleh," I said, "making that sweet music?" "Yes," he replied; "it is a tune I play at dawn and sunset, because at these hours it sounds so sweet that it brings tears to my eyes, so I thought you would like me to play it to you." Well! I thought, I am sorry for those people who imagine our Sarawak natives to be no better than savages.

[1] The roebuck.

SALLEH, A TANJONG CHIEF, PLAYING ON THE NOSE FLUTE, WITH TWO TANJONG ATTENDANTS

CHAPTER XXVII

ON our way down the Rejang we stayed one evening at Sibu. Arriving there about sunset, we took a walk round the Chinese Bazaar to look at the shops and say good-bye to some of our friends. The Chinese are supposed to have been the first people to discover camphor, and Sibu Bazaar is one of the principal dépôts for it in Sarawak. In early days camphor was purchased for about $10 a cattie (1⅓ lb.), but the price has now risen to three times that amount. Chinese merchants all over Sarawak buy this commodity from the natives and send it to Singapore. The camphor seekers in the forests of Sarawak go through a great many superstitious rites in order to find good supplies. Sometimes they stay in the forests for weeks together, having only salt and rice for their sustenance.

The Rejang river is rich in many articles of export: indiarubber, gutta-percha, beeswax, mats, ebony, beads, and geliga or bezoar stones, the latter being found in the stomach of three species of monkeys—wah-wahs, jelu-merahs, and jelu-jangkits. The natives kill these animals with the blow-pipe, and about seven out of every ten are said to contain these valuable and rare stones, highly prized by Chinamen, who buy them at extremely high prices. Bezoar stones are also to be found in porcupines, but they are rarer, and are, in consequence, even dearer than those found in monkeys. A small species of rhinoceros also exists and roams about not far from Kapit Fort; these animals are to be met with near a limestone mountain, called the Mountain of the Moon. The creatures are hunted and killed by the natives for the sake of their horns, which the Chinese scrape into powder, mix with water, and give as a medicine for inflammation; they also boil the dung of these animals and use it as a medicine. The animals are not savage, and only turn upon human beings when wounded.

One of our visits, on this evening at Sibu, was to an old Chinese chemist, who had settled himself in the place when the Rejang was given over to the first white Rajah. His shop was situated in the middle of a row of houses, roofed with wooden shingles, in front of which were wide verandahs with balustrades, floored with planks, where the shopkeepers sat in the cool of the evening, and purchasers wandered about them in comfort all day long, sheltered from sun and rain. The Chinaman was very glad to see us, and Dr. Langmore was interested to meet a colleague, for the old man was supposed to be one of the most skilful doctors in the neighbourhood. He showed Dr. Langmore his grated rhinoceros horn, the powdered bezoar stone, the broth made from sharks' fins, and on one of the counters was a steaming bowl of tamarinds, in readiness for stomachic complaints. He was ending his days in peace and prosperity. His dispensary was thronged from morning to night with patients suffering from all kinds of diseases, nervous and otherwise. The death-rate at Sibu, however, was low, so one imagines the old man's methods were beneficent. Nor was our old friend quite without an eye to the future, for he owned a beautiful coffin made of iron-wood, or bilian, which he kept polished like a looking-glass. It was often put out in the warm, dry air, so that it should be thoroughly well seasoned in case of emergency. The old gentleman would sit on the edge of the coffin smoking his opium pipe after his day's labour—that one solace of hard-working Chinamen, who take one pipe of opium in the evening, just as an abstemious man enjoys his glass of whisky and water before going to bed. From my own experience amongst the people of Sarawak, I can say with truth that opium is not in any way such a curse to the country as are the spirits and "fire water" sold in such large quantities all over the United Kingdom and its colonies, with, apparently, so few restrictions. But to return to our old friend: he would point to his coffin with pride, for he did not dread the time .when the lid would close over him and his place in the world know him no more.

Going back to our bungalow near the Fort, we
17

walked round the other shops in the Bazaar : these were full of beads of dark blue transparent glass, some opaque, ornamented with dabs of black, red, white, and yellow.   These beads are made in Venice, and find ready purchasers amongst the poorer Dyaks, Kayans, and Tanjongs, for they are a fair imitation of ancient beads these people dig up, sometimes by accident, sometimes as the result of dreams.   It is curious how these ancient beads are found, and an interesting account of them may be seen in Dr. Hose's recent book on Sarawak.   The true old beads are regarded with great veneration by the Dyak and Kayan people.   One of my Dyak friends told me that he dreamed if he went to a certain spot in a forest rather distant from his home, and dug under a particular tree, he would find amongst its roots a valuable bead called lukut.   He accordingly went to the spot, dug under the tree, and there found the bead, which he carried round his waist in a little basket, together with bits of rock crystal, stones worn into queer shapes by water, and a peculiar-looking seed covered with red fluff, which was believed to be the hair of a powerful and malignant spirit, named Antu Gergasi.

We bade farewell to the Chinese apothecary and to the bead-finder, who had escorted us to the door of our house, and the next morning we left Sibu on our way to Simanggang.   We entered the Batang Lupar River and steamed by two green mounds, covered with trees, shaped like dumplings, which stand at its entrance. One of these is an island, called the Isle of Birds, where a landslip has up-rooted the great trees on its precipitous side, showing the red soil underneath. On this island is a tomb erected to a Muhammadan lady, who lived a great many years ago in one of the little villages near the coast, and was honoured for her holy life and her incessant prayers to Allah. When she died, she was buried in this little island as a special tribute to her memory. Although a pilgrimage to her tomb requires a tedious journey across the channel dividing the island from the neighbouring coast, the people in this part of the country pay frequent visits to her resting-place, taking with them on each occasion costly silks and satins to lay on her tomb, and thus show the reverence in which she is still held by those who appreciate her holy life.

The passage from the mouth of the Rejang had been so smooth that it was impossible even for me to be sea-sick. The sun was setting, and in front of us the shores of the Batang Lupar were veiled with pink smoke, for it was now in September, and the Dyaks were burning their farms. I saw strange, fitful lights in the western sky, fragments of pale blue framed in golden fluff with ragged edges of copper. A colour, like a fragment of a rainbow, was seen for an instant close by the sea, then disappeared, whilst entanglements of gold and turquoise blue, intricate and delicate, covered the sky. The sun dropping behind the clouds stood out blood-red, like a glorified host; until in a few moments it was hidden behind the sea. A gleam of gold trembled on the water; it vanished, darkness came, and the day was done.

Our arrival at Simanggang was a pleasant one. Our dear friend, Mr. Bailey, who for several years had ruled the district with marked success, and Mr. Kirkpatrick, then Assistant-Resident in the Batang Lupar, were at the wharf to meet us. Bertram and I walked up that sweet-smelling avenue of angsana trees leading to the Fort and to the bungalow where we were to stay, and where we spent a happy time.

A great sadness comes over me now as I write about this river, for since Bertram's and my visit to the Batang Lupar two of the Rajah's most distinguished officers have passed away. In mentioning Simanggang, it would be a great and very ungrateful omission were I not especially to mention these two men—Mr. Frank Maxwell and Mr. Bailey.

Mr. Frank Maxwell lived at Simanggang, in charge of the Fort, for a great many years, and it is almost unnecessary to remind anyone who takes an interest in the Malayan Archipelago how famous the name of Maxwell must for ever be in that part of the world. His father, Sir Benson Maxwell, and his brothers, Sir William and Mr. Robert Maxwell, are also well known for the part they have played in civilizing those far-off Eastern lands. But it is of Mr. Frank Maxwell that I now write, for I am able

HUT CONTAINING EATABLES TO REFRESH THE GOD OF SICKNESS,
BATANG LUPAR RIVER

to speak with authority as to the affection in which all the people of the Batang Lupar hold his name. He joined the Rajah's service as a young man of twenty-two years of age. He first of all learned the methods of Sarawak policy under Mr. Skelton, another of the Rajah's loyal officers, who, alas, was destined to die young. At Mr. Skelton's death, Mr. Maxwell was given charge of this district, and for years he toiled there for the benefit of the people. Head-hunters were busy in those days in the inland country of the Batang Lupar, and many were the expeditions led by him in order to restore peace and trade in the vicinity. A chief, called Lang Endang, gave immense trouble, and at one time menaced in a somewhat serious manner the inhabitants residing in the lower waters of the Batang Lupar River. Now that Mr. Maxwell has passed away, I do not fear his displeasure at pointing out the manner in which he drove these enemies of the Rajah back, thus establishing security and peace in the district. One of these expeditions comes back forcibly to my mind as I write. Mr. Maxwell's health was never very good on account of constant malaria and rheumatism, and once when an expedition was absolutely necessary he was lying crippled with an attack of acute rheumatism in Simanggang Fort. He was carried down to his boat and placed on a mattress, from which he directed the operations necessary against the rebel force. During the arduous river journey he lay almost unable to move hand or foot. Notwithstanding these drawbacks, he led his Dyaks to victory, and when he got back to the Fort and had leisure to be ill in comfort — although still in great pain — he must have felt repaid for his exertions by the grateful affection of the Malays and Dyaks, who, as I have said before, admire above all other things courage and endurance. It was not from Mr. Maxwell that I learned the details of this expedition, but from the Simanggang people themselves.

The same devotion to the country distinguished Mr. Bailey, who was content to live in the Fort situated up that green cliff overlooking the Batang Lupar River for years and years, bereft of European society, with the exception of the English officer under him, straining every nerve to bring the people into civilization, to teach them the benefits of good agriculture, and to keep them as much as possible from the pernicious habit of head-hunting, which seems ingrained in their very bones.

These two names which occur to me as I write are of those who have gone beyond the influence of either praise or blame. Fortunately many of the Rajah's other officers are still alive, and it is only because I have the pleasure of being their friend, and know how much they would dislike being dragged into print, that I refrain from saying all I should like to say about such men as Mr. Bampfylde, Mr. Harry Deshon, and others, who have so nobly followed the example set before them by their chief.

I know I shall be forgiven if I seize the present opportunity of mentioning the names of some of my Englishwomen friends who have also taken an affectionate interest in the lives of the women of our country. The wife of the Bishop of Sarawak, Mrs. Hose, Mrs. Deshon, Mrs. F. Maxwell, Mrs. Buck, and many others were most successful in their sympathetic endeavours to know them well and to become their friends. I wish these ladies could realize how much all who care for Sarawak appreciate their work out there. Mrs. Hose, alas, died some years ago, but her memory still lives in the hearts of the women of Sarawak. Their other Englishwomen friends are often spoken of in Kuching and other places in Sarawak, and the one wish of the women of the country is that they may see them again.

CHAPTER XXVIII

WHILST we were staying at the bungalow at Simanggang, Mr. Bailey sent me a message one morning to the effect that a number of Dyak women, living a little distance in a village up the Batang Lupar, had requested permission to send a deputation to welcome us to the country. I was only too delighted to receive the women, so that Bertram and I stood on the verandah in expectation of their arrival. A little distance up the path, bordered by betel-nut palms, sweet-smelling limes, and other tropical growth we saw a long file of women making their way in our direction, bearing aloft great round trays piled up with fruits and cakes. High silver combs, from which dangled fringes of silver, falling each side of their faces below the ears, decorated their huge coils of hair. Their bodies were cased in innumerable coils of brass rings, and they wore short petticoats of cotton cloth, brown, blue, and white. They wore quantities of anklets and bangles, and their throats were encircled with rows upon rows of beads and gold ornaments. There were about thirty or forty of these women, walking slowly, holding themselves very straight, their eyes cast down, and I noticed the same curious, mysterious, archaic expression on their faces as on those of the Tanjong dancers. They came to the bungalow, passed Bertram and me, and laid their gifts of fruits and cakes on the verandah at the back of our house, then followed us into our sitting-room to have a little talk.

This charming welcome was their way of showing pleasure at our arrival, and when they had taken their places, squatting on the floor, their feet tucked underneath them, and the few moments of silence required on such important occasions had passed, we began our talk, and I asked them about their families and all the news of their village. They told me that not many weeks before, sickness had attacked some members of their community, and that their long house, surrounded by an orchard of bananas, durians, jack fruit, etc., was situated a few yards from the banks of the river. In order to appease the anger of the god of sickness, they had erected a little hut on the river-bank. I felt curious to see this hut, and asked them whether I might pay it a visit. They were pleased with the idea, and these forty women suggested paddling me thither in one of their boats. Accordingly, that afternoon, Bertram and I were conveyed a few reaches up the Batang Lupar by this picturesque crew. It did not take us long to reach the spot, where we saw an open shed, propped on bamboo poles, roofed in with palm leaves. Large plates, some chipped and broken, hung from the roof, and on a platform below were placed cooked rice, pieces of salt fish, and other edibles, together with a gourd of water, to tempt the spirit of the plague to eat his meals there, instead of going further inland to procure his food off human flesh. This custom is, I believe, a universal one amongst some of the tribes in Sarawak. The women assured me that the sickness was stayed by these methods, but the hut had been left there, in case the unwelcome visitor should return at any time for more victims. We were paddled back to the bungalow in the same way as we had come, and the women expressed themselves delighted with the time we had spent together.

That evening we held a large reception in the Fort, at which all my old friends, Malays and Dyaks, were present, Mr. Bailey and Mr. Kirkpatrick being the masters of ceremony on the occasion. One of the Malays present, a Seripa, whom I knew well in her younger days, amused me much, so careful did she seem to be of Bertram's morals. A pretty girl, whose name was Lada (meaning pepper), a Dyak of Sekarrang and the daughter of a fortman, happened to be amongst our guests. Her magnificent hair, her great dark eyes fringed with eyelashes of wonderful length, her little flat nose and well-shaped mouth, her pale yellow complexion, her slim figure, and her graceful movements made her a striking personality at the party. I must own Bertram thought the girl pretty and talked a good deal to her, but in quite a fatherly manner. This conduct, however, on his part, did not please the Seripa, who sat next to me. She objected to his showing attention to a person she considered an " orang kechil " (a little person of no consequence). She told me she was my friend, and therefore competent to teach " Anak Rajah " (a Rajah's child) in the ways he should go. She continued her ejaculations on the subject during the evening. I tried to pacify her, and could only manage to do so by telling her that perhaps she might get an opportunity the following morning of seeing Bertram, and remonstrating with him on his conduct. Meanwhile, poor Bertram was quite unconscious of the displeasure of the Seripa. She was a curious-looking woman, of Arabian descent, and her features were more European than were those of Malays generally. She had been good-looking, and was even then a picturesque figure in her draperies of dark blue and her dark purple scarf, made of gauzy material, flung over her locks, still untouched with grey, but curling in profusion all over her head.

The next morning Ima told me that the Seripa and one or two of her female retinue were prowling round the garden of the bungalow, in order to waylay Bertram as he went out for his morning walk. What happened at the interview, I never quite made out, but, being warned by Ima that the couple had met, I stood on the verandah and watched the proceedings. The angry dame was pouring forth a torrent of words to Bertram, who could only understand about a quarter of all she said. Ima told me, however, that the gist of it was that she (the Seripa) was my friend, and that if Bertram chose to pay attention to any of her relations it would be quite the right thing for a Rajah's son to do, as they were Seripas, but she forbade him to waste his compliments and attentions on people below his rank. I am sorry to say that Bertram did not at all appreciate the friendly interference of the angry Seripa, although when a few days had elapsed, my loyal friend could judge for herself that the matter was not of such serious import after all. By the time we left Simanggang, Bertram and the Seripa had become good friends.

It must be remembered that the greatest pleasure to Malays who have passed their first youth is in teaching others. Their one idea on approaching young people is to "ajar" them. "Baik sahya ajar" (it is well I should teach him) were the words I was perpetually hearing from many Malays during my journeys with Bertram through Sarawak. It shows friendship and interest on their part, and I remember with tenderness and affection the admonitions the dear people used to give me when I first went amongst them in the days of my youth.

CHAPTER XXIX

DURING our stay at Simanggang I saw, as usual, a great many natives, and being interested in the legends of the place, I persuaded my visitors to relate some of these to me. It should be remembered that none of these legends have been written down by themselves, since the Dyaks possess no literature, with the result that they vary in the telling. I cannot say positively that the following legends have not already appeared in print; to my mind, however, their interest lies in their slight difference; every variation goes to show how strongly these legends are embedded in the minds and lives of the people, and should, in their way, help to unfold the secret of their origin.

I found that the strange idea of people becoming petrified by storms and tempests, through laughing or ill-treating animals, was universal amongst the inhabitants of this district. The following are two stories regarding this belief, told me by my friends.

Many years ago there was a little village called Marup, far up the Batang Lupar River. It stood on the banks near its source, and below the village the water rippled over pebbles under the shade of great

trees.   There were deep pools here and there
between the rocks, where fish could be seen swimming
about, and these the village boys caught in their hands.
It was a happy little place, too poor to be attacked
by robbers, and out of the reach of the terrible
head-hunters living nearer the coast.   The orchards
round the village were full of fruit, and the rice-crops
were never known to fail.   The women passed their
time weaving cloths made from the cotton growing
on the trees round their dwellings, or working in the
rice-fields, whilst the men fished, hunted, or went long
journeys in their canoes in search of certain palms,
which they brought home to their women, who worked
them into mats or plaited them into baskets.   One
day a young girl went down to the river with her net.
She filled her basket with fish called by the people
" Ikan Pasit."   The girl took them home, and as
she was preparing them for supper, the smallest fish
jumped out of the cooking pot and touched her
breast.   "What are you doing?" she said to the fish.
" Do you imagine that you are my husband?" and at
this joke she laughed heartily.   The people who were
watching her prepare the meal joined in the laugh,
and the peals of laughter were so loud that the
villagers, hearing the noise, rushed to see what was
the matter, and they too began to laugh.   Suddenly,
a great black pall was seen to rise over the western
hills, and spread over the sky.   A mighty wind blew
accompanied by flashes of lightning and detona-
tions sounding like the fall of great hills.   Then

a stone-rain (hail-storm) began, and soon a terrible
tempest was in progress. The torrents of rain and
hail were so dense that day turned to night. After a
time the rain ceased, but great hailstones beat pitilessly
down on the village until every man, woman, and
child, and every animal, even the houses themselves,
were turned to stone and fell into the river with a
loud crash. When the storm subsided, a deep silence
lay over the valley, and the only traces of that once
happy settlement were great boulders of rock lying
in the bed of the stream.

The girl who had been the first to mock at the
fish was only partly petrified, for her head and neck
remained human and unchanged. She, also, had
fallen into the river, and was embedded like a
rock in the middle of the stream. Thus she lived
for many years, with a living head and neck, and a
body of stone. Whenever a canoe paddled by she
implored its inmates to take their swords and kill her,
but they could make no impression whatever on her
stone body or on her living head. They could not
move the rock, for it was too big, and although they
hacked at her head with axes, swords, and various
other implements, she bore a charmed life, and was
doomed to remain alive. One evening a man
paddled by, carrying his wife's spindle in the bottom
of his canoe. He heard the girl's cries, and tried all
means possible with his axe and his sword to put her
out of her misery; at length in a fit of impotent
despair he seized hold of the spindle and struck her

over the head with it. Suddenly her cries ceased, and her head and neck slowly turned to stone. This legend is known to a great many of the Dyaks living up the Batang Lupar River, and the group of rocks was pointed out to me when we passed by them, if I remember rightly, not far from Lobok Antu.

The other legend is known as the Cat story, and is supposed to have happened to a tribe who lived not far from the lady turned to stone by a spindle. This village was also built on the banks of one of the little streams flowing into the Batang Lupar River. The chief was a proud, haughty man, whose tribe numbered one thousand men, women, and children. He was given the title of " Torrent of Blood," whilst his more famous warriors were also distinguished by similarly splendid names. His house was so large that it had seventy-eight doors (meaning seventy-eight families lived under the same long roof). He was indeed a great man : when he consulted the birds, they were favourable to his wishes, and when he led his warriors to battle, he always returned victorious, with his boats laden with heads, jars, sacks of paddy, and plunder of various kinds. No tribe in Borneo could equal the noise made by his warriors when they gave vent to the terrible head yells, by which they made known to the countryside that they were returning from some successful expedition. Practice had made them perfect, and the mountains, rocks, and valleys resounded with their shouts. When an expedition returned, the women and children stood on the banks to watch the arrival of the boats. The most distinguished warriors' helmets were decorated with hornbill's plumes, and their war-jackets were a mass of feathers. None but renowned head-hunters were allowed to wear the hornbill's plumes, for they were a token of the wearer having captured heads of enemies in battle.

But there was one poor individual who could take no part in either these warlike expeditions, or in the "Begawai Antu" (head feast) given in honour of heads of enemies taken in their wars. Some years before, the poor man's parents had accidentally set fire to one of the houses in the village, and, according to the custom of these Dyaks, such a misfortune entailed the whole of the culprit's family being enslaved. One by one the relations of the poor man had died, until he remained the only slave of the tribe. Indignities were heaped upon him, he was looked upon with great contempt, and made to live in the last room of the village where the refuse was thrown. One day, feeling more desolate than usual, he made friends with a cat belonging to the tribe. He enticed the animal into his miserable room and dressed it up in a scarlet waistband, a war-jacket made of panther's skin, and a cap decorated with hornbill's plumes : in short, in the costume of a distinguished Dyak warrior. He carried the animal to the open verandah in sight of the chiefs and elders who were discussing plans for a fresh expedition, and of the women and young girls husking

18

the paddy. There, before them all, the friendless creature hugged the cat and held it to his heart. He was nearly weeping and tears stood in his eyes, but hard-hearted and scornful, the people pointed at him in derision for owning such a friend, and laughed loudly. The warriors forgot about their war plans and the women about their paddy, in their keen enjoyment of the poor man's misery. Suddenly, he let the cat jump out of his arms, and as it touched the ground it ran like a mad thing in and out of the crowd, dropping here and there the cap, the jacket, and the scarlet waistband. Freed from these trappings, the cat leapt out of the house and disappeared. Then a great storm arose and the stone-rain fell upon the people. The chief of the village, together with all his tribe, were hurled by Antu Ribut into the stream, and they and their houses were turned into those great rocks which anyone can see for himself if he will take the trouble involved in a journey up those many reaches of the Batang Lupar River. The poor despised man found rest and shelter in the general confusion, for he crept inside a bamboo growing near the house, and there he has remained ever since, embedded in its heart.

Dr. Hose has told me that Bukitans and Ukits also believe in the danger of laughing at animals, for he once had a baby maias [1] which learnt to put its arms into the sleeves of a small coat, until it quite got to like the coat. When visiting Dr. Hose at

[1] Orang-outang, a species of monkey.

the Fort these people sometimes saw the creature
slowly putting on his coat, when they hid their
faces and turned away their heads, for fear the
animal should see them laughing at it. When
Dr. Hose asked them why they were afraid to be
seen laughing, they replied, " It is 'mali' (forbidden)
to laugh at an animal, and might cause a tempest."

Here is another legend about people being turned
to stone on account of ingratitude and disrespect
to their parents. Not far from the mouth of the
Batang Lupar River, some miles up the coast, are
rocks standing on the shore and which, according
to my friends, were remains of an ancient village, in
which a man, his wife, and their son once lived.
The parents were exceedingly fond of the boy and
brought him up with especial care. The father
taught him how to make schooners, how to fashion
canoes, and to make nets in order to obtain a
large haul of fish : indeed, he taught the boy all he
knew. When the lad grew up, he started from his
village on a trading expedition in a schooner built
by his father and himself. The parents parted
regretfully with their child, but in their unselfishness
they were only too glad he should go forth in the
world outside their little settlement and make a name
for himself. After many years the son managed to
amass a considerable fortune from his trading expeditions, and returned to the place of his birth to
visit his father and mother who had never for a
moment forgotten the boy so dear to them. But,

so the story goes, when he realized the poverty of their surroundings and their position in the world, his heart grew hard towards them, and he felt ashamed of their low estate. He spoke unkind words to the old couple, who had almost given their life's blood to build up his fortune. One day, after insulting them more than usual, a great storm arose, and father, mother, and son, together with the whole of the inhabitants of the village and their houses, were tossed into the sea and turned into stone.

The Batang Lupar district is rich in legends, and I will tell yet another as related to me by a fortman's wife in Simanggang. Every one living in Simanggang knows the great mass of sandstone and forest, called Lingga Mountain, and all those who have travelled at all (so said the fortman's wife) have seen this Lingga Mountain and know how high and difficult it is to climb, and how a great stretch of country can be seen from its flat and narrow top with the wide expanse of sea stretching from the shores of the Batang Lupar across the great bay of Sarawak to the mountains beyond the town of Kuching. A young Dyak, named Laja, once resided in a village at the foot of this mountain. A beautiful lady, the Spirit of the mountain, one night appeared to him in his dreams, and told him he must rise early the next morning, before the trees on the banks of the river had emerged from the mists of night, and climb Lingga Mountain, where he would find the

safflower (that blossom which has since become so great
a blessing to the Dyak race) at the top.   The vision
went on to explain that this plant would benefit Laja's
tribe, for it could cure most illnesses, more especially
sprains and internal inflammation.   Laja obeyed the
orders of this beautiful lady and started off the next
morning before dawn had broken over the land.   He
had climbed half-way up the mountain when he saw,
just above the fog, the fragment of a rainbow, like a
gigantic orchid painted in the sky, its rose colour
gleaming through the mist and melting away in the
most wonderful moss-green hue.   Seeing the coloured
fragment, Laja knew at once that the Spirit of the
mountain, a king's daughter, was about to descend by
the rainbow to bathe in the mountain stream.   When
the colours had faded from the sky, Laja went his way,
until he reached the top, where he had some difficulty
in finding the safflower on account of its diminutive
size.   After searching for some time, he found the
root and carried it back to his village.   He then
pounded it up and gave it to people who were sick.
But the plant was capricious, for, whilst it cured some,
others derived no benefit from it and died.   Its
successes, however, proved more numerous than its
failures, and every member of the tribe became
anxious to procure a root for himself, although no
one ventured to undertake the journey at the time
as the farming season was in full swing, necessitating
the villagers working hard at their paddy ; moreover,
the place where the plant grew was a long way off

and the climb up the mountain was a somewhat perilous one.

Notwithstanding, a young man, named Simpurei, started off one day in search of the safflower, without telling anyone of his intentions. When he reached half-way up the mountain he saw the rainbow glittering in the sky, but instead of its being a fragment, its arch was perfect, both ends resting on the sides of a hill opposite the mountain. Simpurei realized that the king's daughter must be bathing in the neighbour-hood; nevertheless, he still went on. He heard the sound of water and rustling leaves close by, and, pushing aside a great branch of foliage, peered through, when he saw a woman most divinely beautiful bathing in a pool. She was unclothed, her hair falling down her back until it touched her feet. She threw the water over her head from a bucket of pure gold, and as Simpurei stood staring at this beautiful vision, one of the twigs in his hand broke off. At the sound the girl looked up, and seeing the youth, fled to a great bed of safflowers near which her clothes were lying. As she sped away, one of her hairs became entangled in the bushes and was left hanging there. Simpurei saw it all wet and glistening, like a cobweb left on a branch after a dewy night, and rolling the fragile thread up carefully, put it with the beads, pebbles, pieces of wood, seeds, etc., which he carried about with him as charms, in his sirih bag.

He hastened home, having forgotten the saf-flower in the excitement of this unexpected meeting, but he had scarcely reached his house when he was seized with violent illness. He lingered for some hours, for he had time before he died to relate his adventures to the whole of the village who had immediately come to his house on hearing of his illness. Medicine men were called in, but their remedies were of no avail, and the elders of the tribe showed their wisdom when they decided that his death was a just punishment sent him by the Rajah, the Spirit of the Sun :—for had not Simpurei stood and gazed at his daughter when she was unclothed?

Another legend, which I had from the fortman's wife, telling how the paddy was first brought to Borneo, is a general one all over the country, and is related by many of our people with certain variations. Some generations ago a man dwelt alone by the side of a river in a small hut. One day, after a succession of thunder-storms and heavy rains, he was watching snags and driftwood hurrying down the stream after heavy freshets, owing to which the upper districts of the river had been submerged and a number of people drowned in the flood. A snag, on which perched a milk-white paddy bird, was hurrying to the sea, followed, more leisurely, by a great tree torn up by its roots. This tree got caught in a sandbank and swung to and fro in the current with a portion of its roots above water. The man noticed a strange-looking plant entangled in its roots, and unfastening his canoe from the landing-place near by, he paddled to the spot and took the plant home. It was a delicate-looking thing with leaves of the tenderest green, but thinking it of no use, he threw it in a corner of his hut and soon forgot all about it. When evening came on he unfolded his mat, put up his mosquito-net, and was soon fast asleep. In his dreams, a beautiful being appeared to him and spoke about the plant. This phantom, who seemed more like a spirit than a man, revealed to him that the plant was necessary to the human race, but that it must be watched and cherished, and planted when seven stars were shining together in the sky just before dawn. The man then woke up and, pulling his curtains aside, saw the plant lying in the corner of the hut shrivelled and brown. There he left it, and went to visit a friend living in the neighbourhood, to whom he related what had happened, and went on to say that the spirit of his dreams must be very stupid in telling him to look for seven stars when there were always so many shining in the sky. But his friend was a wise man and able to explain the meaning of his dream. He told him that Patara himself had appeared to him, and that the seven stars were quite different from other stars, as they did not twinkle, but remained still in the heavens, and as they chose their own season for appearing in the sky no one could tell for certain, without their help, when the new plant was to be put in the ground. The friend, being also versed in the law of antus, or spirits, said that the plant found in the roots of the tree was paddy (rice), and that Patara had taken the trouble to say so himself.

After this explanation the man went home, picked up the plant and put it away carefully until another dream should reveal when he was to look out for the seven stars. In due time, under Patara's guidance, the man noticed the "necklace of Pleiades" appearing in the sky. The little plant was then put in the ground, where it grew and multiplied. The people in neighbouring villages also procured roots to plant in their farms, so that the paddy now flourishes all over the country and the people of Sarawak have always enough to eat.

Sarawak people have very beautiful ideas about paddy, and their mythical tales about the food-giving plant remind one of the many legends all over the world relating to Demeter and other earth-mother goddesses. Amongst some tribes, indeed, I fancy, nearly all over Sarawak, the people plant the roots of a lily called Indu Padi (or wife of the Paddy, by Sea Dyaks) in their paddy fields. They treat this flower as though it were the most powerful goddess, and every paddy field belonging to the Dyaks of the Rejang, of the Batang Lupar, of the Sadong, and also of the Land Dyaks near Kuching, possesses a root of this flower.[1] They build little protecting huts over it, and treat its delicate and short life with the utmost care and reverence. I have often tried to get a glimpse of this flower, but have never succeeded. However, a good many of the Rajah's officers, who have lived some time in native houses, and who have witnessed the people's harvest

[1] I believe it to be a species of *Crinum*.

festivals, have given me a description of it. I have always thought it such a beautiful superstition of theirs that of caring for and nurturing the delicate petals of a flower as though its fragile existence were a protection to the well-being of their race. They greatly fear anything happening to the plant, for should it die or shrivel up before the paddy is husked and garnered, it is thought to bode disaster to their tribe.

A chief named Panau, who had a considerable following, often paid me visits in our bungalow at Simanggang. I had known him for years, and, like all Dyaks, he was fond of talking, and a shrewd observer of men and things. He was a reader of character, and when he trusted anyone became their loyal friend. His dark, restless eyes, his smiling face, his swagger, his conceit, his humility, and his kindness always interested me. He had a sense of humour, too, and cracked many jokes of which I did not always catch the sense; this was perhaps fortunate, as Dyak jokes are sometimes Rabelaisian in character. He was greatly interested in my camera, and thought the manner in which I fired at the landscape and caught it in the box nothing short of miraculous. One day I took his portrait, attired in his war-dress. He kept me waiting for some minutes adjusting a warlike pose before I pulled off the cap. " Let those who look upon my picture tremble with fear," he said, as he grasped his spear in one hand and his shield in the other. I took him into the dark room arranged for

PANAU—A SEA DYAK CHIEF

me in our bungalow to see me develop the picture. He looked over my shoulder as I moved the acid over the plate, and when he saw his likeness appear, he gave a yell, screamed out "Antu!" tore open the door, and rushed out, slamming the door behind him. On that account his picture is somewhat fogged. It took some time before he recovered from his fright, but he eventually accepted one of the prints. A great reason I had for enjoying Panau's company was his devotion to my eldest son, Vyner, who had visited Sarawak the previous year. At the time of Bertram's and my stay in Sarawak, Vyner was finishing his education at Cambridge. Panau confided to me that he longed for the time to come when his Rajah Muda would be amongst his people again. It appeared that Vyner had made many peaceful expeditions up the Batang Lupar River with Panau and his tribe. On one occasion Panau informed me he had saved Vyner from being engulfed by the Bore. When, on my return to England, I asked Vyner for details, he told me he did not remember the incident, and thought it must have existed only in Panau's imagination. I daresay Panau, having so often related this imaginary adventure, had come to look upon it as true. At any rate, the Chief was devoted to him, and, knowing how deeply my eldest son appreciates the natives, it was pleasant to realize how much he was esteemed by them in return.

I do not think it would be amiss to relate in this

connection a subsequent adventure that befell Vyner
some years after my stay at the Batang Lupar
River, up one of its tributaries. The Rajah found
himself obliged to send an expedition against a
tribe who had committed many murders in these
inland rivers. The expedition started from Simanggang, with Mr. Harry Deshon in charge of a
force of Dyaks and Malays numbering about eight
thousand, whilst Mr. Bailey and Vyner accompanied
them. For some unexplained reason, cholera broke
out amongst the force just before it had reached the
enemy's country. It was impossible to turn back on
account of the bad impression such a course would
have made on the enemy, so that, in spite of losing
men daily, the expedition had to push on. When the
force reached the enemy's country, a land party was
dispatched to the scene of action. A chosen body
of men, led by Malay chiefs, started on foot for the
interior, leaving the Englishmen and the body of the
force to await their return. During those days of
waiting, the epidemic became most virulent. The
three white men had encamped on a gravel bed, and
the Dyak force remained in their boats close by. As
the days wore on, the air was filled with the screams
and groans of the stricken and dying. Out of six or
seven thousand men who remained encamped by the
shores of the river, about two thousand died of the
plague, and to Vyner's great grief and mine our old
friend Panau was attacked with the disease, and
died in a few hours.

Mr. Deshon and Mr. Bailey have since told me that Vyner's presence helped to keep discipline and hope amongst the force during the awful time. He was always cheerful, they said. It appears that Vyner and his two friends used to sit on the gravel bed and with a grim humour point out to one another where they would like to be buried, in case at any moment they might be carried off by the plague.

When, after having conquered the head-hunters, the attacking party returned to camp, they found the gravel bed strewn with the bodies of the dead and dying. The return journey to Simanggang was terrible, for all along those many miles of water, corpses had to be flung from the boats in such numbers that there was nothing to be done but to leave them floating in the stream. The enemy, subsequently hearing about the catastrophe, hurried to the place where the Rajah's force had been encamped, and finding there so many dead bodies, proceeded to cut off their heads and to carry them home. These people, however, fell victims to their detestable habit, for they caught the cholera and spread it amongst their tribe, with the result that it was almost annihilated. A great stretch of country became infected, and the little paths around Simanggang were littered with the corpses of Chinese, Dyaks, and Malays. Nothing apparently could be done to stop the disease, which disappeared as suddenly as it had come, but this calamitous epidemic destroyed nearly one-quarter of the population.

Happening to be in Italy at the time, I read in an Italian paper that the Rajah's son had died of cholera in Sarawak, as he was leading an expedition into the interior. I hurried to England with my younger son, Harry, who was staying with me at the time, and when we arrived at Dover, placards at the station confirmed the report. Telegrams, however, soon put us out of suspense, but I had spent a terrible day.

CHAPTER XXX

ON our return to Kuching, Bertram and I were anxious to pay a flying visit to a place called Paku, where one of the Rajah's magistrates resides. The people in the neighbourhood are mostly Chinese, and near by are antimony and quicksilver mines worked by the Borneo Company Limited.

We left Kuching in one of the Government launches about eleven o'clock in the morning, and after a few hours' steaming came to a Chinese settlement, called Sigobang, where the land on the banks becomes a broad alluvial plain and where Chinese settlers grow plantations of sugar, that beautiful cane with its emerald green leaves and golden stems. Fresh sugar-cane is a pleasant thing to munch at in a desultory way. You cut through a piece of the stem, slice it into tubes, peel off its thick rind, and when it looks like a stick of white wood you bite into it, suck its juice, and dispose of its filaments in the most convenient way. The paths in the vicinity of towns or villages are always strewn with the vestiges of sugar-cane eaters, who suck in the juice and spit out the filaments as they go. As we steamed up river we saw pepper vines, yams, pineapples, etc., also growing near the banks, and Chinamen clad in short cotton drawers, holding umbrellas over their heads, and using their other hand as they worked in their gardens. Yellow dogs, about the size of fox terriers, rushed out from Chinese houses and yelped at us from doorways; these were evidently Dyak dogs, who are never known to bark. Bamboo wheels stood under open sheds—primitive machines for extracting the sugar juice from the cane. These Chinese houses appeared more substantial than were those of the poorer Malays. They were built level with the ground, and their wooden doors were ornamented with scarlet bands of paper over which were large black Chinese characters. Ducks and geese were swimming about in the river near these settlements.

These small villages being left behind us, the forests once more encroached on the land. The river now became narrower, and rocky banks replaced the mud. The banks were covered with ferns and bamboo grass, the latter weed looking like green lace and shaking at the slightest current of air. Black butterflies fluttered over the grass, and an alligator bird, or bul-bul, was singing on the banks in the sunshine. Clumps of bamboos grew here and there, and great trees hung over the water, clinging to the banks, their branches entangled with parasites and stag's-horn ferns, whilst the reflection of lagerstremias covered with purple spiked flowers, stained the running water.

We reached Busu, the landing-place for Paku, at six in the evening. At this point the stream is

AN ENCAMPMENT UP THE BATANG LUPAR RIVER

THE TUAN MUDA, MR. BAILEY AND THE AUTHOR WITH MALAY AND DYAK CHIEFS

about twenty yards wide. Malay houses, devoid of orchards or gardens, stood on poles amongst the weeds on the banks. On platforms of crazy planks, where Malays husk their paddy, jutting out from these houses, dilapidated coxcombs planted in old kerosene tins struggled to live in their uncongenial surroundings. A path made of single bamboos, dovetailing into each other, led from the cottages to the river. A man on the bank, shouldering a bamboo, came out of one of these houses to fetch water from the river. He was met with a storm of scornful remarks from our crew, as Malay men are supposed to leave water-carrying to the women of their household. A little farther on was the Borneo Company Ltd.'s wharf, whence the antimony and quicksilver is shipped to Kuching and thence to Singapore and Europe. A tramway starts from the landing-place, leading to the mines some miles inland.

We found Mr. Awdry, one of the Rajah's officers and a great friend of ours, awaiting us at the Wharf. We then got into a horse-truck kindly put at our disposal by the Manager of the Mines, furnished with mattresses and pillows, and comfortably travelled over the four miles separating us from the bungalow. Mrs. Awdry met us at the bottom of the hill leading to her house. As we clambered down from the truck, which was pretty high, a concourse of Chinamen, who had come to meet us, started beating their gongs, blowing into instruments sounding like bagpipes, and waving banners, whilst others set fire to piles of crackers, hanging from iron tripods, all along the road. The hill was steep and, as we headed the procession, the orchestra and banner-bearers, in the exuberance of their welcome, followed closely at our heels, so that we were pushed forward by our noisy welcomers, until I found myself racing up the incline like a panting hare, with a crowd of pursuers immediately behind me. The din was fearful, but the people meant well, and, although short of breath from my exertions, I managed to thank them for their kind reception as soon as I reached the top.

From the verandah of the house a great stretch of country could be seen. There were curious-shaped hills of limestone sticking up singly here and there, although, viewed from Kuching, they appear like a chain of mountains. One of them, called Sebigi, stood out from the plain like a great green thumb. Although forest fires are unusual in Sarawak, for droughts are rare, the whole of one of these hills, called Jambusan, was a mass of burnt trees with the limestone showing through the charred stumps. No one knew how the fire had occurred, but it was conjectured that the rubbing together of the bamboos in the wind during the dry weather had caused them to ignite. With the exception of this charred hillock, the house we were in seemed to be the centre of a sea of green waves. Along the valleys were small Chinese gardens, these people, as is well known, being excellent agriculturists. Here were pumpkins, water melons, scarlet runners, sweet potatoes, maize, and a kind of native spinach growing magnificently. There were small ponds on which floated those beautiful pink and white lotuses, the Chinese cultivating the flowers as food for their pigs. A hot spring bubbled up somewhere in the flat ground near by, its temperature being about 100° Fahrenheit. The Chinese and Dyaks of the district bathed in its waters as a cure for rheumatism. English cattle were grazing here and there, and the place looked prosperous and peaceful.

The day after our arrival at Paku an individual named Pa Baniak (meaning Father of plenty) came to see me, accompanied by two members of his tribe. He was a Land Dyak and his village was situated on the steep slope of limestone mountains in the neighbourhood. He was short and stout, and a few white bristles sprouted over his chin. He wore Chinese drawers, a dirty white cotton jacket, and a dark blue handkerchief was twisted round his head. He had wooden discs screwed into the rims of his ears, which, he said, were necessary to his comfort for two reasons : firstly, they made his hearing more acute, and secondly, they pleased the crocodiles. He told us that although he and his tribe were constantly fishing in the main river, he felt sure that none of these monsters would attempt to eat any of them. In response to my inquiry, he related the following story—not, however, before he had risen, coughed, spat out of the verandah, taken hold of the tips of my fingers, passed the back of his hand across his nostrils, and then returned to his place on the floor :—

"Malays are not good people," he said, "and before the first white Rajah came to our country, they did many wicked things. In the time of long ago, a Malay caught a crocodile; this was treacherous of him, because he tied a dog to a wooden hook attached to a long piece of rattan which he made fast to a tree, leaving its loose end floating on the river. The dog howled and attracted a hungry crocodile, who swam joyfully to the spot, and, in spite of the warnings of his friend, the alligator bird, he snapped at the bait. He swallowed the dog and hook at one gulp, when the hook fixed itself in his throat, as the Malay had intended, and the beast could neither swallow the hook nor spit it up, and therefore his jaw was prised open. The Malay, seeing the loose end of the rattan floating down the river, paddled after it, but the beast was too quick for him, and got away from the country near the sea to the country of the Land Dyaks, more inland. A member of Pa Baniak's tribe, passing by in a canoe, noticed the crocodile's open jaw and felt sorry for him. The crocodile begged the man to put his arm down his throat and wrench the hook away. Thinking it might be dangerous, the Dyak did not much like the task, and inquired what the crocodile would do for him in return. 'I promise never to attack or eat any member of your tribe,' said the crocodile.

The man thought this a fair offer, and the compact was made, after which the man removed the hook. The operation over, the crocodile thanked his deliverer, and told him to warn all his people to thrust wooden discs in the cartilage of their ears, so that crocodiles should not mistake them for members of some other tribe."

To prove the truth of this tale, Pa Baniak informed me that, only a few days before our arrival at Paku, a young man of his tribe had been seized by a crocodile as he was taking fruit from his orchard down the river to the Kuching market. With a switch of its tail the animal sent the canoe up in the air, and as its occupant, paddle in hand, was falling into its formidable jaws, the beast noticed the wooden discs, and finding that the man's flesh did not taste nice, he threw him on shore and went away snorting with disgust. Bertram and I made ejaculations of approval at the end of this tale, and Pa Baniak was mightily pleased at the effect he had produced.

Although four or five miles away, the trees on the top of Singghi mountain stood out distinctly that afternoon in the lurid light of an approaching thunder-storm. His thumbs pointing in the direction of the mountain, Pa Baniak said, "Antus live up there, and my tribe has made wooden images of men and women to keep them amused. If ever the trees on the top of Singghi are cut down, leaving the antus without either playground or shelter, they would roam amongst the trees in the plain and tease the people living there." We listened to Pa Baniak's talk for some little time, and he told us many things, as for instance, about the terrible consequences of men eating the flesh of deer, which made them cowards; of the importance of being burned instead of buried in the earth, in order that one's relations could tell by the direction of the smoke whether or no the dead had started for Paradise. But at length we became tired and allowed him to depart. He rose slowly, grunted, scratched himself under his armpits, took a little brass bell off the sirih basket hanging at his waist, and gave it to me. "It will preserve you from lightning, snake bites, and antus," he said. Then, followed by his attendants, he made his way downstairs. Thunder was growling in the distance, and drops of rain were falling as the trio went out of the house, each opening Chinese umbrellas to keep the rain off their naked bodies, for most Sarawak natives imagine that rain falling on their skin brings on malaria. We watched them as they went along the plain in single file; then the rain came down in torrents, blotting them out from view.

CHAPTER XXXI

ONE morning Bertram and I, accompanied by Mr. Frank Maxwell, Mr. Awdry, and Dr. Langmore, started from Kuching in a steam launch on an expedition to Munggo Babi, a Land Dyak settlement. Up the Sadong River we passed Malay villages with palm-leaf houses erected on poles and standing in the mud. A few ragged flags of red, white, blue, and yellow, on long thin sticks, fluttered along the banks near Chinese houses, where women and children set fire to bunches of crackers, for they had somehow got wind of our journey. On the banks grew great, sweet-smelling, white lilies, called by the natives "bungga bakong," but by European scientists *Crinum Northianum*, because they were first made known to European botanists by Miss North's pictures. They looked like crowns of great white stars resting on green and glossy lance-like leaves.

We slept in a Malay house at a village called Gading. The house was made of palm leaves, and the poles supporting it stood on the mud: the whole construction was lashed together by rattans, as no nail or peg is ever used by the poorer Malays in building such humble dwellings. Clean mats were laid upon the floor, and I noticed that one portion of the roof was used as a storeroom, whilst scattered about the floor were large water-jars and cooking-pans. At night, as I lay on a mattress stretched on the floor, I heard the incoming tide gurgling, as it were, under my pillow. Frogs, insects, nightbirds, and all sorts of creatures, grotesque or beautiful, hooted, whistled, and coughed, sounding like the shrill and rough jabbering of drunken men; and there were hummings, moanings, murmurings—the cogitations, so to speak, of spirits of the darkness and evil, all heard as distinctly by me as if I were resting outside in the mud right amongst them. I thought of crocodiles moving through the slime, until I felt terrified, and almost welcomed the homely sensation of being bitten by a flea. Then morning dawned, the sun came out, and with its joyous advent I felt that sense of security we none of us can account for at the dawn of day.

But to return to our journey. We embarked on the launch early. The river soon narrowed, and the banks were full of that beautiful shrub with its enormous deeply-indented leaves, pale yellow flowers as large as soup plates, its clustered, bullet-shaped, carmine-coloured buds, and its open pods revealing seeds of a ravishing coral colour. I am not quite certain, but I think the plant must be a species of Wormia. Then there were screw pines growing near the mud, from which strong fibre can be obtained, their beautiful red fruits nestling in their roots, reminding one of gigantic strawberries. I saw dark green small-leaved shrubs starred over with waxy sweet-smelling blossoms, rather like stephanotis, and mauve, yellow, and pink convolvuli throttled great trees in the entanglement of their embrace. A large grey bird flew from out the lilies, alighted on a piece of driftwood, and was borne down the stream. We passed a place called Tana Mera (red earth) where at a little distance from the bank is the grave of an exceedingly righteous Malay gentleman whom the people called Datu Sumbang Kring. He lived many years ago, but the influence of his holy life still endures, and the people in the neighbourhood are never tired of relating how he taught every one to be kind and good, and how he spread abroad the precepts of that holy book, the Koran. I could not make out how long ago this righteous life was lived, but, according to the people, it was many years before the first Rajah Brooke came to Sarawak.

After passing Tana Mera, snags stuck up in all directions in the bed of the river. Some Land Dyaks from Munggo Babi came to meet us, bringing with them canoes in which we were to accomplish the last stages of our journey. I noticed how different these Land Dyaks were to Kayans, Malays, or Sea Dyaks. They were tall and slender with well-shaped noses, arched eyebrows, more pronounced chins, and their faces were oval and longer than were the faces of the other inhabitants of Sarawak. Their colour, however, was the same, but instead of the bright, laughing, bustling habits of the other people, they wore an expression of profound melancholy.

A Malay Haji had come with them to meet us and to direct proceedings. Our canoes had to be pushed through labyrinths of snags and other impediments barring our progress. At one part of the journey the men in our canoe had to cut down a snag before we could proceed further. When this was accomplished, they began to yell at their success, but the Haji remonstrated with them, and pointing to a tall Tapang tree towering over the jungle near the banks told them that the swarm of bees clinging to its branches would be angry at the noise, so that if the crew did not stop yelling, he feared the insects might attack us. He added, however, that the day being showery, we did not run the same risks as though the day were fine.

Tapang trees rise to a height of over one hundred feet without a branch. Their trunks are smooth and round, and swarms of bees often hang in their branches. Dyaks climb them at night to obtain the wax. The ascent is made by means of bamboo pegs driven into the trunk above the climber's head, so that the ascent is slow, and takes several hours to accomplish. The bees are scared from their nests with a lighted torch, after which the wax is taken with impunity. The wax is sold at Kuching and forms one of the exports of the country. A great hindrance to the Dyaks who go in search of

BATCHELOR HOUSE AT MUNGGO BABI

TUAN MUDA'S RESIDENCE DURING OUR VISIT

this commodity is the little honey bear that roams about the forests of Sarawak, for it is very fond of stealing and eating the honey from these hives. Two or three specimens of this animal are to be seen in the London Zoological Gardens.

Munggo Babi lies at the foot of a mountain two thousand feet high. In order to reach the village we had to leave our canoes at the landing-place and proceed up a path for three miles or so. We found a crowd of young Dyaks drawn up on the banks to meet us, the elders having arranged to receive us at the entrance of their village. These young men wore waist-cloths of bright colours. The women and girls were dressed in short petticoats with rows of silver dollars and silver chains for waistbelts, and round their necks were rows of black, yellow, and red beads. These women do not know how to weave their petticoat stuffs, as do the Sea Dyak women, but buy them from wandering Chinese traders, or obtain them on their visits to the capital. Most of the young girls wore wire rings round the upper part of their arms and also round their legs. These rings all being, apparently, of the same size, impede the circulation and sometimes cause acute suffering, owing to the way the wire sinks into the growing limb. Four Dyaks carried me in a cane chair slung on poles nearly all the way, excepting where the path grew steep, or the way became difficult, when I preferred to trust to my own feet. I might have been a thing of feathers so easily did my four carriers skip along, although my weight was a respectable one. The road led through glades carpeted with various kinds of ferns, some having a bright blue bloom on them as they grew in the shade. We passed three or four round houses neatly thatched with pointed roofs, standing on high ironwood posts round which were placed circular slabs of wood, very large in diameter, as a protection against the rats, these being the barns in which the paddy of the tribe was stored. These granaries were surrounded by groves of bread-fruit, lancat, durians, mangosteens, mangoes, and various other fruit trees. We crossed a stream by walking over large sandstone boulders scattered in its bed, round which the water rushed and foamed.

The elders met us at this spot. One of them was dressed in an old military coat, which had belonged to the South Lancashire regiment. His legs and thighs were bare, and a large piece of turkey twill was twisted round his waist and fell in folds front and back. He held a long slender twig from which floated a diminutive Sarawak flag looking like the petals of a drooping flower. His black beard was well tended and he seemed very proud of it. His hair, long enough to reach below his waist, was tucked up in a chignon under a fillet made of calico bound round his forehead like a crown. The other old men wore long flowing robes of brightly coloured red or blue chintz, patterned over with flowers and birds. One of them wore a large turban, although he was not a Malay; another wore a red-and-yellow head-handkerchief, and two very old, almost toothless, men wore jaunty smoking-caps stuck at the side of their bald heads. These old men stood in a row behind the leader in the military jacket, each holding long thin sticks with a flag at the end, which they agitated gently when we appeared. The oldest chief took hold of my hand and led me over a series of notched poles and narrow trunks of trees, and across a deep muddy ditch leading to the village. The village lay in a green basin, scooped out of the side of a hill. Down a ravine on one side of the village, a little torrent, fed by daily rain, made a refreshing and gurgling sound day and night. Bamboo shoots led up the mountain-side to the uppermost houses on the hill, whence the people obtained water for household purposes, and where they also bathed many times a day.

When we arrived at the houses prepared for us, we climbed up slippery poles with no rails to steady our ascent and where the notches were extremely insignificant. These poles were some twenty feet high, leading to verandahs of planks. My residence turned out to be the head-house of the village and the building of ceremony. It consisted of one large, round room, in which I had to bathe, dress, eat, and sleep, whilst one part was portioned off for our Chinese cook to prepare our food. Another house was prepared for the men of our party; this house was called the "Bachelor House" because none but men were supposed to use it. But to return to my quarters. Seen from outside, the house looked like a large pigeon-cot, propped on high poles, and lashed together with the fibre of the Gemuti palm.[1] It rocked and creaked at the slightest provocation like a ship in a heavy sea. The walls were made of planks, and small apertures served for windows. Screens of dried palm leaves were placed in different parts of the room; one of these recesses was my bed-room and another my bathroom, where a large tub of water always stood ready for my use. The place screened off for my reception-room had a wooden divan of thin planks all round it, finished off with a wooden valance. Our hosts had spared no trouble to make the place habitable, and had even stretched gold brocade across the top of the room, thus forming an improvised ceiling, whilst the posts were wreathed round with smilax and the fronds of betel-nut palms. Just over my bed hung the trophies of the tribe. These were nothing more or less than a large bundle of dried skulls. The Dyaks imagined that the

---

[1] This Borassus Gemuti palm plays a great part in the rural economy of the people in Sarawak. It flourishes in the high upland of the interior, and is very rough and wild-looking. It has a sap obtained from the petals of its flowers, used as sugar by the natives, and out of the liquid, which quickly ferments, is made an intoxicating beverage. Between the trunk and the fronds is a horse-hair-like substance, used for cordage in shipping throughout the Malayan Archipelago. Tinder can be obtained from a fine cotton-like substance which the plant also yields. Its strong, stiff spines are made into pens, used by the people who write on paper; and a great many of the primitive tribes of the interior make their arrows from these prickly points. I believe that the pith of the trunk furnishes a kind of sago. The seeds are enveloped by a poisonous juice to which the Dutch people give the name of "hell water."

brocade had hidden these trophies from my searching
gaze, but I am sorry to say I could see through an
aperture some of the skulls which the tribe had
taken in their battles of long ago, when they rose up
against the tyranny of the Brunei princes, or on the
occasion of the Chinese insurrection, which took place
in the late Rajah Brooke's reign, when a good many
Chinese heads were captured. I noticed that one of
the round objects was larger than the rest, and I asked
questions about it. "Oh," said the chief contemptu-
ously, "that one is only the head of a Chinaman, for
they always have larger heads than we people of the
country!"

At the commencement of our stay one or two
little hitches were experienced, but these were soon
put right. Our Chinese cook gave himself airs, and
informed Mr. Awdry that he could not possibly cook
decent food in such a wilderness of discomfort.
After a good deal of talk between our kind hosts and
the cook, a small outhouse was rigged up for him
and his saucepans.

From the window of my head-house I could see
all the way down the village. I noticed the houses
were built in blocks, placed here and there, some ten
or twelve in a row, in the inequalities of the soil by
the side of the stream. The houses were, of course,
propped up by poles of different heights, and there
were platforms made of split bamboos lashed together
by rattans running down the fronts of these houses,
behind which were covered verandahs. I was told that

there was a fireplace in each house, with shelves above it, where water, oil, salt fish, jars, potted durians, etc., were stored. A raised platform was invariably erected at the end of each room, used as a place to sit on when receiving one's friends, also as a sleeping-place when strangers came to the village. The women looked picturesque with their white shell armlets, brass rings, and silver girdles shining against the dark background of the houses. I noticed that most of them parted their hair, and that the children's heads were not shaved. At sunset in the wooden verandahs the girls of the village prepared food for their pigs, made of paddy husks mixed with water. A special brew was poured into smaller basins and kept for little pigs, which the girls caught from under the houses and threw here and there on to the verandahs. The girls then pushed the little pigs' snouts into the food, whilst with long poles they beat off the cocks and hens anxious to join in the feast. In the evening the elders of the tribe rested under the shade of a banyan tree conversing with one another, whilst pigs grunted under the houses, cocks and hens strutted about the roofs, and dogs ran in and out of doorways—a tiny speck of human and animal life surrounded by gigantic backgrounds of mysterious and unexplored forests and mountains.

These Land Dyaks are very hospitable, and, barring the time of my afternoon siestas or when I retired for the night, my room in the head-house was filled at all times of the day with the élite of the Dyak tribe. Whenever the elders were seated on the wooden divan in front of me, I was struck anew with the unlikeness of these people to the rest of our Sarawak tribes. I could not help thinking they resembled the Cingalese, for they had the same dreamy, soft, and effeminate look.

The chief of the tribe, Mito, was anxious that I should bless his house during my visit, so he gave a feast, to which he invited all the inhabitants of Munggo Babi, as well as those of a neighbouring village. The women came to fetch me from my airy abode, helping me down the notched logs with the greatest care. Their movements were greatly restricted by the tightness of the wire rings round their legs, which prevented them from bending their knees comfortably. As we entered the house, I saw the bones of pigs' jaws hanging in festoons over the doors leading into the inner room as trophies of the chase. The long gallery was decorated with yellow and red cloths, and all the people of the village were squatting in rows down each side. A seat covered with yellow cloth was prepared for me, and the rest of our English party were given raised chairs to sit on. Just in front of me, on the floor, were round brass dishes filled with uncooked rice, and two eggs were laid on the top of each dish. Between the dishes, about twenty in number, were bamboos filled with cooked rice, tasting something like the rice puddings of our childhood The chief came to me with a small basin, filled with water, into which he asked me to place one of my

20

gold rings, so that its goodness might enter into the water ; he then gave me a bead necklace to dip into the basin, after which I had to go up and down the whole length of the gallery, holding the necklace on high, and say, " I wish this house cold and plenty. I wish that the paddy may be fruitful ; that the wives of this village may have many sons ; that sickness may never enter it, and that its people may live in peace and prosperity." A basin of yellow rice was then handed to me, when I had to go through the same ceremony and repeat the same blessing. The contents of the brass dishes were then emptied into baskets and given to me, together with a large box of eggs, which had been left in front of my seat during the proceedings. The party now began in earnest. We ate the rice out of the bamboos, partook of the many cakes and fruits provided for us, and drank tumblers of cocoa-nut milk.

Then came the dances, the gongs and instruments being hung in readiness against the wall. The musicians, their arms over the top of the wooden frames, held the gongs, and drummed at them with their fingers with a will. Two women, with their arms completely hidden under masses of brass rings and white shell armlets, crept forward and touched the tips of my fingers. Then drooping their heads and extending their arms they began to move about slowly. They put their feet close together and shuffled and slid from one side of the room to the other, keeping time to the gongs whilst the little bells tied to their ankles tinkled.

We were told that this was called the Hornbill's dance. The women were very small, slim, and well-made, with pretty expressive eyes, and rather thinner lips than those of the other women of Sarawak, but theirs were so stained with betel-nut juice that in the dim light their mouths looked like large red wounds across their faces.

After the women had danced, two men wound in and out of the people squatting on the floor, and stood before us. Under the folds of their sarongs they wore a circle of plaited rattans, making them stand out like crinolines. Their long hair was twisted up Cingalese fashion, and stood out from the handkerchiefs wound round their heads. They commenced the performance by flapping their arms and gliding about without lifting their feet from the floor. They then advanced and nearly touched one another, when they swiftly retreated, wheeled round one another, their arms describing circles in the air. The sarongs over their crinolines billowed and swayed with their every movement, and the dance gave one the impression of sweeping lines and of space. It was supposed to represent the flight of great hawks through the air, and I thought it beautiful. The dancers were handsome men, with sleek and gentle faces, and very arched eyebrows. All their movements were much more languid than those of the Sea Dyaks.

When the dances were over we sat talking to the people, and I asked a chief what he thought of our language. He said that English people talking was like the song of birds, but the Chinese language was like the hooting of antus. He then told us of a superstition about bamboos. When people die, he said, their flesh goes into the bamboo and their souls enter the bodies of unborn children, when they are born again into the world.

The next morning we were all ready to start on our way back at 7.30, but the people who were to carry our luggage down to the landing-place wanted a good deal of rousing after their dissipation of the night before. However, after severe reprimands from their chief and from the village authorities, they came to assist us with our luggage. An enormous crowd was required for the purpose, one man taking a saucepan, another two plates, a third two bottles of beer, a fourth a handbag, which he carried with both hands, until our luggage was divided among one hundred people or so, walking in Indian file, and forming a procession about half a mile long. A chair had been provided for me, but as the road was slippery (it had been raining the night before) I preferred walking the whole way back to the landing-place.

Before reaching the place where our canoes were awaiting us, one of the chiefs, who had been an entertaining talker and had told us about the bamboo superstition, suddenly darted into the forest on the edge of the path, whence he reappeared with a branch of bamboo he had cut with his parang. He showed me the red sap within the cane. "See there," he said; "this is the burying-place of some human being."

I said good-bye to the chiefs and all the carriers, after which we got into the boat. I carried the bit of bamboo home, and still preserve it amongst my treasures from Sarawak.

We reached Kuching after twenty-four hours' journey, and two days after we embarked on the *Rajah Brooke* for England.

It was a sad day for Bertram and I when we said good-bye to our Malay friends at Kuching. Datu Isa and all her family, accompanied by nearly all the Malay women of the town, came to the Astana to say good-bye. As I stood watching them from the deck of the steamer, congregated as they were near our landing-place, I felt a tightening at my heart, and wondered how many years would elapse before I should see them again. Bertram was really as much touched as I was at leaving them. The *Rajah Brooke* moved away, and slowly rounded the reach which hid the dear people from sight. Many years have gone by since that day, and yet I may say with truth that absence from my people has only increased my love and affection for them, and should my hopes be realized of one day returning to Sarawak, I am sure of finding there the very kindest welcome from the best friends I have in the world.

CHAPTER XXXII

BEFORE closing these notes, it might be as well to give an idea of the position Sarawak occupies with regard to its external relations.

In 1888 a treaty placing Sarawak under British protection, whilst the internal affairs of the country remained immune from British intervention, was drawn up between the British Government and the Rajah. Some years later I had the honour of being received at Windsor by Queen Victoria, and of being presented to Her Majesty as Ranee of Sarawak. The Queen received me in one of the small apartments at Windsor Castle. At first, I naturally felt nervous, but when the Queen inquired kindly about our Sarawak people my feeling of shyness vanished, and I could think of nothing but the Queen's gracious words, and notice that beautiful smile of hers that seemed to illuminate every corner of the room. The Rajah was, at the time, absent in Sarawak, and this prevented his being included in Her Majesty's invitation to Windsor. However, knowing how much the Rajah would appreciate Her Majesty's interest in Sarawak, which after all was a compliment to himself, I telegraphed the news out to our country, where all concerned were much gratified at such a token of the Queen's sympathy.

When King Edward came to the throne, the affairs of Sarawak and status of its ruler apparently interested him. His Majesty, aware of the manner Sarawak was governed, and after having made inquiries as to the prosperity and well-being of its inhabitants, decreed that the Rajahs of Sarawak should be given precedence at the English Court immediately after that of the ruling Princes of India. But even then difficulties arose regarding the position of the Rajah's sons. Our eldest son, although heir-apparent, and our younger sons who are heirs-presumptive, were not allowed to be presented at Court under their Sarawak titles. Our present King, however, a little while ago saw fit to confirm our eldest son's title of Rajah Muda in England, but his brothers, who have also a certain right in the succession, have not been allowed the same privilege at the English Court. We all know that in hereditary properties the younger sons of the actual possessor are recognized as having a legal interest in the possible succession of their father. When one realizes that we are dealing with an hereditary State, the question at stake becomes a doubly important one.

We have had recent and ample opportunities to judge of the dangers which half-civilized nations run at the hands of exploiting commercialism. That

Sarawak should hitherto have escaped such dangers
is infinitely to the honour of the Borneo Company
Ltd., who have never sought to enrich themselves
to the detriment of Sarawak people. Nor must we
forget that immunity from companies of a less
scrupulous character is due to the vigilance and
firmness of the Rajahs of Sarawak, determined as
they were that the people who placed themselves
under their rule should have the benefit of European
contact without any of its often terrible drawbacks.
We must therefore hope that the future Rajah and
his brothers will consolidate a regime which has so
admirably safeguarded the natives under their two
first White Rajahs. It is therefore consonant with
the wisdom of the present Sovereign that he should
have sought to strengthen the position of his
successor, whenever a change in the succession
occurs, by arranging for the assistance of a Consulta-
tive Council who would sit in London, and consisting
of his two younger sons, of two highly distinguished
officials in the Sarawak service, and, if possible, of
an independent Englishman experienced in colonial
government and in matters dealing with primitive
people and their interests. The Rajah is fully aware
that whatever steps he may see fit to take for the
future safety of his people, the more publicly such
precautions are made known, the better it will be for
the success of his schemes. Public opinion is a
mighty lever when used to champion any honest
or righteous cause, and it is with the help of public

opinion that the Rajah may gain the necessary help
in order to realize the fulfilment of his dearest wish—
that being to keep Sarawak for the benefit of its own
people, and, in so doing, from the devastating grasp
of money-grabbing syndicates.

INDEX

Other Oxford Paperbacks for readers interested in South-East Asia, past and present

Cambodia

Angkor: An Introduction
GEORGE COEDÈS

Angkor and the Khmers
MALCOLM MacDONALD

Indonesia

An Artist in Java
JAN POORTENAAR

Bali and Angkor
GEOFFREY GORER

Coolie
MADELON H. LULOFS

Diverse Lives: Contemporary Stories from Indonesia
JEANETTE LINGARD

Flowering Lotus: A View of Java in the 1950s
HAROLD FORSTER

Forgotten Kingdoms in Sumatra
F. M. SCHNITGER

The Head-Hunters of Borneo
CARL BOCK

The Hidden Force*
LOUIS COUPERUS

The Hunt for the Heart: Selected Tales from the Dutch East Indies
VINCENT MAHIEU

In Borneo Jungles
WILLIAM O. KHRON

Island of Bali*
MIGUEL COVARRUBIAS

Java: Facts and Fancies
AUGUSTA DE WIT

Java: The Garden of the East
E. R. SCIDMORE

Java: A Travellers' Anthology
JAMES R. RUSH

Javanese Panorama
H. W. PONDER

The Last Paradise
HICKMAN POWELL

Let It Be
PAULA GOMES

Makassar Sailing
G. E. P. COLLINS

The Malay Archipelago
ALFRED RUSSEL WALLACE

The Outlaw and Other Stories
MOCHTAR LUBIS

The Poison Tree*
E. M. BEEKMAN (Ed.)

Rambles in Java and the Straits in 1852
'BENGAL CIVILIAN' (C. W. KINLOCH)

Rubber
MADELON H. LULOFS

A Tale from Bali*
VICKI BAUM

The Temples of Java
JACQUES DUMARÇAY

Through Central Borneo
CARL LUMHOLTZ

To the Spice Islands and Beyond: Travels in Eastern Indonesia
GEORGE MILLER

Travelling to Bali
ADRIAN VICKERS

Twin Flower: A Story of Bali
G. E. P. COLLINS

Unbeaten Tracks in Islands of the Far East
ANNA FORBES

Witnesses to Sumatra
ANTHONY REID

Yogyakarta: Cultural Heart of Indonesia
MICHAEL SMITHIES

Malaysia

Among Primitive Peoples in Borneo
IVOR H. N. EVANS

An Analysis of Malay Magic
K. M. ENDICOTT

At the Court of Pelesu and Other Malayan Stories
HUGH CLIFFORD

The Best of Borneo Travel
VICTOR T. KING

Borneo Jungle
TOM HARRISSON

The Chersonese with the Gliding Off
EMILY INNES

The Experiences of a Hunter and Naturalist in the Malay Peninsula and Borneo
WILLIAM T. HORNADAY

The Field-Book of a Jungle-Wallah
CHARLES HOSE

Fifty Years of Romance and Research in Borneo
CHARLES HOSE

The Gardens of the Sun
F. W. BURBIDGE

Glimpses into Life in Malayan Malayan Lands
JOHN TURNBULL THOMSON

The Golden Chersonese
ISABELLA BIRD

Illustrated Guide to the Federated Malay States (1923)
C. W. HARISSON

The Malay Magician
RICHARD WINSTEDT

Malay Poisons and Charm Cures
JOHN D. GIMLETTE

My Life in Sarawak
MARGARET BROOKE, THE RANEE OF SARAWAK

Natural Man
CHARLES HOSE

Nine Dayak Nights
W. R. GEDDES

A Nocturne and Other Malayan Stories and Sketches
FRANK SWETTENHAM

Orang-Utan
BARBARA HARRISSON

The Pirate Wind
OWEN RUTTER

Queen of the Head-Hunters
SYLVIA, LADY BROOKE, THE RANEE OF SARAWAK

Six Years in the Malay Jungle
CARVETH WELLS

The Soul of Malaya
HENRI FAUCONNIER

They Came to Malaya
J. M. GULLICK

Wanderings in the Great Forests of Borneo
ODOARDO BECCARI

The White Rajahs of Sarawak
ROBERT PAYNE

Philippines

Little Brown Brother
LEON WOLFF

Singapore

The Manners and Customs of the Chinese
J. D. VAUGHAN

Raffles of the Eastern Isles
C. E. WURTZBURG

Singapore 1941–1942
MASANOBU TSUJI

Travellers' Singapore
JOHN BASTIN

South-East Asia

Adventures and Encounters
J. M. GULLICK

Adventurous Women in South-East Asia
J. M. GULLICK (Ed.)

Explorers of South-East Asia
VICTOR T. KING (Ed.)

Soul of the Tiger*
JEFFREY A. McNEELY and PAUL SPENCER WACHTEL

Thailand

Behind the Painting and Other Stories
SIBURAPHA

Descriptions of Old Siam
MICHAEL SMITHIES

The English Governess at the Siamese Court
ANNA LEONOWENS

The Politician and Other Stories
KHAMSING SRINAWK

The Prostitute
K. SURANGKHANANG

Temples and Elephants
CARL BOCK

To Siam and Malaya in the Duke of Sutherland's Yacht *Sans Peur*
FLORENCE CADDY

Travels in Siam, Cambodia and Laos 1858–1860
HENRI MOUHOT

Vietnam

The General Retires and Other Stories
NGUYEN HUY THIEP

The Light of the Capital: Three Modern Vietnamese Classics
GREG & MONIQUE LOCKHART

*Titles marked with an asterisk have restricted rights.

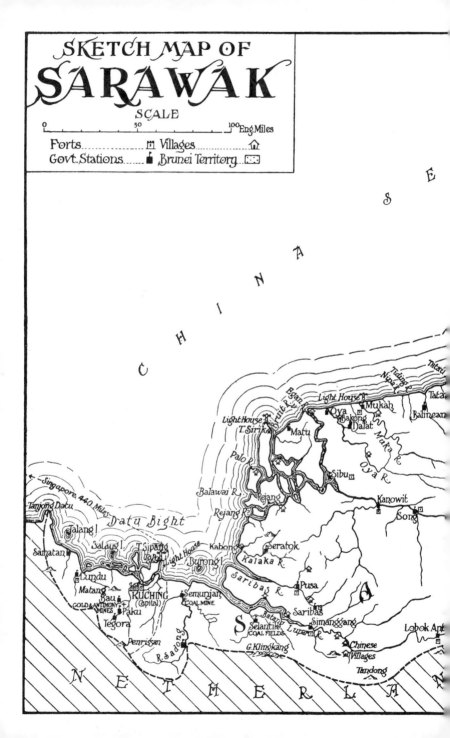